THE ANTI-FEDERALIST PAPERS

DOVER THRIFT EDITIONS

Patrick Henry and Others

DOVER PUBLICATIONS
GARDEN CITY, NEW YORK

DOVER THRIFT EDITIONS

GENERAL EDITOR: SUSAN L. RATTINER
EDITOR OF THIS VOLUME: JIM MILLER

Bibliographical Note

The Anti-Federalist Papers, first published by Dover Publications in 2020, is a new compilation of speeches, essays, and letters from 1787–88 concerning the ratification of the United States Constitution. They have been reprinted from standard sources. The Introduction and explanatory notes preceding each section have been specially prepared for this edition by John Grafton. Spelling, punctuation, and style vagaries, like inconsistent capitalization, derive from the original eighteenth-century sources.

International Standard Book Number

ISBN-13: 978-0-486-84345-2
ISBN-10: 0-486-84345-9

Manufactured in the United States of America
84345905
www.doverpublications.com

Contents

Introduction

WHILE THE WAR against England still raged, the thirteen original colonies drafted their first "Constitution," officially named The Articles of Confederation and Perpetual Union, during the Second Continental Congress in 1777. The Articles of Confederation took force on March 31, 1781, after having been ratified by all thirteen "United States," a slow process that began with Virginia's endorsement in 1777 and ended when Maryland finally joined the fold on February 2, 1781. Eight months later, the British surrender at Yorktown brought the Revolution to a successful close.

It did not take long for the problems inherent in the Articles to become clear to many of the new nation's leading political figures. The Articles were essentially a treaty linking the independent states, not a blueprint for a national government. It provided only for a national legislature; no executive or judicial branches were created. Crucially, no powers to tax were included—funds had to be requested from the states, which generally didn't provide them very generously, and seldom in a timely manner. Because of this, the debts incurred during the Revolution couldn't be paid, and an ongoing national defense could not be financed. Individual states could issue money, which quickly lost value, as did the currency issued by the weak central government. Foreign trade regulations were left to each individual state, so potential foreign trading partners could not be dealt with on a unified basis, and American shipping could not be defended in international waters. Complicating this, each state had one vote and any change to the Articles required unanimous agreement, always hard to obtain, and any major legislation required nine of 13 votes to pass, also hard to obtain. Events such as Shays' Rebellion, an uprising of angry Revolutionary War veterans and other citizens against aggressive state tax collectors in Massachusetts in 1786–87, while eventually put down after a struggle, convinced many that these concerns were not simply theoretical, and a way had to be found to provide for more effective government.

A crucial step was taken when delegates from five states—New Jersey, New York, Pennsylvania, Delaware, and Virginia—met at Mann's Tavern in Annapolis, Maryland, in September 1786, to discuss improving conditions caused by the trade barriers between states which were widely seen as stifling the growth of commerce in the new nation. All the states had been invited to send representatives to Annapolis. Several sent delegates who were, however, unable to get to Annapolis in time for the meeting, and others took no action at all. The ones who were there unanimously sent a report back to the national Congress calling for a larger convention to be held the following May in Philadelphia, and expressing the hope that more states would send delegates then and that perhaps more items could be discussed than just trade issues. From this beginning the Constitutional Convention of 1787 was called into existence.

The 1787 Philadelphia Convention got off to a slow start when delegates from several states were unable to arrive in time for the planned May 14 opening. By May 25, a quorum of representatives from seven states had arrived and the proceedings could begin. The venue was the Pennsylvania State House, also known as Independence Hall, where the Declaration of Independence had been signed 11 years before. George Washington was elected President of the Convention, and it was decided to keep the proceedings confidential until the end. Despite the heat of the Philadelphia summer, the windows were nailed shut to preserve the total privacy in which the delegates wanted to have their debates.

It became clear early in the discussions that there was momentum to go beyond the idea of trying to fix what the Articles of Confederation had created, and toward the forming of a new national government. Many of the delegates came with experience in this area: individual states had each drafted new Constitutions of their own during the period of the Revolution, and delegates had previously grappled with many of the same issues on the state level that now arose on the national scene.

New York's Alexander Hamilton and Virginia's James Madison were the leading proponents for the creation of a document that would create a whole new federal government. Madison's Virginia

Plan, circulated early in the proceedings, outlined a new federal government with three branches--executive, judicial, and legislative. In midsummer, a logjam was averted by the Connecticut Compromise, which proposed that the composition of the new national legislature's lower house, the House of Representatives, would be determined by the population of each state—the larger states therefore having the most representatives—while the upper house, or Senate, would give each state, regardless of population, the same number of members. As the days and weeks went by, many other contentious issues were gradually dealt with—would there be a single chief executive, or a panel of more than one in charge?—how would slaves be counted?—how would the President be elected, and how long would members of each legislative body serve?—how would judges be appointed, and would there be an impeachment process?—any many more. After weeks of debate and many compromises, large and small, the new Constitution was signed by 39 delegates, representing a substantial majority, on September 17, 1787.

This volume includes a number of excerpts from the debates at the Philadelphia Convention of 1787 as recorded by James Madison in his *Notes of Debates in the Federal Convention of 1787*, first published in book form only in the 1830s. Madison's *Notes* are an essential source for the thinking then current on both sides of the great national debate, and reading them allows us to go back and follow the Convention's progress issue by issue, throughout the long summer. The Federalists on one side argued for the benefits a more powerful national government would bring; the Anti-Federalists on the other side, concerned about the freedoms the original states and individuals might lose under the new Constitution, argued against it.

The national debate over all of these issues provoked an immense war of words, a battle, essentially, of dueling newspaper columns in every city and state throughout the new republic, and in many smaller towns as well. This battle went into high gear as the nation as a whole started to consider whether to ratify the new Constitution that the Philadelphia Convention had brought forth. The Federalists and their leading advocates made their case not only in the justly famous series of Federalist Papers by Hamilton, Madison, and John Jay, which have been widely read and studied since they first appeared in the newspapers during the battle over ratification, but in many other articles and essays during those contentious years. The spokesmen for the anti-Federalists were less organized and more diffuse than their Federalist counterparts. They didn't function as an organized group or coordinated committee, but they also made their case, and made it effectively in newspaper pieces of their own, many of which raise points that still resonate with considerable numbers of American voters even today, and which certainly had an impact on the outcome of events at the time. The anti-Federalists didn't win the immediate battle—after an arduous and lengthy process, the new Constitution which came out of the 1787 Philadelphia Convention was ratified on June 21, 1788, when Rhode Island became the ninth state to sign. Following the necessary elections, the new government of the United States opened for business in New York on March 4, 1789. However, the greatest victory of the anti-Federalists was yet to come.

During the debates at the Philadelphia Convention, there had been many arguments for and against what came to be called the Bill of Rights. Three delegates who were present on September 17, 1787—George Mason, Edmund Randolph, and Elbridge Gerry, refused to sign the new Constitution, largely because it lacked a bill of rights. Federalists generally argued that a bill of rights wasn't needed because the Constitution only granted to the Federal Government the powers it specifically enumerated; anti-Federalists felt an explicit list of rights reserved to individuals was necessary to protect the freedoms they had fought for in the Revolution.

As the ratification process continued in every state, the argument over the Bill of Rights took a primary role. Some states ratified the new Constitution while expressing that they did so in anticipation that such a Bill would soon be forthcoming. At a crucial juncture one of the wisest of the Founding Fathers, Virginia's James Madison, originally an opponent of the idea of a Bill of Rights, came to the realization that the Federalists needed to get out in front of this issue before the whole Constitutional effort was jeopardized. Madison, then a member of the House of Representatives, drafted 17 proposed amendments to the Constitution, taking as a primary source the 1776 Virginia Declaration of Rights, written by George Mason. The Senate whittled the list down to 12. By December 15, 1791, three-fourths of the States had ratified 10 of these amendments, and so they took their place in the Constitutional framework of the new nation as the Bill of Rights. Now explicitly protected were freedom of religion, speech, press, assembly and petition, the right to keep and bear arms to maintain a well-regulated militia, the right to due process of law, and freedom from self-incrimination and double jeopardy.

Admirers of the Bill of Rights can certainly thank the anti-Federalists for having made this process necessary and for working to bring it to a successful conclusion. It was surely their greatest legacy. This unequivocal establishment of the rule of law and every citizen's entitlement to these vital protections was a victory for the anti-Federalists even as the Constitution they first opposed took effect as the Federalists planned. In a sense, both sides won, a rarity in history.

Who were the anti-Federalist writers? It was a mixed group: some were famous, some were virtually unknown, most preferred to publish anonymously, and some of those have been able to retain their anonymity indefinitely and are identified by scholars today either not at all or only conjecturally. They were from the North and the South, farmers, soldiers, and merchants, richer and poorer, slave owners and not. This volume includes speeches by Patrick Henry, famous revolutionary orator, planter, first Governor of Virginia, and Melancton Smith, a New York merchant, a man fairly well known in his time but not to many casual readers of history today. Many of the Anti-Federalist essays which appeared in newspapers during the ratification debate and are reprinted in this volume were published under pseudonyms, often pseudonyms referring to characters in Roman history. The best evidence holds that the essays first published under the name "Cato" were by Melancton Smith, those by "Brutus" were likely by Smith, or Robert Yates, a New York attorney, or John Williams, a General in the New York militia; those by "Centinel" were by Samuel Bryan, a figure in Pennsylvania politics; and those by "Federal Farmer" were by Smith, or Richard Henry Lee, a leading Virginia political figure, or Mercy Otis Warren, a Massachusetts political writer. Also included in this volume are some essays published during the Constitutional ratification debates under the name "John DeWitt." This pseudonym was an homage to a famous seventeenth-century Dutch patriot Johan De Witt (1625–1672) who defended the rights of citizens against an oppressive government, but the actual identity of the eighteenth-century American "DeWitt" remains a mystery.

The concerns of the anti-Federalists centered on freedom and power. Having fought a war for independence from what they considered a despotic monarchy answerable to no one, the anti-Federalists feared creating a central power in the new United States that might come to resemble another version of the British crown they despised. Dividing power among the 13 original states seemed like a better idea than concentrating it in the hands of a stronger central government. No doubt the universally respected George Washington's decision to run for President, and his well-known total lack of interest in becoming anything like a British king, allayed some, but not all, of those fears. The anti-Federalists were concerned that the individual states would eventually give up all of their rights to the new central government—no doubt investing in states' rights seemed like a surer way to guarantee individual freedoms. This debate has resonated throughout American history, and still goes on in the twenty-first century.

JOHN GRAFTON

QUALIFICATIONS FOR SUFFRAGE

August 7, 10

The proposition was debated that qualifications for voting for members of the House of Representatives in the new Congress should be the same in each state as the qualifications for voting for the part of their own legislature that had the most members. Gouverneur Morris of New York tried to pass a resolution limiting the right to vote for members of Congress to freeholders (landowners). It was defeated by a wide margin, 7–1.

MR. WILSON. This part of the Report was well considered by the Committee, and he did not think it could be changed for the better. It was difficult to form any uniform rule of qualifications for all the States. Unnecessary innovations he thought too should be avoided. It would be very hard and disagreeable for the same persons at the same time, to vote for representatives in the State Legislature and to be excluded from a vote for those in the National Legislature.

MR. GOUVERNEUR MORRIS. Such a hardship would be neither great nor novel. The people are accustomed to it and not dissatisfied with it, in several of the States. In some the qualifications are different for the choice of the Governor and Representatives; in others for different Houses of the Legislature. Another objection against the clause as it stands is that it makes the qualifications of the National Legislature depend on the will of the States, which he thought not proper.

MR. ELLSWORTH thought the qualifications of the electors stood on the most proper footing. The right of suffrage was a tender point, and strongly guarded by most of the State Constitutions. The people will not readily subscribe to the National Constitution if it should subject them to be disfranchised. The States are the best Judges of the circumstances and temper of their own people.

1

COLONEL MASON. The force of habit is certainly not attended to by those gentlemen who wish for innovations on this point. Eight or nine States have extended the right of suffrage beyond the freeholders, what will the people there say, if they should be disfranchised. A power to alter the qualifications would be a dangerous power in the hands of the Legislature.

MR. BUTLER. There is no right of which the people are more jealous than that of suffrage. Abridgments of it tend to the same revolution as in Holland where they have at length thrown all power into the hands of the Senates, who fill up vacancies themselves, and form a rank aristocracy.

MR. DICKINSON had a very different idea of the tendency of vesting the right of suffrage in the freeholders of the Country. He considered them as the best guardians of liberty; and the restriction of the right to them as a necessary defence against the dangerous influence of those multitudes without property and without principle with which our Country like all others, will in time abound. As to the unpopularity of the innovation it was in his opinion chimerical. The great mass of our Citizens is composed at this time of freeholders, and will be pleased with it.

MR. ELLSWORTH. How shall the freehold be defined? Ought not every man who pays a tax, to vote for the representative who is to levy and dispose of his money? Shall the wealthy merchants and manufacturers, who will bear a full share of the public burdens be not allowed a voice in the imposition of them—taxation and representation ought to go together.

MR. GOUVERNEUR MORRIS. He had long learned not to be the dupe of words. The sound of Aristocracy therefore had no effect on him. It was the thing, not the name, to which he was opposed, and one of his principal objections to the Constitution as it is now before us, is that it threatens this Country with an Aristocracy. The aristocracy will grow out of the House of Representatives. Give the votes to people who have no property, and they will sell them to the rich who will be able to buy them. We should not confine our attention to the present moment. The time is not distant when this Country will abound with mechanics and manufacturers who will receive their bread from their employers. Will such men be the secure and faithful Guardians of liberty? Will they be the impregnable barrier against aristocracy?—He was as little duped by the association of the words "taxation and Representation." The man who does not give his vote freely is not represented. It is the man who dictates the vote.

Children do not vote. Why? because they want prudence, because they have no will of their own. The ignorant and the dependent can be as little trusted with the public interest. He did not conceive the difficulty of defining "freeholders" to be insuperable. Still less that the restriction could be unpopular. Nine-tenths of the people are at present freeholders and these will certainly be pleased with it. As to Merchants, etc., if they have wealth and value the right they can acquire it. If not they don't deserve it.

COLONEL MASON. We all feel too strongly the remains of ancient prejudices, and view things too much through a British medium. A Freehold is the qualification in England, and hence it is imagined to be the only proper one. The true idea in his opinion was that every man having evidence of attachment to and permanent common interest with the Society ought to share in all its rights and privileges. Was this qualification restrained to freeholders? Does no other kind of property but land evidence a common interest in the proprietor? Does nothing besides property mark a permanent attachment? Ought the merchant, the monied man, the parent of a number of children whose fortunes are to be pursued in his own Country, to be viewed as suspicious characters, and unworthy to be trusted with the common rights of their fellow Citizens.

MR. MADISON. The right of suffrage is certainly one of the fundamental articles of republican Government, and ought not to be left to be regulated by the Legislature. A gradual abridgment of this right has been the mode in which Aristocracies have been built on the ruins of popular forms. Whether the Constitutional qualification ought to be a freehold, would with him depend much on the probable reception such a change would meet with in States where the right was now exercised by every description of people. In several of the States a freehold was now the qualification. Viewing the subject in its merits alone, the freeholders of the Country would be the safest depositories of Republican liberty. In future times a great majority of the people will not only be without landed, but any other sort of, property. These will either combine under the influence of their common situation; in which case, the rights of property and the public liberty, will not be secure in their hands: or which is more probable, they will become the tools of opulence and ambition, in which case there will be equal danger on another side. The example of England had been misconceived [by Colonel Mason]. A very small proportion of the Representatives are there chosen by freeholders. The greatest part are chosen by the Cities and boroughs, in many of which the qualification of suffrage is as low as it is in any one of the United States and it was in the boroughs and Cities rather than the Counties, that bribery most prevailed, and the influence of the Crown on elections was most dangerously exerted.

DR. FRANKLIN. It is of great consequence that we should not depress the virtue and public spirit of our common people; of which they displayed a great deal during the war, and which contributed principally to the favorable issue of it. He related the honorable refusal of the American seamen who were carried in great numbers into the British Prisons during the war, to redeem themselves from misery or to seek their fortunes, by entering on board the Ships of the Enemies to their Country; contrasting their patriotism with a contemporary instance in which the British seamen made prisoners by the Americans, readily entered on the ships of the latter on being promised a share of the prizes that might be made out of their own Country. This proceeded he said from the different manner in which the common people were treated in America and Great Britain. He did not think that the elected had any right in any case to narrow the privileges of the electors. He quoted as arbitrary the British Statute setting forth the danger of tumultuous meetings, and under that pretext narrowing the right of suffrage to persons having freeholds of a certain value; observing that this Statute was soon followed by another under the succeeding Parliament subjecting the people who had no votes to peculiar labors and hardships. He was persuaded also that such a restriction as was proposed would give great uneasiness in the populous States. The sons of a substantial farmer, not being themselves freeholders, would not be pleased at being disfranchised, and there are a great many persons of that description.

MR. MERCER. The Constitution is objectionable in many points, but in none more than the present. He objected to the footing on which the qualification was put, but particularly to the *mode of election* by the people. The people can not know and judge of the characters of Candidates. The worse possible choice will be made. He quoted the case of the Senate in Virginia as an example in point. The people in Towns can unite their votes in favor of one favorite; and by that means always prevail over the people of the Country, who being dispersed will scatter their votes among a variety of candidates.

MR. RUTLEDGE thought the idea of restraining the right of suffrage to the freeholders a very unadvised one. It would create division among the people and make enemies of all those who should be excluded.

*The debate continued on August 10 with discussion of the qualifications
for serving as members of Congress. There was a strong faction for
having a "wealth requirement" for membership in Congress, but
the members were unable to foresee any possibility of agreeing on
what would be a suitable amount. Benjamin Franklin is recorded
as having opposed the whole idea, pointing out that some of
the worst rogues he had ever encountered in his long life were the
richest . . .*

MR. PINCKNEY. The Committee as he had conceived were instructed to report the proper qualifications of property for the members
of the National Legislature; instead of which they have referred the
task to the National Legislature itself. Should it be left on this
footing, the first Legislature will meet without any particular
qualifications of property: and if it should happen to consist of rich
men they might fix such qualifications as may be too favorable to
the rich; if of poor men, an opposite extreme might be run into.
He was opposed to the establishment of an undue aristocratic
influence in the Constitution but he thought it essential that the
members of the Legislature, the Executive, and the Judges, should
be possessed of competent property to make them independent and
respectable. It was prudent when such great powers were to be
trusted to connect the tie of property with that of reputation in
securing a faithful administration. The Legislature would have the
fate of the Nation put into their hands. The President would also
have a very great influence on it. The Judges would have not only
important causes between Citizen and Citizen but also, where
foreigners are concerned. They will even be the Umpires between
the United States and individual States as well as between one State
and another. Were he to fix the quantum of property which should
be required, he should not think of less than one hundred thousand
dollars for the President, half of that sum for each of the Judges,
and in like proportion for the members of the National Legislature.
He would however leave the sums blank. His motion was that the
President of the United States, the Judges, and members of the
Legislature should be required to swear that they were respectively
possessed of a cleared unincumbered Estate to the amount of ——
in the case of the President etc., etc.

MR. RUTLEDGE seconded the motion; observing that the Committee
had reported no qualifications because they could not agree on any
among themselves, being embarrassed by the danger on one side of

displeasing the people by making them high, and on the other of rendering them nugatory by making them low.

MR. ELLSWORTH. The different circumstances of different parts of the U.S. and the probable difference between the present and future circumstances of the whole, render it improper to have either *uniform* or *fixed* qualifications. Make them so high as to be useful in the Southern States, and they will be inapplicable to the Eastern States. Suit them to the latter, and they will serve no purpose in the former. In like manner what may be accommodated to the existing State of things among us, may be very inconvenient in some future state of them. He thought for these reasons that it was better to leave this matter to the Legislative discretion than to attempt a provision for it in the Constitution.

DR. FRANKLIN expressed his dislike of every thing that tended to debase the spirit of the common people. If honesty was often the companion of wealth, and if poverty was exposed to peculiar temptation, it was not less true that the possession of property increased the desire of more property. Some of the greatest rogues he was ever acquainted with, were the richest rogues. We should remember the character which the Scripture requires in Rulers, that they should be men hating covetousness. This Constitution will be much read and attended to in Europe, and if it should betray a great partiality to the rich, will not only hurt us in the esteem of the most liberal and enlightened men there, but discourage the common people from removing into this Country. . . .

Note written by Madison, probably in 1787, giving a longer account of his views on qualifications for suffrage.

NO. 1. IN CONVENTION OF
AUGUST 7TH, 1787

As appointments for the General Government here contemplated will, in part, be made by the State Governments, all the Citizens in States where the right of suffrage is not limited to the holders of property, will have an indirect share of representation in the General Government. But this does not satisfy the fundamental principle that men can not be justly bound by laws in making which they have no part. Persons and property being both essential objects of Government, the most that either can claim, is such a structure of it, as will leave a reasonable security for the other. And the most obvious provision, of this double character, seems to be that of confining to the holders of property the object deemed least secure in popular Governments, the right of suffrage for one of the two Legislative branches. This is not without example among us, as well as other constitutional modifications, favoring the influence of property in the Government. But the U.S. have not reached the Stage of Society in which conflicting feelings of the class with, and the class without property, have the operation natural to them in Countries fully peopled. The most difficult of all political arrangements is that of so adjusting the claims of the two classes as to give security to each, and to promote the welfare of all. The federal principle—which enlarges the sphere of power without departing from the elective bases of and controls in various ways the propensity in small republics to rash measures and the facility of forming and executing them, will be found the best expedient yet tried for solving the problem.

Note written by Madison in the 1820s presenting his views on suffrage more fully. He was guided by two principles—first that the people, meaning average citizens, should have a role in making the laws by which they were to be governed. Thus giving too much weight to property ownership would exclude too many people from the process. And in America, unlike Europe, he believed that poor people could reasonably hope of one day being property owners and thus should always have a strong role in the political process.

No. 2 [1821–1829?]

The right of suffrage is a fundamental Article in Republican Constitutions. The regulation of it is, at the same time, a task of peculiar delicacy. Allow the right exclusively to property, and the rights of persons may be oppressed. The feudal polity alone sufficiently proves it. Extend it equally to all, and the rights of property or the claims of justice may be overruled by a majority without property, or interested in measures of injustice. Of this abundant proof is afforded by other popular Governments and is not without examples in our own, particularly in the laws impairing the obligation of contracts.

In civilized communities, property as well as personal rights is an essential object of the laws, which encourage industry by securing the enjoyment of its fruits: that industry from which property results, and that enjoyment which consists not merely in its immediate use, but in its posthumous destination to objects of choice and of kindred affection.

In a just and a free Government, therefore, the rights both of property and of persons ought to be effectually guarded. Will the former be so in case of a universal and equal suffrage? Will the latter be so in case of a suffrage confined to the holders of property?

As the holders of property have at stake all the other rights common to those without property, they may be the more restrained from infringing, as well as the less tempted to infringe the rights of the latter. It is nevertheless certain, that there are various ways in which the rich may oppress the poor; in which property may oppress liberty; and that the world is filled with examples. It is necessary that the poor should have a defence against the danger.

On the other hand, the danger to the holders of property can not be disguised, if they be undefended against a majority without property. Bodies of men are not less swayed by interest than individuals, and are less controlled by the dread of reproach and the other motives felt by individuals. Hence the liability of the rights of property, and of the impartiality of laws affecting it, to be violated by Legislative majorities having an interest real or supposed in the injustice: Hence agrarian laws, and other leveling schemes: Hence the cancelling or evading of debts, and other violations of contracts. We must not shut our eyes to the nature of man, nor to the light of experience. Who would rely on a fair decision from three individuals if two had an interest in the case opposed to the rights of the third? Make the number as great as you please, the impartiality will not be increased, nor any further security against injustice be obtained, than what may result from the greater difficulty of uniting the wills of a greater number.

In all Government there is a power which is capable of oppressive exercise. In Monarchies and Aristocracies oppression proceeds from a want of sympathy and responsibility in the Government towards the people. In popular Governments the danger lies in an undue sympathy among individuals composing a majority, and a want of responsibility in the majority of the minority. The characteristic excellence of the political System of the U.S. arises from a distribution and organization of its powers which at the same time that they secure the dependence of the Government on the will of the nation, provides better guards than are found in any other popular Government against interested combinations of a Majority against the rights of a Minority.

The United States have a precious advantage also in the actual distribution of property particularly the landed property; and in the universal hope of acquiring property. This latter peculiarity is among the happiest contrasts in their situation to that of the old world, where no anticipated change in this respect, can generally inspire a like sympathy with the rights of property. There may be at present, a Majority of the Nation, who are even freeholders, or the heirs, or aspirants to Freeholds. And the day may not be very near when such will cease to make up a Majority of the community. But they can not always so continue. With every admissible subdivision of the Arable lands, a populousness not greater than that of England or France, will reduce the holders to a Minority. And whenever the Majority shall be without landed or other equivalent property and without the means or hope of acquiring it, what is to secure the rights of property against the danger from an equality and universality of suffrage, vesting compleat power over property in hands without a share in it: not to speak of a danger in the mean time from a dependence of an increasing number on the wealth of a few? In other Countries this dependence results in some from the relations between Land-lords and Tenants in others both from that source, and from the relations between wealthy capitalists and indigent labourers. In the U.S. the occurrence must happen from the last source; from the connection between the great Capitalists in Manufacturers and Commerce and the numbers employed by them. Nor will accumulations of Capital for a certain time be precluded by our laws of descent and of distribution; such being the enterprize inspired by free Institutions, that great wealth in the hands of individuals and associations, may not be infrequent. But it may be observed, that the opportunities, may be diminished, and the permanency defeated by the equalizing tendency of the laws.

No free Country has ever been without parties, which are a natural offspring of Freedom. An obvious and permanent division of every people is into the owners of the Soil, and the other inhabitants. In a certain sense the Country may be said to belong to the former. If each landholder has an exclusive property in his share, the Body of Landholders have an exclusive property in the whole. As the Soil becomes subdivided, and actually cultivated by the owners, this view of the subject derives force from the principle of natural law, which vests in individuals an exclusive right to the portions of ground with which they have incorporated their labour and improvements. Whatever may be the rights of others derived from their birth in the Country, from their interest in the high ways and other parcels left open for common use, as well as in the national Edifices and monuments; from their share in the public defence, and from their concurrent support of the Government it would seem unreasonable to extend the right so far as to give them when become the majority, a power of Legislation over the landed property without the consent of the proprietors. Some shield against the invasion of their rights would not be out of place in a just and provident System of Government. The principle of such an arrangement has prevailed in all Governments where peculiar privileges or interests held by a part were to be secured against violation, and in the various associations where pecuniary or other property forms the stake. In the former case a defensive right has been allowed; and if the arrangement be wrong, it is not in the defense, but in the kind of privilege to be defended. In the latter case, the shares of suffrage, allotted to individuals have been with acknowledged justice apportioned more or less to their respective interests in the Common Stock.

These reflections suggest the expediency of such a modification of Government as would give security to the part of the Society having most at stake and being most exposed to danger. Three modifications present themselves.

1. *Confining* the right of suffrage to freeholders, and to such as hold an equivalent property, convertible of course into freeholds. The objection to this regulation is obvious. It violates the vital principle of free Government that those who are to be bound by laws, ought to have a voice in making them. And the violation would be more strikingly unjust as the lawmakers become the minority: The regulation would be as unpropitious also as it would be unjust. It would engage the numerical and physical force in a constant struggle against the public authority; unless kept down by a standing army fatal to all parties.

2. Confining the right of suffrage for one Branch to the holders of property, and for the other Branch to those without property. This arrangement which would give a mutual defence, where there might be mutual danger of encroachment, has an aspect of equality and fairness. But it would not be in fact either equal or fair, because the rights to be defended would be unequal, being on one side those of property as well as of persons, and on the other those of

persons only. The temptation also to encroach though in a certain degree mutual, would be felt more strongly on one side than on the other. It would be more likely to beget an abuse of the Legislative Negative in extorting concessions at the expence of property, than the reverse: the division of the State into the two Classes, with distinct and independent Organs of power, and without any intermingled Agency whatever, might lead to contests and antipathies not dissimilar to those between the Patricians and Plebeians at Rome.

3. Confining the right of electing one Branch of the Legislature to freeholders, and admitting all others to a common right with holders of property, in electing the other Branch. This would give a defensive power to holders of property, and to the class also without property when becoming a majority of electors, without depriving them in the mean time of a participation in the public Councils. If the holders of property would thus have a twofold share of representation, they would have at the same time a twofold stake in it, the rights of property as well as of persons the twofold object of political institutions. And if no exact and safe equilibrium can be introduced, it is more reasonable that a preponderating weight should be allowed to the greater interest than to the lesser. Experience alone can decide how far the practice in this case would accord with the Theory. Such a distribution of the right of suffrage was tried in New York and has been abandoned whether from experienced evils or party calculations, may possibly be a question. It is still on trial in N. Carolina, with what practical indications is not known. It is certain that the trial, to be satisfactory ought to be continued for no inconsiderable period; untill in fact the non freeholders should be the majority.

4. Should Experience or public opinion require an equal and universal suffrage for each branch of the Government such as prevails generally in the U.S. a resource favorable to the rights of landed and other property, when its possessors become the Minority, may be found in an enlargement of the Election Districts for one branch of the Legislature and a prolongation of its period of service. Large districts are manifestly favorable to the election of persons of general respectability, and of probable attachment to the rights of property, over competitors depending on the personal solicitations practicable on a contracted theatre. And although an ambitious candidate, of personal distinction, might occasionally recommend himself to popular choice by espousing a popular though unjust object, it might rarely happen to many districts at the same time.

The tendency of a longer period of service would be, to render the Body more stable in its policy, and more capable of stemming popular currents taking a wrong direction, till reason and justice could regain their ascendancy.

5. Should even such a modification as the last be deemed inadmissible, and universal suffrage and very short periods of elections within contracted spheres be required for each branch of the Government, the security for the holders of property when the minority, can only be derived from the ordinary influence possessed by property, and the superior information incident to its holders; from the popular sense of justice enlightened and enlarged by a diffusive education; and from the difficulty of combining and effectuating unjust purposes throughout an extensive country; a difficulty essentially distinguishing the U.S. and even most of the individual States, from the small communities where a mistaken interest or contagious passion, could readily unite a majority of the whole under a factious leader, in trampling on the rights of the Minor party.

Under every view of the subject, it seems indispensable that the Mass of Citizens should not be without a voice, in making the laws which they are to obey, and in choosing the Magistrates, who are to administer them, and if the only alternative be between an equal and universal right of suffrage for each branch of the Government and a confinement of the *entire* right to a part of the Citizens, it is better that those having the greater interest at stake namely that of property and persons both, should be deprived of half their share in the Government; than, that those having the lesser interest, that of personal rights only, should be deprived of the whole.

CITIZENSHIP FOR IMMIGRANTS

August 9

On August 9 the Convention debated a motion to require immigrants to be citizens for 14 years for eligibility to serve in the Senate, and this sparked a lively debate on the role of immigrants in the new country. Most of the members who took part were opposed to creating large obstacles to full participation in the country's new government, and were opposed to making the new Constitution in any way an instrument of illiberality. The view was clearly expressed that a country that stood for freedom should not be too restrictive; but there were delegates, such as Gouverneur Morris, representing Pennsylvania, who were distrustful of foreigners and the allegiances they might bring with them.

MR. GOUVERNEUR MORRIS moved to insert 14 instead of 4 years citizenship as a qualification for Senators: urging the danger of admitting strangers into our public Councils. MR. PINCKNEY seconded him.

MR. ELLSWORTH was opposed to the motion as discouraging meritorious aliens from emigrating to this Country.

MR. PINCKNEY. As the Senate is to have the power of making treaties and managing our foreign affairs, there is peculiar danger and impropriety in opening its door to those who have foreign attachments. He quoted the jealousy of the Athenians on this subject who made it death for any stranger to intrude his voice into their Legislative proceedings.

COLONEL MASON highly approved of the policy of the motion. Were it not that many not natives of this Country had acquired great merit during the revolution, he should be for restraining the eligibility into the Senate, to natives.

MR. MADISON was not averse to some restrictions on this subject; but could never agree to the proposed amendment. He thought any restriction however in the *Constitution* unnecessary, and improper; unnecessary because the National Legislature is to have the right of regulating naturalization, and can by virtue thereof fix different periods of residence as conditions of enjoying different privileges of Citizenship: Improper because it will give a tincture of illiberality to the Constitution: because it will put it out of the power of the National Legislature even by special acts of naturalization to confer the full rank of Citizens on meritorious strangers and because it will discourage the most desireable class of people from emigrating to the United States. Should the proposed Constitution have the intended effect of giving stability and reputation to our Governments great numbers of respectable Europeans: men who love liberty and wish to partake its blessings, will be ready to transfer their fortunes hither. All such would feel the mortification of being marked with suspicious incapacitations though they should not covet the public honors. He was not apprehensive that any dangerous number of strangers would be appointed by the State Legislatures, if they were left at liberty to do so: nor that foreign powers would make use of strangers as instruments for their purposes. Their bribes would be expended on men whose circumstances would rather stifle than excite jealousy and watchfulness in the public.

MR. BUTLER was decidedly opposed to the admission of foreigners without a long residence in the Country. They bring with them, not only attachments to other Countries; but ideas of Government so distinct from ours that in every point of view they are dangerous. He acknowledged that if he himself had been called into public life within a short time after his coming to America, his foreign habits, opinions, and attachments would have rendered him an improper agent in public affairs. He mentioned the great strictness observed in Great Britain on this subject.

DR. FRANKLIN was not against a reasonable time, but should be very sorry to see any thing like illiberality inserted in the Constitution. The people in Europe are friendly to this Country. Even in the Country with which we have been lately at war, we have now and had during the war, a great many friends not only among the people at large but in both houses of Parliament. In every other Country in Europe all the people are our friends. We found in the course of the Revolution that many strangers served us faithfully—and that many natives took part against their Country. When foreigners after looking about for some other Country in which they can obtain more happiness, give a preference to ours, it is a proof of attachment which ought to excite our confidence and affection.

MR. RANDOLPH did not know but it might be problematical whether emigrations to this Country were on the whole useful or not: but he could never agree to the motion for disabling them for 14 years to participate in the public honours. He reminded the Convention of the language held by our patriots during the Revolution, and the principles laid down in all our American Constitutions. Many foreigners may have fixed their fortunes among us under the faith of these invitations. All persons under this description, with all others who would be affected by such a regulation, would enlist themselves under the banners of hostility to the proposed System. He would go as far as seven years, but no farther.

MR. WILSON said he rose with feelings which were perhaps peculiar; mentioning the circumstance of his not being a native, and the possibility, if the ideas of some gentlemen should be pursued, of his being incapacitated from holding a place under the very Constitution, which he had shared in the trust of making. He remarked the illiberal complexion which the motion would give to the System, and the effect which a good system would have in inviting meritorious foreigners among us, and the discouragement and mortification they must feel from the degrading discrimination, now proposed. He had himself experienced this mortification. On his removal into Maryland, he found himself, from defect of residence, under certain legal incapacities which never ceased to produce chagrin, though he assuredly did not desire and would not have accepted the offices to which they related. To be appointed to a place may be a matter of indifference. To be incapable of being appointed, is a circumstance grating and mortifying.

MR. GOUVERNEUR MORRIS. The lesson we are taught is that we should be governed as much by our reason, and as little by our feelings as possible. What is the language of Reason on this subject? That we should not be polite at the expence of prudence. There was a moderation in all things. It is said that some tribes of Indians, carried their hospitality so far as to offer to strangers their wives and daughters. Was this a proper model for us? He would admit them to his house, he would invite them to his table, would provide for them comfortable lodgings; but would not carry the complaisance so far as, to bed them with his wife. He would let them worship at the same altar, but did not choose to make Priests of them. He ran over the privileges which emigrants would enjoy among us, though they should be deprived of that of being eligible to the great offices of Government; observing that they exceeded the privileges allowed to foreigners in any part of the world; and that as every Society from a great nation down to a club had the right of declaring the conditions on which new members should be admitted, there could be no room for complaint. As to those philosophical gentlemen, those citizens of the World as they call themselves, he owned he did not wish to see any of them in our public Councils. He would not trust them. The men who can shake off their attachments to their own Country can never love any other. These attachments are the wholesome prejudices which uphold all Governments. Admit a Frenchman into your Senate, and he will study to increase the commerce of France: an Englishman, he will feel an equal bias in favor of that of England. It has been said that the Legislatures will not choose foreigners, at least improper ones. There was no knowing what Legislatures would do. Some appointments made by them, proved that every thing ought to be apprehended from the cabals practised on such occasions. He mentioned the case of a foreigner who left this State in disgrace, and worked himself into an appointment from another to Congress.

SLAVERY AND THE CONSTITUTION

August 21, 22

A contentious issue at the Philadelphia Convention was between delegates from northern states who wanted to abolish the slave trade and delegates from southern states who wanted to continue to allow it. Ultimately, one of the several compromises that paved the way for completion of the new Constitution was reached when New England states agreed to allow the slave trade to continue, while southern states agreed to drop a proposal that laws regarding commercial regulation receive a two-thirds majority in Congress.

MR. L. MARTIN proposed to vary the Sect: 4. art. VII. so as to allow a prohibition or tax on the importation of slaves. 1. as five slaves are to be counted as 3 free men in the apportionment of Representatives; such a clause would leave an encouragement to this trafic. 2. slaves weakened one part of the Union which the other parts were bound to protect: the privilege of importing them was therefore unreasonable. 3. it was inconsistent with the principles of the revolution and dishonorable to the American character to have such a feature in the Constitution.

MR. RUTLEDGE did not see how the importation of slaves could be encouraged by this Section. He was not apprehensive of insurrections and would readily exempt the other States from the obligation to protect the Southern against them.—Religion and humanity had nothing to do with this question. Interest alone is the governing principle with nations. The true question at present is whether the Southern States shall or shall not be parties to the Union. If the Northern States consult their interest, they will not oppose the

17

increase of Slaves which will increase the commodities of which they will become the carriers.

MR. ELLSWORTH was for leaving the clause as it stands. Let every State import what it pleases. The morality or wisdom of slavery are considerations belonging to the States themselves. What enriches a part enriches the whole, and the States are the best judges of their particular interest. The old confederation had not meddled with this point, and he did not see any greater necessity for bringing it within the policy of the new one. . . .

MR. PINCKNEY. South Carolina can never receive the plan if it prohibits the slave trade. In every proposed extension of the powers of the Congress, that State has expressly and watchfully excepted that of meddling with the importation of negroes. If the States be all left at liberty on this subject, S. Carolina may perhaps by degrees do of herself what is wished, as Virginia and Maryland have already done.

MR. SHERMAN was for leaving the clause as it stands. He disapproved of the slave trade; yet as the States were now possessed of the right to import slaves, as the public good did not require it to be taken from them, and as it was expedient to have as few objections as possible to the proposed scheme of Government, he thought it best to leave the matter as we find it. He observed that the abolition of Slavery seemed to be going on in the United States and that the good sense of the several States would probably by degrees compleat it. He urged on the Convention the necessity of despatching its business.

COLONEL MASON. This infernal traffic originated in the avarice of British Merchants. The British Government constantly checked the attempts of Virginia to put a stop to it. The present question concerns not the importing States alone but the whole Union. The evil of having slaves was experienced during the late war. Had slaves been treated as they might have been by the Enemy, they would have proved dangerous instruments in their hands. But their folly dealt by the slaves, as it did by the Tories. He mentioned the dangerous insurrections of the slaves in Greece and Sicily; and the instructions given by Cromwell to the Commissioners sent to Virginia, to arm the servants and slaves, in case other means of obtaining its submission should fail. Maryland and Virginia he said had already prohibited the importation of slaves expressly. North Carolina had done the same in substance. All this would be in vain if South Carolina and Georgia be at liberty to import. The Western people are already calling out for slaves for their new lands, and will fill that Country with slaves if they can be got through South Carolina and Georgia.

Slavery discourages arts and manufactures. The poor despise labor when performed by slaves. They prevent the immigration of Whites, who really enrich and strengthen a Country. They produce the most pernicious effect on manners. Every master of slaves is born a petty tyrant. They bring the judgment of heaven on a Country. As nations can not be rewarded or punished in the next world they must be in this. By an inevitable chain of causes and effects providence punishes national sins, by national calamities. He lamented that some of our Eastern brethren had from a lust of gain embarked in this nefarious traffic. As to the States being in possession of the Right to import, this was the case with many other rights, now to be properly given up. He held it essential in every point of view that the General Government should have power to prevent the increase of slavery.

Mr. Ellsworth. As he had never owned a slave, he could not judge of the effects of slavery on character: He said however that if it was to be considered in a moral light we ought to go farther and free those already in the Country.—As slaves also multiply so fast in Virginia and Maryland that it is cheaper to raise than import them, whilst in the sickly rice swamps foreign supplies are necessary, if we go no farther than is urged, we shall be unjust towards South Carolina and Georgia. Let us not intermeddle. As population increases poor laborers will be so plenty as to render slaves useless. Slavery in time will not be a speck in our Country. Provision is already made in Connecticut for abolishing it. And the abolition has already taken place in Massachussets. As to the danger of insurrections from foreign influence, that will become a motive to kind treatment of the slaves.

Mr. Pinckney. If slavery be wrong, it is justified by the example of all the world. He cited the case of Greece, Rome and other ancient States; the sanction given by France, England, Holland and other modern States. In all ages one half of mankind have been slaves. If the Southern States were let alone they will probably of themselves stop importations. He would himself as a Citizen of South Carolina vote for it. An attempt to take away the right as proposed will produce serious objections to the Constitution which he wished to see adopted.

General Pinckney declared it to be his firm opinion that if himself and all his colleagues were to sign the Constitution and use their personal influence, it would be of no avail towards obtaining the assent of their Constituents. South Carolina and Georgia cannot do without slaves. As to Virginia she will gain by stopping the importations. Her slaves will rise in value, and she has more than she wants. It would be unequal to require South Carolina and Georgia to confederate on such unequal terms. He said the Royal assent before the Revolution had never been refused to South Carolina as to Virginia. He contended that the importation of slaves would be for the interest of the whole Union. The more slaves, the more produce to employ the carrying trade; the more consumption also, and the more of this, the more of revenue for the common treasury. He admitted it to be reasonable that slaves should be dutied like other imports, but should consider a rejection of the clause as an exclusion of South Carolina from the Union.

MR. BALDWIN had conceived national objects alone to be before the Convention, not such as like the present were of a local nature. Georgia was decided on this point. That State has always hitherto supposed a General Government to be the pursuit of the central States who wished to have a vortex for every thing—that her distance would preclude her from equal advantage—and that she could not prudently purchase it by yielding national powers. From this it might be understood in what light she would view an attempt to abridge one of her favorite prerogatives. If left to herself, she may probably put a stop to the evil. As one ground for this conjecture, he took notice of the sect of which he said was a respectable class of people, who carried their ethics beyond the mere *equality of men*, extending their humanity to the claims of the whole animal creation.

MR. WILSON observed that if South Carolina and Georgia were themselves disposed to get rid of the importation of slaves in a short time as had been suggested, they would never refuse to Unite because the importation might be prohibited. As the Section now stands all articles imported are to be taxed. Slaves alone are exempt. This is in fact a bounty on that article.

MR. GERRY thought we had nothing to do with the conduct of the States as to Slaves, but ought to be careful not to give any sanction to it.

MR. DICKINSON considered it as inadmissible on every principle of honor and safety that the importation of slaves should be authorised to the States by the Constitution. The true question was whether the national happiness would be promoted or impeded by the importation, and this question ought to be left to the National Government not to the States particularly interested. If England and France permit slavery, slaves are at the same time excluded from both those Kingdoms. Greece and Rome were made unhappy by their slaves. He could not believe that the Southern States would refuse to confederate on the account apprehended; especially as the power was not likely to be immediately exercised by the General Government.

MR. WILLIAMSON stated the law of North Carolina on the subject, to wit that it did not directly prohibit the importation of slaves. It imposed a duty of £5 on each slave imported from Africa, £10 on each from elsewhere, and £50 on each from a State licensing manumission. He thought the Southern States could not be members of the Union if the clause should be rejected, and that it was wrong to force any thing down, not absolutely necessary, and which any State must disagree to.

MR. KING thought the subject should be considered in a political light only. If two States will not agree to the Constitution as stated on one side, he could affirm with equal belief on the other, that great and equal opposition would be experienced from the other States. He remarked on the exemption of slaves from duty whilst every other import was subjected to it, as an inequality that could not fail to strike the commercial sagacity of the Northern and middle States.

MR. LANGDON was strenuous for giving the power to the General Government. He could not with a good conscience leave it with the States who could then go on with the traffic, without being restrained by the opinions here given that they will themselves cease to import slaves.

GENERAL PINCKNEY thought himself bound to declare candidly that he did not think South Carolina would stop her importations of slaves in any short time, but only stop them occasionally as she now does. He moved to commit the clause that slaves might be made liable to an equal tax with other imports which he thought right and which would remove one difficulty that had been started.

MR. RUTLEDGE. If the Convention thinks that North Carolina, South Carolina and Georgia will ever agree to the plan, unless their right to import slaves be untouched, the expectation is vain. The people of those States will never be such fools as to give up so important an interest. . . .

ELECTION AND POWERS OF THE PRESIDENT

September 4, 5, 6

By early September, the Philadelphia Convention had largely approved many features of the new Constitution as it was eventually proposed to the states for ratification, but issues remained concerning the election and powers of the President, and the nature of the powers shared by the President with the Senate. On September 4, a committee presented a report which included many features close to those that were finally adopted: the electoral college, four-year terms for President and Vice President, impeachment by the House followed by trial in the Senate, and the appointment and treaty-making powers of the President with the "advice and consent" of the Senate. In the first excerpt below, Gouverneur Morris explained this committee's proposals.

MR. GOUVERNEUR MORRIS said he would give the reasons of the Committee and his own. The First was the danger of intrigue and faction if the appointment should be made by the Legislature. 2. The inconveniency of an ineligibility required by that mode in order to lessen its evils. 3. The difficulty of establishing a Court of Impeachments, other than the Senate which would not be so proper for the trial nor the other branch for the impeachment of the President, if appointed by the Legislature. 4. No body had appeared to be satisfied with an appointment by the Legislature. 5. Many were anxious even for an immediate choice by the people. 6. The indispensible necessity of making the Executive independent of the Legislature.—As the Electors would vote at the same time throughout the U.S. and at so great a distance from each other, the great evil of cabal was avoided. It would be impossible also to corrupt them. A conclusive reason for making the Senate instead of the Supreme Court the Judge of impeachments, was that the latter was to try the President after the trial of the impeachment.

COLONEL MASON confessed that the plan of the Committee had removed some capital objections, particularly the danger of cabal and corruption. It was liable however to this strong objection, that nineteen times in twenty the President would be chosen by the Senate, an improper body for the purpose.

MR. BUTLER thought the mode not free from objections, but much more so than an election by the Legislature, where as in elective monarchies, cabal faction and violence would be sure to prevail.

MR. PINCKNEY stated as objections to the mode 1. that it threw the whole appointment in fact into the hands of the Senate. 2. The Electors will be strangers to the several candidates and of course unable to decide on their comparative merits. 3. It makes the Executive re-eligible which will endanger the public liberty. 4. It makes the same body of men which will in fact elect the President his Judges in case of an impeachment.

MR. WILLIAMSON had great doubts whether the advantage of re-eligibility would balance the objection to such a dependence of the President on the Senate for his reappointment. He thought at least the Senate ought to be restrained to the *two* highest on the list.

MR. GOUVERNEUR MORRIS said the principal advantage aimed at was that of taking away the opportunity for cabal. The President may be made if thought necessary ineligible on this as well as on any other mode of election. Other inconveniences may be no less redressed on this plan than any other.

MR. BALDWIN thought the plan not so objectionable when well considered, as at first view. The increasing intercourse among the people of the States, would render important characters less and less unknown; and the Senate would consequently be less and less likely to have the eventual appointment thrown into their hands.

MR. WILSON. This subject has greatly divided the House, and will also divide people out of doors. It is in truth the most difficult of all on which we have had to decide. He had never made up an opinion on it entirely to his own satisfaction. He thought the plan on the whole a valuable improvement on the former. It gets rid of one great evil, that of cabal and corruption; and Continental Characters will multiply as we more and more coalesce, so as to enable the electors in every part of the Union to know and judge of them. It clears the way also for a discussion of the question of re-eligibility on its own merits, which the former mode of election seemed to forbid. He thought it might be better however to refer the eventual appointment to the Legislature than to the Senate, and to confine it to a smaller number than five of the Candidates. The eventual election by the Legislature would not open cabal anew, as it would be restrained to certain designated objects of choice, and as these must have had the previous sanction of a number of the States: and if the election be made as it ought as soon as the votes of the electors are opened and it is known that no one has a majority of the whole, there can be little danger of corruption. Another reason for preferring the Legislature to the Senate in this business, was that the House of Representatives will be so often changed as to be free from the influence and faction to which the permanence of the Senate may subject that branch.

MR. RANDOLPH preferred the former mode of constituting the Executive, but if the change was to be made, he wished to know why the eventual election was referred to the *Senate* and not to the *Legislature?* He saw no necessity for this and many objections to it. He was apprehensive also that the advantage of the eventual appointment would fall into the hands of the States near the Seat of Government.

MR. GOUVERNEUR MORRIS said the *Senate* was preferred because fewer could then, say to the President, you owe your appointment to us. He thought the President would not depend so much on the Senate for his re-appointment as on his general good conduct. . . .

The following are excerpts from the debate as it continued on September 5 and 6.

The Report made yesterday as to the appointment of the Executive being taken up. MR. PINCKNEY renewed his opposition to the mode, arguing 1. that the electors will not have sufficient knowledge of the fittest men, and will be swayed by an attachment to the eminent men of their respective States. Hence secondly the dispersion of the votes would leave the appointment with the Senate, and as the President's reappointment will thus depend on the Senate he will be the mere creature of that body. 3. He will combine with the Senate against the House of Representatives. 4. This change in the mode of election was meant to get rid of the ineligibility of the President a second time, whereby he will become fixed for life under the auspices of the Senate. . . .

COLONEL MASON admitted that there were objections to an appointment by the Legislature as originally planned. He had not yet made up his mind, but would state his objections to the mode proposed by the Committee. 1. It puts the appointment in fact into the hands of the Senate, as it will rarely happen that a majority of the whole votes will fall on any one candidate: and as the Existing President will always be one of the five highest, his re-appointment will of course depend on the Senate. 2. Considering the powers of the President and those of the Senate, if a coalition should be established between these two branches, they will be able to subvert the Constitution.—The great objection with him would be removed by depriving the Senate of the eventual election. He accordingly moved to strike out the words "if such number be a majority of that of the electors."

MR. WILLIAMSON seconded the motion. He could not agree to the clause without some such modification. He preferred making the highest though not having a majority of the votes, President, to a reference of the matter to the Senate. Referring the appointment to the Senate lays a certain foundation for corruption and aristocracy.

MR. GOUVERNEUR MORRIS thought the point of less consequence than it was supposed on both sides. It is probable that a majority of votes will fall on the same man. As each elector is to give two votes, more than one quarter will give a majority. Besides as one vote is to be given to a man out of the State, and as this vote will not be thrown away, one half of the votes will fall on characters eminent and generally known. Again if the President shall have given satisfaction, the votes will turn on him of course, and a majority of them will reappoint him, without resort to the Senate: If he should be disliked, all disliking him, would take care to unite their votes so as to ensure his being supplanted. . . .

MR. WILSON said that he had weighed carefully the report of the Committee for remodelling the constitution of the Executive; and on combining it with other parts of the plan, he was obliged to consider the whole as having a dangerous tendency to aristocracy; as throwing a dangerous power into the hands of the Senate. They will have in fact, the appointment of the President, and through his dependence on them, the virtual appointment to offices; among others the offices of the Judiciary Department. They are to make Treaties; and they are to try all impeachments. In allowing them thus to make the Executive and Judiciary appointments, to be the Court of impeachments, and to make Treaties which are to be laws of the land, the Legislative, Executive and Judiciary powers are all blended in one branch of the Government. The power of making Treaties involves the case of subsidies, and here as an additional evil, foreign influence is to be dreaded. According to the plan as it now stands, the President will not be the man of the people as he ought to be, but the Minion of the Senate. He cannot even appoint a tide-waiter without the Senate. He had always thought the Senate too numerous a body for making appointments to office. The Senate, will moreover in all probability be in constant Session. They will have high salaries. And with all those powers, and the President in their interest, they will depress the other branch of the Legislature, and aggrandize themselves in proportion. Add to all this, that the Senate sitting in conclave, can by holding up to their respective States various and improbable candidates, contrive so to scatter their votes, as to bring the appointment of the President ultimately before themselves. Upon the whole, he thought the new mode of appointing the President, with some amendments, a valuable improvement; but he could never agree to purchase it at the price of the ensuing parts of the Report, nor befriend a system of which they make a part.

MR. GOUVERNEUR MORRIS expressed his wonder at the observations of Mr. Wilson so far as they preferred the plan in the printed Report to the new modification of it before the House, and entered into a comparative view of the two, with an eye to the nature of Mr. Wilson's objections to the last. By the first the Senate he observed had a voice in appointing the President out of all the Citizens of the United States; by this they were limited to five candidates previously nominated to them, with a probability of being barred altogether by the successful ballot of the Electors. Here surely was no increase of power. They are now to appoint Judges nominated to them by the President. Before they had the appointment without any agency whatever of the President. Here again was surely no additional power. If they are to make Treaties as the plan now stands, the power was the same in the printed plan. If they are to try impeachments, the Judges must have been triable by them before. Wherein then lay the dangerous tendency of the innovations to establish an aristocracy in the Senate? As to the appointment of officers, the weight of sentiment in the House, was opposed to the exercise of it by the President alone; though it was not the case with himself. If the Senate would act as was suspected, in misleading the States into a fallacious disposition of their votes for a President, they would, if the appointment were withdrawn wholly from them, make such representations in their several States where they have influence, as would favor the object of their partiality.

MR. WILLIAMSON replying to Mr. Morris: observed that the aristocratic complexion proceeds from the change in the mode of appointing the President which makes him dependent on the Senate.

MR. CLYMER said that the aristocratic part to which he could never accede was that in the printed plan, which gave the Senate the power of appointing to offices.

MR. HAMILTON said that he had been restrained from entering into the discussions by his dislike of the Scheme of Government in General; but as he meant to support the plan to be recommended, as better than nothing, he wished in this place to offer a few remarks. He liked the new modification, on the whole, better than that in the printed Report. In this the President was a Monster elected for seven years, and ineligible afterwards; having great powers, in appointments to office, and continually tempted by this constitutional disqualification to abuse them in order to subvert the Government. Although he should be made re-eligible, still if appointed by the Legislature, he would be tempted to make use of corrupt influence to be continued in office. It seemed peculiarly desireable therefore that some other mode of election should be devised. Considering the different views of different States, and the different districts, Northern, Middle, and Southern, he concurred with those who thought that the votes would not be concentered, and that the appointment would consequently in the present mode devolve on the Senate. The nomination to offices will give great weight to the President. Here then is a mutual connection and influence, that will perpetuate the President, and aggrandize both him and the Senate. What is to be the remedy? He saw none better than to let the highest number of ballots, whether a majority or not, appoint the President. What was the objection to this? Merely that too small a number might appoint. But as the plan stands, the Senate may take the candidate having the smallest number of votes, and make him President.

OPPOSITION TO THE CONSTITUTION

September 7, 10, 15

As the debate on the new Constitution was winding down in September 1787, with agreements finally in place on most of the new Constitution's provisions, and many delegates eager to return to their home states, three delegates expressed their dissatisfaction with the Constitution as written and declared that they would not be signing it in its present form—Elbridge Gerry of Massachusetts, and Edmund Randolph and George Mason of Virginia. Reprinted here are excerpts from speeches by all three men delivered between September 7 and 15.

COLONEL MASON thought the office of vice president an encroachment on the rights of the Senate; and that it mixed too much the Legislative and Executive, which as well as the Judiciary departments, ought to be kept as separate as possible. He took occasion to express his dislike of any reference whatever of the power to make appointments to either branch of the Legislature. On the other hand he was averse to vest so dangerous a power in the President alone. As a method for avoiding both, he suggested that, a privy Council of six members to the president should be established; to be chosen for six years by the Senate, two out of the Eastern, two out of the middle, and two out of the Southern quarters of the Union, and to go out in rotation two every second year; the concurrence of the Senate to be required only in the appointment of Ambassadors, and in making treaties, which are more of a legislative nature. This would prevent the constant sitting of the Senate which he thought dangerous, as well as keep the departments separate and distinct. It would also save the expence of constant sessions of the Senate. He had he said always considered the Senate as too unwieldy and expensive for appointing officers, especially the smallest, such as tidewaiters etc. He had not reduced his idea to writing, but it could be easily done if it should be found acceptable. . . .

MR. RANDOLPH took this opportunity to state his objections to the System. They turned on the Senate's being made the Court of Impeachment for trying the Executive—on the necessity of three quarters instead of two thirds of each house to overrule the negative of the President—on the smallness of the number of the Representative branch—on the want of limitation to a standing army—on the general clause concerning necessary and proper laws—on the want of some particular restraint on navigation acts—on the power to lay duties on exports—on the Authority of the General Legislature to interpose on the application of the *Executives* of the States—on the want of a more definite boundary between the General and State Legislatures—and between the General and State Judiciaries—on the unqualified power of the President to pardon treasons—on the want of some limit to the power of the Legislature in regulating their own compensations. With these difficulties in his mind, what course he asked was he to pursue? Was he to promote the establishment of a plan which he verily believed would end in Tyranny? He was unwilling he said to impede the wishes and Judgment of the Convention, but he must keep himself free, in case he should be honored with a seat in the Convention of his State, to act according to the dictates of his judgment. The only mode in which his embarrassments could be removed, was that of submitting the plan to Congress to go from them to the State Legislatures, and from these to State Conventions having power to adopt, reject or amend; the process to close with another General Convention with full power to adopt or reject the alterations proposed by the State Conventions, and to establish finally the Government. . . .

MR. RANDOLPH [commenting] on the indefinite and dangerous power given by the Constitution to Congress, expressing the pain he felt at differing from the body of the Convention, on the close of the great and awful subject of their labours, and anxiously wishing for some accommodating expedient which would relieve him from his embarrassments, made a motion importing "that amendments to the plan might be offered by the State Conventions, which should be submitted to and finally decided on by another general Convention." Should this proposition be disregarded, it would he said be impossible for him to put his name to the instrument. Whether he should oppose it afterwards he would not then decide but he would not deprive himself of the freedom to do so in his own State, if that course should be prescribed by his final judgment.

COLONEL MASON seconded and followed Mr. Randolph in animadversions on the dangerous power and structure of the Government, concluding that it would end either in monarchy, or a tyrannical aristocracy; which, he was in doubt, but one or other, he was sure. This Constitution had been formed without the knowledge or idea of the people. A second Convention will know more of the sense of the people, and be able to provide a system more consonant to it. It was improper to say to the people, take this or nothing. As the Constitution now stands, he could neither give it his support or vote in Virginia; and he could not sign here what he could not support there. With the expedient of another Convention as proposed, he could sign. . . .

MR. GERRY stated the objections which determined him to withhold his name from the Constitution. 1. The duration and re-eligibility of the Senate. 2. The power of the House of Representatives to conceal their journals. 3. The power of Congress over the places of election. 4. The unlimited power of Congress over their own compensations. 5. Massachusetts has not a due share of Representatives allotted to her. 6. Three fifths of the Blacks are to be represented as if they were freemen. 7. Under the power over commerce, monopolies may be established. 8. The vice president being made head of the Senate. He could however he said get over all these, if the rights of the Citizens were not rendered insecure 1. By the general power of the Legislature to make what laws they may please to call necessary and proper. 2. Raise armies and money without limit. 3. To establish a tribunal without juries, which will be a Star-chamber as to Civil cases. Under such a view of the Constitution, the best that could be done he conceived was to provide for a second general Convention.

OBJECTIONS TO THE CONSTITUTION
OF GOVERNMENT FORMED BY THE
CONVENTION

November

George Mason was one of the Virginia delegates to the Convention and author of the "Declaration of Rights" in the Virginia Constitution of 1776. His "Objections to the Constitution," largely focusing on the absence of a Bill of Rights, was widely circulated during the Federalist/Anti-Federalist debate on ratification.

There is no Declaration of Rights; and the Laws of the general Government being paramount to the Laws and Constitutions of the several States, the Declarations of Rights in the separate States are no Security. Nor are the people secured even in the Enjoyment of the Benefits of the common law: which stands here upon no other Foundation than its having been adopted by the respective Acts forming the Constitutions of the several States.

In the House of Representatives there is not the Substance, but the Shadow only of Representation; which can never produce proper Information in the Legislature, or inspire Confidence in the People: the Laws will therefore be generally made by Men little concerned in, and unacquainted with their Effects and Consequences.[1]

The Senate have the Power of altering all Money Bills and of originating Appropriations of Money and the Salaries of the Officers of their own Appointment in Conjunction with the President of

---

[1] This Objection has been in some Degree lessened by an Amendment, often before refused, and at last made by an Erasure, after the Engrossment upon Parchment, of the word *forty*, and inserting *thirty*, in the Third Clause of the Second Section of the First Article. (Mason)

31

the United States; although they are not the Representatives of the People, or amenable to them.

These with their other great Powers (viz. their Power in the Appointment of Ambassadors and all public Officers, in making Treaties, and in trying all Impeachments) their Influence upon and Connection with the supreme Executive from these Causes, their Duration of Office, and their being a constant existing Body almost continually sitting, joined with their being one complete Branch of the Legislature, will destroy any Balance in the Government, and enable them to accomplish what Usurpations they please upon the Rights and Liberties of the People.

The Judiciary of the United States is so constructed and extended, as to absorb and destroy the Judiciaries of the several States; thereby rendering Law as tedious, intricate, and expensive, and Justice as unattainable, by a great part of the Community, as in England, and enabling the Rich to oppress and ruin the Poor.

The President of the United States has no constitutional Council (a thing unknown in any safe and regular Government): he will therefore be unsupported by proper Information and Advice; and will generally be directed by Minions and Favorites—or He will become a Tool to the Senate—or a Council of State will grow out of the principal Officers of the great Departments; the worst and most dangerous of all Ingredients for such a Council, in a free Country; for they may be induced to join in any dangerous or oppressive Measures, to shelter themselves, and prevent an Inquiry into their own Misconduct in Office; whereas had a constitutional Council been formed (as was proposed) of six Members; viz. two from the Eastern, two from the Middle, and two from the Southern States, to be appointed by Vote of the States in the House of Representatives, with the same Duration and Rotation of Office as the Senate, the Executive would always have had safe and proper Information and Advice, the President of such a Council might have acted as Vice President of the United States, pro tempore, upon any Vacancy or Disability of the chief Magistrate; and long continued Sessions of the Senate would in a great Measure have been prevented.

From this fatal Defect of a constitutional Council has arisen the improper Power of the Senate, in the Appointment of public Officers, and the alarming Dependence and Connection between that Branch of the Legislature, and the supreme Executive.

Hence also sprung that unnecessary and dangerous Officer, the Vice President; who for want of other Employment, is made President of the Senate; thereby dangerously blending the executive and legislative Powers; besides always giving to some one of the States an unnecessary and unjust Preeminence over the others.

The President of the United States has the unrestrained Power of granting Pardon for Treason; which may be sometimes exercised to screen from Punishment those whom he had secretly instigated to commit the Crime, and thereby prevent a Discovery of his own Guilt.

By declaring all Treaties supreme Laws of the Land, the Executive and the Senate have in many Cases, an exclusive Power of Legislation; which might have been avoided by proper Distinctions with Respect to Treaties, and requiring the Assent of the House of Representatives, where it could be done with Safety.

By requiring only a Majority to make all commercial and navigation Laws, the five Southern States (whose Produce and Circumstances are totally different from that of the eight Northern and Eastern States) will be ruined; for such rigid and premature Regulations may be made, as will enable the Merchants of the Northern and Eastern States not only to demand an exorbitant Freight, but to monopolize the Purchase of the Commodities at their own Price, for many years: to the great Injury of the landed Interest, and Impoverishment of the People: and the Danger is the greater, as the Gain on one Side will be in Proportion to the Loss on the other. Whereas requiring two-thirds of the members present in both Houses would have produced mutual moderation, promoted the general Interest, and removed an insuperable Objection to the Adoption of the Government.

Under their own Construction of the general Clause at the End of the enumerated powers the Congress may grant Monopolies in Trade and Commerce, constitute new Crimes, inflict unusual and severe Punishments, and extend their Power as far as they shall think proper; so that the State Legislatures have no Security for the Powers now presumed to remain to them; or the People for their Rights.

There is no Declaration of any kind for preserving the Liberty of the Press, the Trial by Jury in civil Causes; nor against the Danger of standing Armies in time of Peace.

The State Legislatures are restrained from laying Export Duties on their own Produce.

The general Legislature is restrained from prohibiting the further Importation of Slaves for twenty-odd Years; though such Importations render the United States weaker, more vulnerable, and less capable of Defense.

Both the general Legislature and the State Legislatures are expressly prohibited making ex post facto Laws; though there never was, or can be a Legislature but must and will make such Laws, when necessity and the public Safety require them; which will hereafter be a Breach of all the Constitutions in the Union, and afford precedents for other Innovations.

This Government will commence in a moderate Aristocracy; it is at present impossible to foresee whether it will, in its Operation, produce a Monarchy, or a corrupt oppressive Aristocracy; it will most probably vibrate some Years between the two, and then terminate in the one or the other.

RICHARD HENRY LEE, LETTER TO EDMUND RANDOLPH WITH OBJECTIONS TO THE CONSTITUTION

16 October 1787

During the national debate over ratification, Virginia's Richard Henry Lee wrote to the Governor of Virginia, Edmund Randolph, outlining his objections to the new Constitution. It can be seen in this important letter that many of the anti-Federalist objections to the Constitution—such as the lack of guarantees of freedom of religion, freedom of the press, the right to assembly and petition, the right to a jury trial, prohibition of unreasonable searches and seizures of property—concerned individual rights that would later, very much in response to the debate over these points during the ratification period, be permanently protected in American law under the Bill of Rights.

Richard Henry Lee (1732–1794) was a planter, merchant, politician, and member of the Virginia political aristocracy. At the Second Continental Congress in 1776, it was Lee who offered the motion to declare independence from Great Britain.

Edmund Randolph (1753–1813) was a delegate from Virginia to the Constitutional Convention of 1787 and was Governor of Virginia from 1786 to 1788.

It having been found from universal experience, that the most expressed declarations and reservations are necessary to protect the just rights and liberty of mankind from the silent powerful and ever active conspiracy of those who govern; and it appearing to be the sense of the good people of America, by the various bills or declarations of rights whereon the government of the greater number of states are founded: that such precautions are necessary to restrain and regulate the exercise of the great powers given to the rulers. In conformity with these principles, and from respect for the public sentiment on this subject, it is submitted, that the new Constitution proposed for the government of the United States be bottomed upon a declaration or bill of rights, clearly and precisely stating the principles upon which this social compact is founded, to wit:

(1)   that the rights of conscience in matters of religion ought not to be violated,

(2)   that the freedom of the press shall be secured,

(3)   that the trial by jury in criminal and civil cases, and the modes prescribed by the common law for the safety of life in criminal prosecutions shall be held sacred,

(4)   that standing armies in times of peace are dangerous to liberty, and ought not to be permitted unless assented to by two-thirds of the members composing each house of the legislature under the new Constitution,

(5)   that the elections should be free and frequent,

(6)   that the right administration of justice should be secured by the independence of the judges,

(7)   that excessive bail, excessive fines, or cruel and unusual punishments should not be demanded or inflicted,

(8)   that the right of the people to assemble peaceably for the purpose of petitioning the legislature shall not be prevented,

(9)   that the citizens shall not be exposed to unreasonable searches, seizure of their persons, houses, papers or property,

(10) and it is necessary for the good of society, that the administration of government be conducted with all possible maturity of judgment, for which reason it has been the practice of civilized nations and so determined by every state in the Union, that a council of state or privy council should be appointed to advise and assist in the arduous business assigned to the executive power. Therefore let the new Constitution be so amended as to admit the appointment of a privy council to consist of eleven members chosen by the president, but responsible for the advice they may give. For which purpose the advice given shall be entered in a council book, and signed by the giver in all affairs of great moment, and that the counselors act under an oath of office. In order to prevent the dangerous blending of the legislative and executive powers, and to secure responsibility, the privy, and not the senate, shall be joined with the president

in the appointment of all officers civil and military under the new Constitution, that the Constitution be so altered as not to admit the creation of a vice president, when duties as assigned may be discharged by the privy council, except in the instance of proceedings in the senate, which may be supplied by a speaker chosen from the body of senators by themselves as usual, that so may be avoided the establishment of a great officer of state, who is sometimes to be joined with the legislature, and sometimes administer the government, rendering responsibility difficult, besides giving unjust and needless pre-eminence to that state from whence this officer may have come,

(11) that such parts of the new Constitution be amended as provide imperfectly for the trial of criminals by a jury of the vicinage, and so supply the omission of a jury trial in civil causes or disputes about property between individuals, whereby the common law is directed, and as generally it is secured by the several state constitutions,

(12) that such parts of the new Constitution be amended as permit the vexatious and oppressive callings of citizens from their own country, and all controversies between citizens of different states and between citizens and foreigners, to be tried in a far distant court, and as it may be without a jury, whereby in a multitude of cases, the circumstances of distance and expense, may compel numbers to submit to the most unjust and ill founded demand,

(13) that in order to secure the rights of the people more effectually from violation, the power and respectability of the House of Representatives be increased, by increasing the number of delegates to that house where the popular interest must chiefly depend for protection,

(14) that the Constitution be so amended as to increase the number of votes necessary to determine questions in cases where a bare majority may be seduced by strong motives of interest to injure and oppress the minority of the community as in commercial regulations, where advantage may be taken of circumstances to ordain rigid and premature laws that will in effect amount to monopolies, to the great impoverishment of those states whose peculiar situation expose them to such injuries

"JOHN DEWITT," ESSAYS I, II, AND III

22 October 1787 / 27 October 1787 /
5 November 1787

*Addressed "To the Free Citizens of the Commonwealth of Massachusetts,"
the as yet unidentified Massachusetts political philosopher who adopted
the pseudonym "John DeWitt" (see Introduction), published five letters
in the Boston* American Herald *between October and December 1787,
which effectively presented the anti-Federalist case against a more powerful
central government for the new United States of America. The first three of
his letters, published on October 22, 27, and November 5, are reprinted
here. Despite his efforts, the Massachusetts Ratifying Convention voted
to ratify on February 6, 1788—the sixth state to ratify—by the fairly
close vote of 187 to 168.*

I
22 OCTOBER, 1787

To the Free Citizens of the Commonwealth of Massachusetts:

Whoever attentively examines the history of America, and compares
it with that of other nations, will find its commencement, its growth,
and its present situation, without a precedent.

It must ever prove a source of pleasure to the Philosopher, who ranges
the explored parts of this inhabitable globe, and takes a comparative
view, as well of the rise and fall of those nations, which have been and
are gone, as of the growth and present existence of those which are now
in being, to close his prospect with this Western world. In proportion
as he loves his fellow creatures, he must here admire and approve;

for while they have severally laid their foundations in the blood and slaughter of three, four, and sometimes, ten successive generations, from their passions have experience, every misery to which human nature is subject, and at this day present striking features of usurped power, unequal justice, and despotic tyranny. America stands completely systemised without any of these misfortunes.—On the contrary, from the first settlement of the country, the necessity of civil associations, founded upon equality, consent, and proportionate justice have ever been universally acknowledged.—The means of education always attended to, and the fountains of science brought within the reach of poverty.—Hitherto we have commenced society, and advanced in all respects resembling a family, without partial affections, or even a domestic bickering: And if we consider her as an individual, instead of an undue proportion of violent passions and bad habits, we must set her down possessed of reason, genius and virtue.—I premise these few observations because there are too many among us of narrow minds, who live in the practice of blasting the reputation of their own country.—They hold it as a maxim, that virtues cannot grow in their own soil.—They will appreciate those of a man, they know nothing about, because he is an exotic; while they are sure to depreciate those much more brilliant in their neighbours, because they are really acquainted with and know them.

Civil society is a blessing.—It is here universally known as such.—The education of every child in this country tends to promote it.—There is scarcely a citizen in America who does not wish to bring it, consistent with our situation and circumstances, to its highest state of improvement.—Nay, I may say further, that the people in general aim to effect this point, in a peaceable, laudable, and rational way. These assertions are proved by stubborn facts, and I need only resort to that moment, when, in contest with a powerful enemy, they paid such an unprecedented attention to civilization, as to select from among themselves their different conventions, and form their several constitutions, which, for their beautiful theoretical structure, caught the admiration of our enemies, and secured to us the applause of the world.—We at this day feel the effects of this disposition, and now live under a government of our own choice, constructed by ourselves, upon unequivocal principles, and requires but to be well administered to make us as happy under it as generally falls to the lot of humanity. The disturbances in the course of the year past cannot be placed as an objection to the principle I advance.—They took their rise in idleness, extravagance and misinformation, a want of knowledge of our several finances, a universal delusion at the close of the war, and in consequence thereof, a pressure of embarrassments, which checked, and in many cases, destroyed that disposition of forbearance, which ought to be exercised towards each other. These were added to the accursed practice of letting money at usury, and some few real difficulties and grievances, which our late situation unavoidably brought upon us. The issue of them, however, rather proves the position for, a very few irreclaimables excepted, we find even an anxiety to hearken to reason pervading all classes—industry and frugality increasing, and the advantages arising from good, wholesome laws, confessed by every one.—Let who will gain say it. I am confident we are in a much better situation, in all respects, than we were at this period the last year; and as fast as can be expected, consistent with the passions and habits of a free people, of men who will think for themselves, coalescing, as a correspondent observes in a late paper, under a firm, wise and efficient government. The powers vested in Congress have hitherto been found inadequate.—Who are those that have been against investing them? The people of this Commonwealth have very generally supposed it expedient, and the farmer equally with the merchant have taken steps to effect it.—A Convention from the different States for that sole purpose hath been appointed of their most respectable citizens—respectable indeed I may say for their equity, for their literature, and for their love of their country.— Their proceedings are now before us for our approbation.—The eagerness with which they have been received by certain classes of our fellow citizens, naturally forces upon us this question: Are we to adopt this Government, without an examination?—Some there are, who, literally speaking, are for pressing it upon us at all events. The name of the man who but lisps a sentiment in objection to it, is to be handed to the printer, by the printer to the public, and by the public he is to be led to execution. They are themselves stabbing its reputation. For my part, I am a stranger to the necessity for all this haste! Is it not a subject of some small importance? Certainly it is.— Are not your lives, your liberties and properties intimately involved in it?—Certainly they are. Is it a government for a moment, a day, or a year? By no means—but for ages—. Altered it may possibly be, but it is easier to correct before it is adopted.—Is it for a family, a state, or a small number of people? It is for a number no less respectable than three millions. Are the enemy at our gates, and have we not time to consider it? Certainly we have. Is it so simple in its form as to be comprehended instantly?—Every letter, if I may be allowed the expression, is an idea. Does it consist of but few additions to our present confederation, and those which have been from time to time described among us, and known to be necessary?—Far otherwise. It is a compleat system of government, and armed with every power, that a people in any circumstances ought to bestow. It is a path newly struck out, and a new set of ideas are introduced that have neither occurred or been digested.—A government for national purposes, preserving our constitution entire, hath been the only plan hitherto agitated. I do not pretend to say, but it is in theory the most unexceptionable, and in practice will be the most conducive to our happiness of any possible to be adopted:—But it ought to undergo a candid and strict examination. It is the duty of every one in the Commonwealth to communicate his sentiments to his neighbour, divested of passion, and equally so of prejudices. If they are honest and he is a real friend to his country, he will do it and embrace every opportunity to do it. If thoroughly looked into before it is adopted, the people will be more apt to approve of it in practice, and every man is a TRAITOR to himself and his posterity, who shall ratify it with his signature, without first endeavouring to understand it.—We are but yet in infancy; and we had better proceed slow than too fast.—It is much easier to dispense powers, than recall them.—The present generation will not be drawn into any system; they are too enlightened; they have not forfeited their right to a share in government, and they ought to enjoy it.

Some are heard to say, "When we consider the men who made it, we ought to take it for sterling, and without hesitation—that they were the collected wisdom of the States, and had no object but the general good."—I do not doubt all this, but facts ought not to be winked out of sight:—They were delegated from different States, and nearly equally represented, though vastly disproportionate both in wealth and numbers. They had local prejudices to combat, and in many instances, totally opposite interests to consult. Their situations, their habits, their extent, and their particular interest, varied each from the other. The gentlemen themselves acknowledge that they have been less rigid upon some points, in consequence of those difficulties than they otherwise should have been.—Others again tell you that the Convention is or will be dissolved; that we must take their proceedings in whole or reject them.—But this surely cannot be a reason for their speedy adoption; it rather works the other way. If evils are acknowledged in the composition, we ought, at least, to see whose shoulders are to bear the most; to compare ours with those of other States, and take care that we are not saddled with more than our proportion: That the citizens of Philadelphia are running mad after it, can be no argument for us to do the like:—Their situation is almost contrasted with ours; they suppose themselves a central State; they expect the perpetual residence of Congress, which of itself alone will ensure their aggrandizement: We, on the contrary, are sure to be near one of the extremes; neither the loaves or fishes will be so plenty with us, or shall we be so handy to procure them.

We are told by some people, that upon the adopting this New Government, we are to become every thing in a moment:—Our foreign and domestic debts will be as a feather; our ports will be crowded with the ships of all the world, soliciting our commerce and our produce: Our manufactures will increase and multiply; and, in short, if we STAND STILL, our country, notwithstanding, will be like the blessed Canaan, a land flowing with milk and honey. Let us not deceive ourselves; the only excellency of any government is in exact proportion to the administration of it:—Idleness and luxury will be as much a bane as ever; our passions will be equally at war with us then as now; and if we have men among us trying with all their ability to undermine our present Constitution, these very persons will direct their force to sap the vitals of the new one.—

Upon the whole, my fellow countrymen, I am as much a federal man as any person: In a federal union lies our political salvation.—To preserve that union, and make it respectable to foreign opticks, the National Government ought to be armed with all necessary powers; but the subject I conceive of infinite delicacy, and requires both ability and reflection. In discussing points of such moment, America has nothing to do with passions or hard words; every citizen has an undoubted right to examine for himself, neither ought he to be ill treated and abused, because he does not think at the same moment exactly as we do. It is true, that many of us have but our liberties to lose, but they are dearly bought, and are not the least precious in estimation:—In the mean time, is it not of infinite consequence, that we pursue inflexibly that path, which I feel persuaded we are now approaching, wherein we shall discourage all foreign importations; shall see the necessity of greater economy and industry; shall smile upon the husbandman, and reward the industrious mechanic; shall promote the growth of our own country, and wear the produce of our own farms; and, finally, shall support measures in proportion to their honesty and wisdom, without any respect to men. Nothing more is wanted to make us happy at home, and respectable abroad.

John DeWitt.

II
27 OCTOBER 1787

To the Free Citizens of the Commonwealth of Massachusetts:

In my last address upon the proceedings of the Federal Convention, I endeavored to convince you of the importance of the subject, that it required a cool, dispassionate examination, and a thorough investigation, previous to its adoption—that it was not a mere revision and amendment of our first Confederation, but a compleat System for the future government of the United States, and I may now add in preference to, and in exclusion of, all others heretofore adopted.— It is not TEMPORARY, but in its nature, PERPETUAL.—It is not designed that you shall be annually called, either to revise, correct, or renew it; but, that your posterity shall grow up under, and be governed by it, as well as ourselves.—It is not so capable of alterations as you would at the first reading suppose; and I venture to assert, it never can be, unless by force of arms. The fifth article in the proceedings, it is true, expressly provides for an alteration under certain conditions, whenever "it shall be ratified by the Legislatures of three fourths of the several States, or by Conventions in three fourths thereof, as the one or the other mode of ratification may be proposed by Congress."— Notwithstanding which, such are the *"heterogeneous materials from which this System was formed,"* such is the difference of interest, different manners, and different local prejudices, in the different parts of the United States, that to obtain that majority of three fourths to any one single alteration, essentially affecting this or any other State, amounts to an absolute impossibility. The conduct of the Delegates in dissolving the Convention, plainly speaks this language, and no other.—Their sentiments in their Letter to his Excellency the President of Congress are—that this Constitution was the result of a spirit of amity—that the parties came together disposed to concede as much as possible each to the other—that mutual concessions and compromises did, in fact, take place, and all those which could, consistent with the peculiarity of their political situation. Their dissolution enforces the same sentiment, by confining you to the alternative of taking or refusing their doings in the gross. In this view, who is there to be found among us, who can seriously assert, that this Constitution, after ratification and being practised upon, will be so easy of alteration? Where is the probability that a future Convention, in any future day, will be found possessed of a greater spirit of amity and mutual concession than the present? Where is the probability that three fourths of the States in that Convention, or three fourths of the Legislatures of the different States, whose interests differ scarcely in nothing short of every thing, will be so very ready or willing materially to change any part of this System, which shall be to the emolument of an individual State only? No, my fellow-citizens, as you are now obliged to take it in the whole, so you must hereafter administer it in whole, without the prospect of change, unless by again reverting to a state of Nature, which will be ever opposed with success by those who approve of the Government in being.

That the want of a Bill of Rights to accompany this proposed System, is a solid objection to it, provided there is nothing exceptionable in the System itself, I do not assert.—If, however, there is at any time, a propriety in having one, it would not have been amiss here. A people, entering into society, surrender such a part of their natural rights, as shall be necessary for the existence of that society. They are so precious in themselves, that they would never be parted with, did not the preservation of the remainder require it. They are entrusted in the hands of those, who are very willing to receive them, who are naturally fond of exercising of them, and whose passions are always striving to make a bad use of them.—They are conveyed by a written compact, expressing those which are given up, and the mode in which those reserved shall be secured. Language is so easy of explanation, and so difficult is it by words to convey exact ideas, that the party to be governed cannot be too explicit. The line cannot be drawn with too much precision and accuracy. The necessity of this accuracy and this precision encreases in proportion to the greatness of the sacrifice and the numbers who make it.—That a Constitution for the United States does not require a Bill of Rights, when it is considered, that a Constitution for an individual State would, I cannot conceive.— The difference between them is only in the numbers of the parties concerned; they are both a compact between the Governors and Governed, the letter of which must be adhered to in discussing their powers. That which is not expressly granted, is of course retained.

The Compact itself is a recital upon paper of that proportion of the subject's natural rights, intended to be parted with, for the benefit of adverting to it in case of dispute. Miserable indeed would be the situation of those individual States who have not prefixed to their Constitutions a Bill of Rights, if, as a very respectable, learned Gentleman at the Southward observes, "the People, when they established the powers of legislation under their separate Governments, invested their Representatives with every right and authority which they did not, in explicit terms, reserve; and therefore upon every question, respecting the jurisdiction of the House of Assembly, if the Frame of Government is silent, the jurisdiction of the House of Assembly, if the Frame of Government is silent, the jurisdiction is efficient and complete." [From James Wilson's speech of October 6, 1787] In other words, those powers which the people by their Constitutions expressly give them, they enjoy by positive grant, and those remaining ones, which they never meant to give them, and which the Constitutions say nothing about, they enjoy by tacit implication, so that by one means and by the other, they became possessed of the whole.—This doctrine is but poorly calculated for the meridian of America, where the nature of compact, the mode of construing them, and the principles upon which society is founded, are so accurately known and universally diffused. That insatiable thirst for unconditional controul over our fellow-creatures, and the facility of sounds to convey essentially different ideas, produced the first Bill of Rights ever prefixed to a Frame of Government. The people, although fully sensible that they reserved every tittle of power they did not expressly grant away, yet afraid that the words made use of, to express those rights so granted might convey more than they originally intended, they chose at the same moment to express in different language those rights which the agreement did not include, and which they never designed to part with, endeavoring thereby to prevent any cause for future altercation and the intrusion into society of that doctrine of tacit implication which has been the favorite theme of every tyrant from the origin of all governments to the present day.

The proceedings of the Convention are now handed to you by your Legislature, and the second Wednesday in January is appointed for your final answer. To enable you to give that with propriety; that your future reflections may produce peace, however opposed the present issue of your present conduct may be to your present expectations, you must determine, that, in order to support with dignity the Federal Union, it is proper and fit, that the present Confederation shall be annihilated:—That the future Congress of the United States shall be armed with the powers of Legislation, Judgment and Execution.—That annual elections in this Congress shall not be known, and the most powerful body, the Senate, in which a due proportion of representation is not preserved, and in which the smallest State has equal weight with the largest, be the longest in duration:—That it is not necessary for the public good, that persons habituated to the exercise of power should ever be reminded from whence they derive it, by a return to the station of private citizens, but that they shall at all times at the expiration of the term for which they were elected to an office, be capable of immediate re-election to that same office:—That you will hereafter risk the probability of having the Chief Executive Branch chosen from among you; and that it is wholly indifferent, both to you and your children after you, whether this future Government shall be administered within the territories of your own State, or at the distance of four thousand miles from them.—You must also determine, that they shall have the exclusive power of imposts and the duties on imports and exports, the power of laying excises and other duties, and the additional power of laying internal taxes upon your lands, your goods, your chattels, as well as your persons at their sovereign pleasure:—That the produce of these several funds shall be appropriated to the use of the United States, and collected by their own officers, armed with a military force, if a civil aid should not prove sufficient:—That the power of organizing, arming and disciplining the militia shall be lodged in them, and this through fear that they shall not be sufficiently attentive to keeping so respectable a body of men as the yeomanry of this Commonwealth, compleatly armed, organized and disciplined; they shall have also the power of raising, supporting and establishing a standing army in time of peace in your several towns, and I see not why in your several houses:—That should an insurrection or an invasion, however small, take place, in Georgia, the extremity of the Continent, it is highly expedient they should have the power of suspending the writ of Habeas Corpus in Massachusetts, and as long as they shall judge the public safety requires it:—You must also say, that your present Supreme Judicial Court shall be an Inferior Court to a Continental Court, which is to be inferior to the Supreme Court of the United States:—That from an undue bias which they are supposed to have for the citizens of their own States, they shall not be competent to determine title to your real estate, disputes which may arise upon a protested Bill of Exchange, a simple note of hand, or book debt, wherein your citizens shall be unfortunately involved with disputes of such or any other kind, with citizens either of other States or foreign States: In all such cases they shall have a right to carry their causes to the Supreme Court of the United States, whether for delay only or vexation; however distant from the place of your abode, or inconsistent with your circumstances:—That such appeals shall be extended to matters of fact as well as law, and a trial of the cause by jury you shall not have a right to insist upon.—In short, my fellow-citizens, previous to a capacity of giving a compleat answer to these proceedings, you must determine that the Constitution of your Commonwealth, which is instructive, beautiful and consistent in practice, which has been justly admired in Europe, as a model of perfection, and which the present Convention have affected to imitate, a Constitution which is especially calculated for your territory, and is made conformable to your genius, your habits, the mode of holding your estates, and your particular interests, shall be reduced in its powers to those of a City Corporation:—The skeleton of it may remain, but its vital principle shall be transferred to the new Government: Nay, you must go still further, and agree to invest the new Congress with powers, which you have yet thought proper to withhold from your own present Government.—All these, and more, which are contained in the proceedings of the Federal Convention, may be highly proper and necessary.—In this overturn of all individual governments, in this new-fashioned set of ideas, and in this total dereliction of those sentiments which animated us in 1775, the Political Salvation of the United States may be very deeply interested, but BE CAUTIOUS.

John DeWitt.

III
5 NOVEMBER 1787

To the Free Citizens of the Commonwealth of Massachusetts:

Civil liberty, in all countries, hath been promoted by a free discussion of publick measures, and the conduct of publick men. The FREEDOM OF THE PRESS hath, in consequence thereof, been esteemed one of its safe guards. That freedom gives the right, at all times, to every citizen to lay his sentiments, in a decent manner, before the people. If he will take that trouble upon himself, whether they are in point or not, his countrymen are obliged to him for so doing; for, at least, they lead to an examination of the subject upon which he writes.—If any possible situation makes it a duty, it is our present important one, for in the course of sixty or ninety days you are to approve of or reject the present proceedings of your Convention, which, if established, will certainly effect, in a greater or less degree, during the remainder of your lives, those privileges which you esteem dear to you, and not improbably those of your children for succeeding ages. Now therefore is unquestionably the proper time to examine it, and see if it really is what, upon paper, it appears to be. If with your eyes open, you deliberately accept it, however different it may prove in practice from what it appears in theory, you will have nobody to blame but yourselves; and what is infinitely worse, as I have before endeavoured to observe to you, you will be wholly without a remedy. It has many zealous advocates, and they have attempted, at least as far as their modesty would permit, to monopolize our gazettes, with their encomiums upon it. With the people they have to manage, I would hint to them, their zeal is not their best weapon, and exertions of such a kind, artful attempts to seize the moment, do seldom tend either to elucidate and explain principles, or ensure success. Such conduct ought to be an additional stimulus for those persons who are not its professed admirers, to speak their sentiments with freedom however unpopular.—Such conduct ought to inspire caution, for as a man is invariably known by his company, so is the tendency of principles known by their advocates.—Nay, it ought to lead you to enquire who are its advocates? Whether ambitious men throughout America, waiting with impatience to make it a stepping stone to posts of honour and emolument, are not of this class? Whether men who openly profess to be tired of republican governments, and sick to the heart of republican measures; who daily ridicule a government of choice, and pray ardently for one of force, are not of the same class? And, whether there are not men among us, who disapprove of it only because it is not an absolute monarchy, but who, upon the whole, are among its advocates?—In such examinations as these, you cannot mispend a proportion of the sixty days.

All contracts are to be construed according to the meaning of the parties at the time of making them. By which is meant, that mutual communications shall take place, and each shall explain to the other their ideas of the contract before them.—If any unfair practices are made use of, if its real tendency is concealed by either party, or any advantage taken in the execution of it, it is in itself fraudulent and may be avoided. There is no difference in the constitution of government.—Consent it is allowed is the spring.—The form is the mode in which the people choose to direct their affairs, and the magistrates are but trustees to put that mode in force.—It will not be denied, that this people, of any under Heaven, have a right of living under a government of their own choosing.—That government, originally consented to, which is in practice, what it purports to be in theory, is a government of choice;

on the contrary, that which is essentially different in practice, from its appearance in theory, however it may be in letter a government of choice, it never can be so in spirit. Of this latter kind appear to me to be the proceedings of the Federal Convention.—They are presented as a Frame of Government purely Republican, and perfectly consistent with the individual governments in the Union. It is declared to be constructed for national purposes only, and not calculated to interfere with domestic concerns. You are told, that the rights of the people are very amply secured, and when the wheels of it are put in motion, it will wear a milder aspect than its present one. Whereas the very contrary of all this doctrine appears to be true. Upon an attentive examination you can pronounce it nothing less, than a government which, in a few years, will degenerate to a complete Aristocracy, armed with powers unnecessary in any case to bestow, and which in its vortex swallows up every other Government upon the Continent. In short, my fellow-citizens, it can be said to be nothing less than a hasty stride to Universal Empire in this Western World, flattering, very flattering to young ambitious minds, but fatal to the liberties of the people. The cord is strained to the very utmost.—There is every spice of the SIC JUBEO possible in the composition. Your consent is requested, because it is essential to the introduction of it; after having received confirmation, your complaints may increase the whistling of the wind, and they will be equally regarded.

It cannot be doubted at this day by any men of common sense, that there is a charm in politicks. That persons who enter reluctantly into office become habitated, grow fond of it, and are loath to resign it.—They feel themselves flattered and elevated, and are apt to forget their constituents, until the time returns that they again feel the want of them.—They uniformly exercise all the powers granted to them, and ninety-nine in a hundred are for grasping at more. It is this passionate thirst for power, which has produced different branches to exercise different departments and mutual checks upon those branches. The aristocratical hath ever been found to have the most influence, and the people in most countries have been particularly attentive in providing checks against it. Let us see if it is the case here.—A President, a Senate, and a House of Representatives are proposed. The Judicial Department is at present out of the question, being separated excepting in impeachments. The Legislative is divided between the People who are the Democratical, and the Senate who are the Aristocratical part, and the Executive between the same Senate and the President who represents the Monarchial Branch.—In the construction of this System, their interests are put in opposite scales. If they are exactly balanced, the Government will remain perfect; if there is a prepondency, it will firmly prevail. After the first four years, each Senator will hold his seat for the term of six years. This length of time will be amply sufficient of itself to remove any checks that he may have upon his independency, from the fear of a future election. He will consider that it is a serious portion of his life after the age of thirty; that places of honour and trust are not generally obtained unsolicited. The same means that placed him there may be again made use of; his influence and his abilities arising from his opportunities, will, during the whole term increase those means; he will have a complete negative upon all laws that shall be general, or that shall favor individuals, and a voice in the appointment of all officers in the United States.—Thus habituated to power, and living in the daily practice of granting favors and receiving solicitations, he may hold himself completely independent of the people, and at the same time ensure his election. If there remains even a risque, the blessed assistance of a little well-distributed money, will remove it.

With respect to the Executive, the Senate excepting in nomination, have a negative upon the President, and if we but a moment attended to their situation and to his, and to the power of persuasion over the human mind, especially when employed in behalf of friends and favorites, we cannot hesitate to say, that he will be infinitely less apt to disoblige them, than they to refuse him. It is far easier for twenty to gain over one, than one twenty; besides, in the one case, we can ascertain where the denial comes from, and the other we cannot. It is also highly improbable but some of the members, perhaps a major part, will hold their seats during their lives. We see it daily in our own Government, and we see it in every Government we are acquainted with, however many the cautions, and however frequent the elections.

These considerations, added to their share above mentioned in the Executive department must give them a decided superiority over the House of Representatives.—But that superiority is greatly enhanced, when we consider the difference of time for which they are chosen. They will have become adepts in the mystery of administration, while the House of Representatives may be composed perhaps two thirds of members, just entering into office, little used to the course of business, and totally unacquainted with the means made use of to accomplish it.—Very possible also in a country where they are total strangers.— But, my fellow-citizens, the important question here arises, who are this House of Representatives? "A representative Assembly, says the celebrated Mr. Adams, is the sense of the people, and the perfection of the portrait, consists in the likeness."—Can this Assembly be said to contain the sense of the people?—Do they resemble the people in any one single feature?—Do you represent your wants, your grievances, your wishes, in person? If that is impracticable, have you a right to send one of your townsmen for that purpose?—Have you a right to send one from your county? Have you a right to send more than one for every thirty thousand of you? Can he be presumed knowing to your different, peculiar situations—your abilities to pay publick taxes, when they ought to be abated, and when increased? Or is there any possibility of giving him information? All these questions must be answered in the negative. But how are these men to be chosen? Is there any other way than by dividing the Senate into districts? May not you as well at once invest your annual Assemblies with the power of choosing them—where is the essential difference? The nature of the thing will admit of none. Nay, you give them the power to prescribe the mode. They may invest it in themselves.—If you choose them yourselves, you must take them upon credit, and elect those persons you know only by common fame. Even this privilege is denied you annually, through fear that you might withhold the shadow of control over them. In this view of the System, let me sincerely ask you, where is the people in this House of Representatives?—Where is the boasted popular part of this much admired System?—Are they not cousins-german in every sense to the Senate? May they not with propriety be termed an Assistant Aristocratical Branch, who will be infinitely more inclined to co-operate and compromise with each other, than to be the careful guardians of the rights of their constituents? Who is there among you would not start at being told, that instead of your present House of Representatives, consisting of members chosen from every town, your future Houses were to consist of but ten in number, and these to be chosen by districts?—What man among you would betray his country and approve of it? And yet how infinitely preferable to the plan proposed?—In the one case the elections would be annual, the persons elected would reside in the center of you, their interests would be yours, they would be subject to your immediate control, and nobody to consult in their deliberations.—But in the other, they are chosen for double the time, during which, however well disposed, they become strangers to the very people choosing them, they reside at a distance from you, you have no control over them, you cannot observe their conduct, and they have to consult and finally be guided by twelve other States, whose interests are, in all material points, directly opposed to yours. Let me again ask you, What citizen is there in the Commonwealth of Massachusetts, that would deliberately consent laying aside the mode proposed, that the several Senates of the several States, should be the popular Branch, and together, form one National House of Representatives?—And yet one moment's attention will evince to you, that this blessed proposed Representation of the People, this apparent faithful Mirror, this striking Likeness, is to be still further refined, and more Aristocratical four times told.—Where now is the exact balance which has been so diligently attended to? Where lies the security of the people? What assurances have they that either their taxes will not be exacted but in the greatest emergencies, and then sparingly, or that standing armies will be raised and supported for the very plausible purpose only of cantoning them upon their frontiers? There is but one answer to these questions.— They have none. Nor was it intended by the makers they should have, for meaning to make a different use of the latter, they never will be at a loss for ways and means to expend the former. They do not design to beg a second time. Knowing the danger of frequent applications to the people, they ask for the whole at once, and are now by their conduct, teazing and absolutely haunting of you into a compliance.—If you choose all these things should take place, by all means gratify them. Go, and establish this Government, which is unanimously confessed imperfect, yet incapable of alteration. Intrust it to men, subject to the same unbounded passions and infirmities as yourselves, possessed with an insatiable thirst for power, and many of them, carrying in them vices, tho' tinsel'd and concealed, yet, in themselves, not less dangerous than those more naked and exposed. But in the mean time, add an additional weight to the stone that now covers the remains of the Great WARREN and MONTGOMERY; prepare an apology for the blood and treasure, profusely spent to obtain those rights which you now so timely part with. Conceal yourselves from the ridicule of your enemies, and bring your New England spirits to a level with the contempt of mankind. Henceforth you may sit yourselves down with propriety, and say, Blessed are they that never expect, for they shall not be disappointed.

John DeWitt.

ANTI-FEDERALIST NO. 1
GENERAL INTRODUCTION: A DANGEROUS PLAN OF BENEFIT ONLY TO THE "ARISTOCRATICK COMBINATION"

Boston Gazette and Country Journal

26 November 1787

Evidence that the passions aroused by the new Constitution could run deep, the Boston Gazette and Country Journal *published this Anti-Federalist diatribe against the wealthy, the bankers, and the lawyers who, the author clearly felt, were the groups who would most profit from the new plan of government. Invoking the spirit of the Revolutionary heroes of 1775, not yet very far in the past, the author urged his readers to be concerned for their rights. He wrote, "I had rather be a free citizen of the small republic of Massachusetts, than an oppressed subject of the great American empire."*

I am pleased to see a spirit of inquiry burst the band of constraint upon the subject of the new plan for consolidating the governments of the United States, as recommended by the late Convention. If it is suitable to the genius and habits of the citizens of these states, it will bear the strictest scrutiny. The people are the grand inquest who have a right to judge of its merits.

The hideous daemon of Aristocracy has hitherto had so much influence as to bar the channels of investigation, preclude the people from inquiry and extinguish every spark of liberal information of its qualities. At length the luminary of intelligence begins to beam its effulgent rays upon this important production; the deceptive mists cast before the eyes of the people by the delusive machinations of its

53

interested advocates begins to dissipate, as darkness flies before the burning taper; and I dare venture to predict, that in spite of those mercenary declaimers, the plan will have a candid and complete examination.

Those furious zealots who are for cramming it down the throats of the people, without allowing them either time or opportunity to scan or weigh it in the balance of their understandings, bear the same marks in their features as those who have been long wishing to erect an aristocracy in this commonwealth [of Massachusetts]. Their menacing cry is for a rigid government, it matters little to them of what kind, provided it answers that description. As the plan now offered comes something near their wishes, and is the most consonant to their views of any they can hope for, they come boldly forward and demand its adoption.

They brand with infamy every man who is not as determined and zealous in its favor as themselves. They cry aloud the whole must be swallowed or none at all, thinking thereby to preclude any amendment; they are afraid of having it abated of its present rigid aspect. They have strived to overawe or seduce printers to stifle and obstruct a free discussion, and have endeavored to hasten it to a decision before the people can duly reflect upon its properties. In order to deceive them, they incessantly declare that none can discover any defect in the system but bankrupts who wish no government, and officers of the present government who fear to lose a part of their power. These zealous partisans may injure their own cause, and endanger the public tranquility by impeding a proper inquiry; the people may suspect the whole to be a dangerous plan, from such covered and designing schemes to enforce it upon them.

Compulsive or treacherous measures to establish any government whatever, will always excite jealousy among a free people: better remain single and alone, than blindly adopt whatever a few individuals shall demand, be they ever so wise. I had rather be a free citizen of the small republic of Massachusetts, than an oppressed subject of the great American empire. Let all act understandingly or not at all. If we can confederate upon terms that wilt secure to us our liberties, it is an object highly desirable, because of its additional security to the whole. If the proposed plan proves such an one, I hope it will be adopted, but if it will endanger our liberties as it stands, let it be amended; in order to which it must and ought to be open to inspection and free inquiry.

The inundation of abuse that has been thrown out upon the heads of those who have had any doubts of its universal good qualities, have been so redundant, that it may not be improper to scan the characters of its most strenuous advocates. It will first be allowed that many undesigning citizens may wish its adoption from the best motives, but these are modest and silent, when compared to the greater number, who endeavor to suppress all attempts for investigation. These violent partisans are for having the people gulp down the gilded pill blindfolded, whole, and without any qualification whatever.

These consist generally, of the noble order of C[incinnatu]s, holders of public securities, men of great wealth and expectations of public office, Bankers and Lawyers: these with their train of dependents form the Aristocratick combination. The Lawyers in particular, keep up an incessant declamation for its adoption; like greedy gudgeons they long to satiate their voracious stomachs with the golden bait. The numerous tribunals to be erected by the new plan of consolidated empire, will find employment for ten times their present numbers; these are the loaves and fishes for which they hunger. They will probably find it suited to their habits, if not to the habits of the people. There may be reasons for having but few of them in the State Convention, lest their own interest should be too strongly considered. The time draws near for the choice of Delegates. I hope my fellow-citizens will look well to the characters of their preference, and remember the Old Patriots of 75; they have never led them astray, nor need they fear to try them on this momentous occasion.

A Federalist

THE ADDRESS AND REASONS OF DISSENT OF THE MINORITY OF THE CONVENTION OF THE STATE OF PENNSYLVANIA TO THEIR CONSTITUENTS

18 December 1787

A more elaborate denunciation of the new Constitution and exposition of the anti-Federalist point of view may be found in this essay, dated December 18, 1787. It was first published in the Pennsylvania Packet and Daily Advertiser, *and widely circulated in 1787–88. The authorship of this piece has not been definitely established, but it was possibly Samuel Bryan, not a member of the Pennsylvania Convention, but the son of a prominent Pennsylvania anti-Federalist.*

It was not until after the termination of the late glorious contest, which made the people of the United States an independent nation, that any defect was discovered in the present confederation. It was formed by some of the ablest patriots in America. It carried us successfully through the war; and the virtue and patriotism of the people, with their disposition to promote the common cause, supplied the want of power in Congress.

The requisition of Congress for the five *percent,* impost was made before the peace, so early as the first of February, 1781, but was prevented taking effect by the refusal of one state; yet it is probable every state in the union would have agreed to this measure at that period, had it not been for the extravagant terms in which it was demanded. The requisition was new molded in the year 1783, and accompanied with an additional demand of certain supplementary funds for twenty-five years. Peace had now taken place, and the United States found themselves laboring under a considerable foreign and domestic debt, incurred during the war. The requisition of 1783 was commensurate with the interest of the debt, as it was then calculated; but it has been more accurately ascertained since that time. The domestic debt has been found to fall several millions of dollars short of the calculation, and it has lately been considerably diminished by large sales of the western lands. The states have been called on by Congress annually for supplies until the general system of finance proposed in 1783 should take place.

It was at this time that the want of an efficient federal government was first complained of, and that the powers vested in Congress were found to be inadequate to the procuring of the benefits that should result from the union. The impost was granted by most of the states, but many refused the supplementary funds; the annual requisitions were set at naught by some of the states, while others complied with them by legislative acts, [but] were tardy in their payments, and Congress found themselves incapable of complying with their engagements, and supporting the federal government. It was found that our national character was sinking in the opinion of foreign nations. The Congress could make treaties of commerce, but could not enforce the observance of them. We were suffering from the restrictions of foreign nations, who had shackled our commerce, while we were unable to retaliate: and all now agreed that it would be advantageous to the union to enlarge the powers of Congress; that they should be enabled in the amplest manner to regulate commerce, and to lay and collect duties on the imports throughout the United States. With this view a convention was first proposed by Virginia, and finally recommended by Congress for the different states to appoint deputies to meet in convention, "for the purposes of revising and amending the present articles of confederation, so as to make them adequate to the exigencies of the union." This recommendation the legislatures of twelve states complied with so hastily as not to consult their constituents on the subject; and though the different legislatures had no authority from their constituents for the purpose, they probably apprehended the necessity would justify the measure; and none of them extended their ideas at that time further than "revising and amending the present articles of confederation." Pennsylvania by the act appointing deputies expressly confined their powers to this object; and though it is probable that some of the members of the assembly of this state had at that time in contemplation to annihilate the present confederation as well as the constitution of Pennsylvania, yet the plan was not sufficiently matured to communicate it to the public.

The majority of the legislature of this commonwealth, were at that time under the influence of the members from the city of Philadelphia. They agreed that the deputies sent by them to convention should have no compensation for their services, which determination was calculated to prevent the election of any member who resided at a distance from the city. It was in vain for the minority to attempt electing delegates to the convention, who understood the circumstances, and the feelings of the people, and had a common interest with them. They found a disposition in the leaders of the majority of the house to choose themselves and some of their dependants. The minority attempted to prevent this by agreeing to vote for some of the leading members, who they knew had influence enough to be appointed at any rate, in hopes of carrying with them some respectable citizens of Philadelphia, in whose principles and integrity they could have more confidence; but even in this they were disappointed, except in one member; the eighth member was added at a subsequent session of the assembly.

The Continental convention met in the city of Philadelphia at the time appointed. It was composed of some men of excellent characters; of others who were more remarkable for their ambition and cunning, than their patriotism; and of some who had been opponents to the independence of the United States. The delegates from Pennsylvania were, six of them, uniform and decided opponents to the constitution of this commonwealth. The convention sat upward of four months. The doors were kept shut, and the members brought under the most solemn engagements of secrecy.[1] Some of those who opposed their going so far beyond their powers, retired, hopeless, from the convention, others had the firmness to refuse signing the plan altogether; and many who did sign it, did it not as a system they wholly approved, but as the best that could be then obtained, and notwithstanding the time spent on this subject, it is agreed on all hands to be a work of haste and accommodation.

While the gilded chains were forging in the secret conclave, the meaner instruments of despotism without, were busily employed in alarming the fears of the people with dangers which did not exist, and exciting their hopes of greater advantages from the expected plan than even the best government on earth could produce.

---

[1] The Journals of the conclave are still concealed. (Minority)

The proposed plan had not many hours issued forth from the womb of suspicious secrecy, until such as were prepared for the purpose, were carrying about petitions for people to sign, signifying their approbation of the system, and requesting the legislature to call a convention. While every measure was taken to intimidate the people against opposing it, the public papers seethed with the most violent threats against those who should dare to think for themselves, and *tar and feathers* were liberally promised to all those who would not immediately join in supporting the proposed government be it what it would. Under such circumstances petitions in favor of calling a convention were signed by great numbers in and about the city, before they had leisure to read and examine the system, many of whom, now they are better acquainted with it, and have had time to investigate its principles, are heartily opposed to it. The petitions were speedily handed into the legislature.

Affairs were in this situation when on the 28th of September last a resolution was proposed to the assembly by a member of the house who had been also a member of the federal convention, for calling a state convention, to be elected within *ten* days for the purpose of examining and adopting the proposed constitution of the United States, though at this time the house had not received it from Congress. This attempt was opposed by a minority, who after offering every argument in their power to prevent the precipitate measure, without effect, absented themselves from the house as the only alternative left them, to prevent the measure taking place previous to their constituents being acquainted with the business—That violence and outrage which had been so often threatened was now practiced; some of the members were seized the next day by a mob collected for the purpose, and forcibly dragged to the house, and there detained by force while the quorum of the legislature, *so formed,* completed their resolution. We shall dwell no longer on this subject, the people of Pennsylvania have been already acquainted therewith. We would only further observe that every member of the legislature, previously to taking his seat, by solemn oath or affirmation, declares, "that he will not do or consent to any act or thing whatever that shall have a tendency to lessen or abridge their rights and privileges, as declared in the constitution of this state." And that constitution which they are so solemnly sworn to support cannot legally be altered but by a recommendation of the council of censors, who alone are authorized to propose alterations and amendments, and even these must be published at least *six months,* for the consideration of the people.—The proposed system of government for the United States, if adopted, will [alter] and may annihilate the constitution of Pennsylvania; and therefore the legislature had no authority whatever to recommend the calling a convention for that purpose. This proceeding could not be considered as binding on the people of this commonwealth. The house was formed by violence, some of the members composing it were detained there by force, which alone would have vitiated any proceedings, to which they were otherwise competent; but had the legislature been legally formed, this business was absolutely without[2] their power.

In this situation of affairs were the subscribers elected members of the convention of Pennsylvania. A convention called by a legislature in direct violation of their duty, and composed in part of members, who were compelled to attend for that purpose, to consider of a constitution proposed by a convention of the United States, who were not appointed for the purpose of framing a new form of government, but whose powers were expressly confined to altering and amending the present articles of confederation.—Therefore the members of the continental convention in proposing the plan acted as individuals, and not as deputies from Pennsylvania.[3] The assembly who called the state convention acted as individuals, and not as the legislature of Pennsylvania; nor could they or the convention chosen on their recommendation have authority to do any [act] or thing, that can alter or annihilate the constitution of Pennsylvania (both of which will be done by the new constitution) nor are their proceedings in our opinion, at all binding on the people.

The election for members of the convention was held at so early a period and the want of information was so great, that some of us did not know of it until after it was over, and we have reason to believe that great numbers of the people of Pennsylvania have not yet had an opportunity of sufficiently examining the proposed constitution—We apprehend that no change can take place that will affect the internal government or constitution of this commonwealth, unless a majority

---

[2] [I.e., beyond.]

[3] The continental convention in direct violation of the thirteenth article of the confederation, have declared, "that the ratification of nine states shall be sufficient for the establishment of this constitution, between the states so ratifying the same."—Thus has the plighted faith of the states been sported with! They had solemnly engaged that the confederation now subsisting should be inviolably preserved by each of them, and the union thereby formed, should be perpetual, unless the same should be altered by mutual consent. (Minority)

of the people should evidence a wish for such a change; but on examining the number of votes given for members of the present state convention, we find that of upward of *seventy thousand* freemen who are entitled to vote in Pennsylvania, the whole convention has been elected by about *thirteen thousand* voters, and though *two-thirds* of the members of the convention have thought proper to ratify the proposed constitution, yet those *two-thirds* were elected by the votes of only *six thousand and eight hundred* freemen.

In the city of Philadelphia and some of the eastern counties, the junto that took the lead in the business agreed to vote for none but such as would solemnly promise to adopt the system *in toto,* without exercising their judgment. In many of the counties the people did not attend the elections as they had not an opportunity of judging of the plan. Others did not consider themselves bound by the call of a set of men who assembled at the statehouse in Philadelphia, and assumed the name of the legislature of Pennsylvania; and some were prevented from voting by the violence of the party who were determined at all events to force down the measure. To such lengths did the tools of despotism carry their outrage, that in the night of the election for members of convention, in the city of Philadelphia, several of the subscribers (being then in the city to transact your business) were grossly abused, ill-treated, and insulted while they were quiet in their lodgings, though they did not interfere, nor had anything to do with the said election, but, as they apprehend, because they were supposed to be adverse to the proposed constitution, and would not tamely surrender those sacred rights, which you had committed to their charge.

The convention met, and the same disposition was soon manifested in considering the proposed constitution, that had been exhibited in every other stage of the business. We were prohibited by an express vote of the convention, from taking any question on the separate articles of the plan, and reduced to the necessity of adopting or rejecting *in toto.*—It is true the majority permitted us to debate on each article, but restrained us from proposing amendments.— They also determined not to permit us to enter on the minutes our reasons of dissent against any of the articles, nor even on the final question our reasons of dissent against the whole. Thus situated we entered on the examination of the proposed system of government, and found it to be such as we could not adopt, without, as we conceived, surrendering up your dearest rights. We offered our objections to the convention, and opposed those parts of the plan, which, in our opinion, would be injurious to you, in the best manner we were able; and closed our arguments by offering the following propositions to the convention.

1. The right of conscience shall be held inviolable; and neither the legislative, executive, nor judicial powers of the United States shall have authority to alter, abrogate, or infringe any part of the constitution of the several states, which provide for the preservation of liberty in matters of religion.

2. That in controversies respecting property, and in suits between man and man, trial by jury shall remain as heretofore, as well in the federal courts, as in those of the several states.

3. That in all capital and criminal prosecutions, a man has a right to demand the cause and nature of his accusation, as well in the federal courts, as in those of the several states; to be heard by himself and his counsel; to be confronted with the accusers and witnesses; to call for evidence in his favor, and a speedy trial by an impartial jury of his vicinage, without whose unanimous consent, he cannot be found guilty, nor can he be compelled to give evidence against himself; and that no man be deprived of his liberty, except by the law of the land or the judgment of his peers.

4. That excessive bail ought not to be required, nor excessive fines imposed, nor cruel nor unusual punishments inflicted.

5. That warrants unsupported by evidence, whereby any officer or messenger may be commanded or required to search suspected places, or to seize any person or persons, his or their property, not particularly described, are grievous and oppressive, and shall not be granted either by the magistrates of the federal government or others.

6. That the people have a right to the freedom of speech, of writing and publishing their sentiments, therefore, the freedom of the press shall not be restrained by any law of the United States.

7. That the people have a right to bear arms for the defense of themselves and their own state, or the United States, or for the purpose of killing game; and no law shall be passed for disarming the people or any of them, unless for crimes committed, or real danger of public injury from individuals; and as standing armies in the time of peace are dangerous to liberty, they ought not to be kept up: and that the military shall be kept under strict subordination to and be governed by the civil powers.

8. The inhabitants of the several states shall have liberty to fowl and hunt in seasonable times, on the lands they hold, and on all other lands in the United States not enclosed, and in like manner to

fish in all navigable waters, and others not private property, without being restrained therein by any laws to be passed by the legislature of the United States.

9. That no law shall be passed to restrain the legislatures of the several states from enacting laws for imposing taxes, except imposts and duties on goods imported or exported, and that no taxes, except imposts and duties upon goods imported and exported, and postage on letters shall be levied by the authority of Congress.

10. That the house of representatives be properly increased in number; that elections shall remain free; that the several states shall have power to regulate the elections for senators and representatives, without being controlled either directly or indirectly by any interference on the part of the Congress; and that elections of representatives be annual.

11. That the power of organizing, arming, and disciplining the militia (the manner of disciplining the militia to be prescribed by Congress) remain with the individual states, and that Congress shall not have authority to call or march any of the militia out of their own state, without the consent of such state, and for such length of time only as such state shall agree.

That the sovereignty, freedom, and independency of the several states shall be retained, and every power, jurisdiction, and right which is not by this constitution expressly delegated to the United States in Congress assembled.

12. That the legislative, executive, and judicial powers be kept separate; and to this end that a constitutional council be appointed, to advise and assist the president, who shall be responsible for the advice they give, hereby the senators would be relieved from almost constant attendance; and also that the judges be made completely independent.

13. That no treaty which shall be directly opposed to the existing laws of the United States in Congress assembled, shall be valid until such laws shall be repealed, or made conformable to such treaty; neither shall any treaties be valid which are in contradiction to the constitution of the United States, or the constitutions of the several states.

14. That the judiciary power of the United States shall be confined to cases affecting ambassadors, other public ministers, and consuls; to cases of admiralty and maritime jurisdiction; to controversies to which the United States shall be a party; to controversies between two or more states—between a state and citizens of different states—between citizens claiming lands under grants of different states; and between

a state or the citizens thereof and foreign states, and in criminal cases, to such only as are expressly enumerated in the constitution, and that the United States in Congress assembled, shall not have power to enact laws, which shall alter the laws of descents and distribution of the effects of deceased persons, the titles of lands or goods, or the regulation of contracts in the individual states.

After reading these propositions, we declared our willingness to agree to the plan, provided it was so amended as to meet those propositions, or something similar to them: and finally moved the convention to adjourn, to give the people of Pennsylvania time to consider the subject, and determine for themselves; but these were all rejected, and the final vote was taken, when our duty to you induced us to vote against the proposed plan, and to decline signing the ratification of the same.

During the discussion we met with many insults, and some personal abuse; we were not even treated with decency, during the sitting of the convention, by the persons in the gallery of the house; however, we flatter ourselves that in contending for the preservation of those invaluable rights you have thought proper to commit to our charge, we acted with a spirit becoming freemen, and being desirous that you might know the principles which actuated our conduct, and being prohibited from inserting our reasons of dissent on the minutes of the convention, we have subjoined them for your consideration, as to you alone we are accountable. It remains with you whether you will think those inestimable privileges, which you have so ably contended for, should be sacrificed at the shrine of despotism, or whether you mean to contend for them with the same spirit that has so often baffled the attempts of an aristocratic faction, to rivet the shackles of slavery on you and your unborn posterity.

Our objections are comprised under three general heads of dissent, viz.

WE Dissent, first, because it is the opinion of the most celebrated writers on government, and confirmed by uniform experience, that a very extensive territory cannot be governed on the principles of freedom, otherwise than by a confederation of republics, possessing all the powers of internal government; but united in the management of their general, and foreign concerns.

If any doubt could have been entertained of the truth of the foregoing principle, it has been fully removed by the concession of *Mr. Wilson,* one of [the] majority on this question, and who was one of the deputies in the late general convention. In justice to him, we will give his own words; they are as follows, viz. "The extent of country for which the new constitution was required, produced another difficulty in the business of the federal convention. It is the opinion of some celebrated writers, that to a small territory, the democratical; to a middling territory (as Montesquieu has termed it) the monarchial; and to an extensive territory, the despotic form of government is best adapted. Regarding then the wide and almost unbounded jurisdiction of the United States, at first view, the hand of despotism seemed necessary to control, connect, and protect it; and hence the chief embarrassment rose. For, we know that, although our constituents would cheerily submit to the legislative restraints of a free government, they would spurn at every attempt to shackle them with despotic power."—And again in another part of his speech he continues.—"Is it probable that the dissolution of the state governments, and the establishment of one *consolidated empire* would be eligible in its nature, and satisfactory to the people in its administration? I think not, as I have given reasons to show that so extensive a territory could not be governed, connected, and preserved, but by the *supremacy of despotic power.* All the exertions of the most potent emperors of Rome were not capable of keeping that empire together, which in extent was far inferior to the dominion of America."

We dissent, secondly, because the powers vested in Congress by this constitution, must necessarily annihilate and absorb the legislative, executive, and judicial powers of the several states, and produce from their ruins one consolidated government, which from the nature of things will be *an iron-handed despotism,* as nothing short of the supremacy of despotic sway could connect and govern these United States under one government.

As the truth of this position is of such decisive importance, it ought to be fully investigated, and if it is founded to be clearly ascertained; for, should it be demonstrated, that the powers vested by this constitution in Congress will have such an effect as necessarily to produce one consolidated government, the question then will be reduced to this short issue, viz. whether satiated with the blessings of liberty; whether repenting of the folly of so recently asserting their inalienable rights, against foreign despots at the expense of so much blood and treasure, and such painful and arduous struggles, the people of America are now willing to resign every privilege of freemen, and submit to the dominion of an absolute government, that will embrace all America in one chain of despotism; or whether they will with virtuous indignation, spurn at the shackles prepared for them, and confirm their liberties by a conduct becoming freemen.

That the new government will not be a confederacy of states, as it ought, but one consolidated government, founded upon the destruction of the several governments of the states, we shall now show.

The powers of Congress under the new constitution, are complete and unlimited over the *purse* and the *sword,* and are perfectly independent of, and supreme over, the state governments; whose intervention in these great points is entirely destroyed. By virtue of their power of taxation, Congress may command the whole, or any part of the property of the people. They may impose what imposts upon commerce; they may impose what land taxes, poll taxes, excises, duties on all written instruments, and duties on every other article that they may judge proper; in short, every species of taxation, whether of an external or internal nature is comprised in section the 8th, of article the 1st, viz. "The Congress shall have power to lay and collect taxes, duties, imposts, and excises, to pay the debts, and provide for the common defense and general welfare of the United States."

As there is no one article of taxation reserved to the state governments, the Congress may monopolize every source of revenue, and thus indirectly demolish the state governments, for without funds they could not exist, the taxes, duties, and excises imposed by Congress may be so high as to render it impracticable to levy further sums on the same articles; but whether this should be the case or not, if the state governments should presume to impose taxes, duties, or excises, on the same articles with Congress, the latter may abrogate and repeal the laws whereby they are imposed, upon the allegation that they interfere with the due collection of their taxes, duties, or excises, by virtue of the following clause, part of section 8th, article 1st. viz. "To make all laws which shall be necessary and proper for carrying into execution the foregoing powers, and all other powers vested by this constitution in the government of the United States, or in any department or officer thereof."

The Congress might gloss over this conduct by construing every purpose for which the state legislatures now lay taxes, to be for the *"general welfare,"* and therefore as of their jurisdiction.

And the supremacy of the laws of the United States is established by article 6th, viz. "That this constitution and the laws of the United

States, which shall be made in pursuance thereof, and *all treaties* made, or which shall be made, under the authority of the United States, shall be the *supreme law of the land;* and *the judges in every state shall be bound thereby; anything in the constitution or laws of any state to the contrary notwithstanding."* It has been alleged that the words "pursuant to the constitution," are a restriction upon the authority of Congress; but when it is considered that by other sections they are invested with every efficient power of government, and which may be exercised to the absolute destruction of the state governments, without any violation of even the forms of the constitution, this seeming restriction, as well as every other restriction in it, appears to us to be nugatory and delusive; and only introduced as a blind upon the real nature of the government. In our opinion, "pursuant to the constitution," will be coextensive with the *will* and *pleasure* of Congress, which, indeed, will be the only limitation of their powers.

We apprehend that two coordinate sovereignties would be a solecism in politics. That therefore as there is no line of distinction drawn between the general, and state governments; as the sphere of their jurisdiction is undefined, it would be contrary to the nature of things, that both should exist together, one or the other would necessarily triumph in the fullness of dominion. However the contest could not be of long continuance, as the state governments are divested of every means of defense, and will be obliged by "the supreme law of the land" *to yield at discretion.*

It has been objected to this total destruction of the state governments, that the existence of their legislatures is made essential to the organization of Congress; that they must assemble for the appointment of the senators and president-general of the United States. True, the state legislatures may be continued for some years, as boards of appointment, merely, after they are divested of every other function, but the framers of the constitution foreseeing that the people will soon be disgusted with this solemn mockery of a government without power and usefulness, have made a provision for relieving them from the imposition, in section 4th, of article 1st, viz. "The times, places, and manner of holding elections for senators and representatives, shall be prescribed in each state by the legislature thereof; *but the Congress may at any time, by law make or alter such regulations; except as to the place of choosing senators."*

As Congress have the control over the time of the appointment of the president-general, of the senators, and of the representatives of the United States, they may prolong their existence in office, for life, by postponing the time of their election and appointment, from period to period, under various pretenses, such as an apprehension of invasion, the factious disposition of the people, or any other plausible pretense that the occasion may suggest; and having thus obtained life-estates in the government, they may fill up the vacancies themselves, by their control over the mode of appointment; with this exception in regard to the senators, that as the place of appointment for them, must, by the constitution, be in the particular state, they may depute some body in the respective states, to fill up the vacancies in the senate, occasioned by death, until they can venture to assume it themselves. In this manner, may the only restriction in this clause be evaded. By virtue of the foregoing section, when the spirit of the people shall be gradually broken; when the general government shall be firmly established, and when a numerous standing army shall render opposition vain, the Congress may complete the system of despotism, in renouncing all dependence on the people, by continuing themselves and [their] children in the government.

The celebrated *Montesquieu,* in his Spirit of Laws, volume 1, page 12th, says, "That in a democracy there can be no exercise of sovereignty, but by the suffrages of the people, which are their will; now the sovereign's will is the sovereign himself; the laws therefore, which establish the right of suffrage, are fundamental to this government. In fact, it is as important to regulate in a republic in what manner, by whom, and concerning what suffrages are to be given, as it is in a monarchy to know who is the prince, and after what manner he ought to govern." The *time, mode,* and *place* of the election of representatives, senators and president-general of the United States, ought not to be under the control of Congress, but fundamentally ascertained and established.

The new constitution, consistently with the plan of consolidation, contains no reservation of the rights and privileges of the state governments, which was made in the confederation of the year 1778, by article the 2nd, viz. "That each state retains its sovereignty, freedom, and independence, and every power, jurisdiction, and right, which is not by this confederation expressly delegated to the United States in Congress assembled."

The legislative power vested in Congress by the foregoing recited sections, is so unlimited in its nature; may be so comprehensive and boundless [in] its exercise, that this alone would be amply sufficient to annihilate the state governments, and swallow them up in the grand vortex of general empire.

The judicial powers vested in Congress are also so various and extensive, that by legal ingenuity they may be extended to every case, and thus absorb the state judiciaries, and when we consider the decisive influence that a general judiciary would have over the civil polity of the several states, we do not hesitate to pronounce that this power, unaided by the legislative, would effect a consolidation of the states under one government.

The powers of a court of equity, vested by this constitution, in the tribunals of Congress; powers which do not exist in Pennsylvania, unless so far as they can be incorporated with jury trial, would, in this state, greatly contribute to this event. The rich and wealthy suitor would eagerly lay hold of the infinite makes,[4] perplexities, and delays, which a court of chancery, with the appellate powers of the supreme court in fact as well as law would furnish him with, and thus the poor man being plunged in the bottomless pit of legal discussion, would drop his demand in despair.

In short, consolidation pervades the whole constitution. It begins with an annunciation that such was the intention. The main pillars of the fabric correspond with it, and the concluding paragraph is a confirmation of it. The preamble begins with the words, "We the people of the United States," which is the style of a compact between individuals entering into a state of society, and not that of a confederation of states. The other features of consolidation, we have before noticed.

Thus we have fully established the position, that the powers vested by this constitution in Congress, will effect a consolidation of the states under one government, which even the advocates of this constitution admit, could not be done without the sacrifice of all liberty.

We dissent, Thirdly, Because if it were practicable to govern so extensive a territory as these United States includes, on the plan of a consolidated government, consistent with the principles of liberty and the happiness of the people, yet the construction of this constitution is not calculated to attain the object, for independent of the nature of the case, it would of itself, necessarily, produce a despotism, and that not by the usual gradations, but with the celerity that has hitherto only attended revolutions effected by the sword.

To establish the truth of this position, a cursory investigation of the principles and form of this constitution will suffice.

---

[4] [*Make* can mean a fraud or swindle.]

The first consideration that this review suggests, is the omission of a BILL OF RIGHTS ascertaining and fundamentally establishing those inalienable and personal rights of men, without the full, free, and secure enjoyment of which there can be no liberty, and over which it is not necessary for a good government to have the control. The principal of which are the rights of conscience, personal liberty by the clear and unequivocal establishment of the writ of *habeas corpus*, jury trial in criminal and civil cases, by an impartial jury of the vicinage or county, with the common-law proceedings, for the safety of the accused in criminal prosecutions; and the liberty of the press, that scourge of tyrants, and the grand bulwark of every other liberty and privilege; the stipulations heretofore made in saving of them in the state constitutions, are entirely superseded by this constitution.

The legislature of a free country should be so formed as to have a competent knowledge of its constituents, and enjoy their confidence. To produce these essential requisites, the representation ought to be fair, equal, and sufficiently numerous, to possess the same interests, feelings, opinions, and views, which the people themselves would possess, were they all assembled; and so numerous as to prevent bribery and undue influence, and so responsible to the people, by frequent and fair elections, as to prevent their neglecting or sacrificing the views and interests of their constituents, to their own pursuits.

We will now bring the legislature under this constitution to the test of the foregoing principles, which will demonstrate, that it is deficient in every essential quality of a just and fair representation.

The house of representatives is to consist of sixty-five members; that is one for about every fifty-thousand inhabitants, to be chosen every two years. Thirty-three members will form a quorum for doing business, and seventeen of these, being the majority, determine the sense of the house.

The senate, the other constituent branch of the legislature, consists of twenty-six members, being *two* from each state, appointed by their legislatures every six years—fourteen senators make a quorum; the majority of whom, eight, determines the sense of the body; except in judging on impeachments, or in making treaties, or in expelling a member, when two-thirds of the senators present, must concur.

The president is to have the control over the enacting of laws, so far as to make the concurrence of *two*-thirds of the representatives and senators present necessary, if he should object to the laws.

Thus it appears that the liberties, happiness, interests, and great concerns of the whole United States, may be dependent upon the integrity, virtue, wisdom, and knowledge of twenty-five or twenty-six men.—How inadequate and unsafe a representation! Inadequate, because the sense and views of three or four millions of people diffused over so extensive a territory comprising such various climates, products, habits, interests, and opinions, cannot be collected in so small a body; and besides, it is not a fair and equal representation of the people even in proportion to its number, for the smallest state has as much weight in the senate as the largest, and from the smallness of the number to be chosen for both branches of the legislature; and from the mode of election and appointment, which is under the control of Congress; and from the nature of the thing, men of the most elevated rank in life will alone be chosen. The other orders in the society, such as farmers, traders, and mechanics, who all ought to have a competent number of their best-informed men in the legislature, will be totally unrepresented.

The representation is unsafe, because in the exercise of such great powers and trusts, it is so exposed to corruption and undue influence, by the gift of the numerous places of honor and emolument, at the disposal of the executive; by the arts and address of the great and designing; and by direct bribery.

The representation is moreover inadequate and unsafe, because of the long terms for which it is appointed, and the mode of its appointment, by which Congress may not only control the choice of the people, but may so manage as to divest the people of this fundamental right, and become self-elected.

The number of members in the house of representatives *may* be increased to one for every thirty-thousand inhabitants. But when we consider, that this cannot be done without the consent of the senate, who from their share in the legislative, in the executive, and judicial departments, and permanency of appointment, will be the great efficient body in this government, and whose weight and predominance would be abridged by an increase of the representatives, we are persuaded that this is a circumstance that cannot be expected. On the contrary, the number of representatives will probably be continued at sixty-five, although the population of the country may swell to treble what it now is; unless a revolution should effect a change.

We have before noticed the judicial power as it would effect a consolidation of the states into one government; we will now examine it, as it would affect the liberties and welfare of the people, supposing such a government were practicable and proper.

The judicial power, under the proposed constitution, is founded on the well-known principles of the *civil law,* by which the judge determines both on law and fact, and appeals are allowed from the inferior tribunals to the superior, upon the whole question; so that *facts* as well as *law,* would be reexamined, and even new facts brought forward in the court of appeals and to use the words of a very eminent Civilian—"The cause is many times another thing before the court of appeals, than what it was at the time of the first sentence."

That this mode of proceeding is the one which must be adopted under this constitution, is evident from the following circumstances:— First. That the trial by jury, which is the grand characteristic of the common law, is secured by the constitution, only in criminal cases.—Second. That the appeal from both *law* and *fact* is expressly established, which is utterly inconsistent with the principles of the common law, and trials by jury. The only mode in which an appeal from law and fact can be established, is, by adopting the principles and practice of the civil law; unless the United States should be drawn into the absurdity of calling and swearing juries, merely for the purpose of contradicting their verdicts, which would render juries contemptible and worse than useless.—Third. That the courts to be established would decide on all cases *of law and equity,* which is a well-known characteristic of the civil law, and these courts would have conusance[5] not only of the laws of the United States and of treaties, and of cases affecting ambassadors, but of all cases of *admiralty and maritime jurisdiction,* which last are matters belonging exclusively to the civil law, in every nation in Christendom.

Not to enlarge upon the loss of the invaluable right of trial by an unbiased jury, so dear to every friend of liberty, the monstrous expense and inconveniences of the mode of proceeding to be adopted, are such as will prove intolerable to the people of this country. The lengthy proceedings of the civil law courts in the chancery of England, and in the courts of Scotland and France, are such that few men of moderate fortune can endure the expense of; the poor man must therefore submit to the wealthy. Length of purse will too often prevail against right and justice. For instance, we are told by the learned judge *Blackstone,* that a question only on the property of an ox of the value of *three* guineas, originating under the civil law proceedings in Scotland, after many interlocutory orders and sentences below, was carried at length from the court of sessions, the highest

---

[5] [I.e., cognizance.]

court in that part of Great Britain, by way of *appeal* to the house of lords, where the question of law and fact was finally determined. He adds, that no pique or spirit could in the court of king's bench or common pleas at Westminster, have given continuance to such a cause for a tenth part of the time, nor have cost a twentieth part of the expense. Yet the costs in the courts of king's bench and common pleas in England, are infinitely greater than those which the people of this country have ever experienced. We abhor the idea of losing the transcendent privilege of trial by jury, with the loss of which, it is remarked by the same learned author, that in Sweden, the liberties of the commons were extinguished by an aristocratic senate; and that *trial by jury* and the liberty of the people went out together. At the same time we regret the intolerable delay, the enormous expenses, and infinite vexation to which the people of this country will be exposed from the voluminous proceedings of the courts of civil law, and especially from the appellate jurisdiction, by means of which a man may be drawn from the utmost boundaries of this extensive country to the seat of the supreme court of the nation to contend, perhaps with a wealthy and powerful adversary. The consequence of this establishment will be an absolute confirmation of the power of aristocratical influence in the courts of justice; for the common people will not be able to contend or struggle against it.

Trial by jury in criminal cases may also be excluded by declaring that the libeller for instance shall be liable to an action of debt for a specified sum thus evading the common-law prosecution by indictment and trial by jury. And the common course of proceeding against a ship for breach of revenue laws by information (which will be classed among civil causes) will at the civil law be within the resort of a court, where no jury intervenes. Besides, the benefit of jury trial, in cases of a criminal nature, which cannot be evaded, will be rendered of little value, by calling the accused to answer far from home; there being no provision that the trial be by a jury of the neighborhood or country. Thus an inhabitant of Pittsburgh, on a charge of crime committed on the banks of the Ohio, may be obliged to defend himself at the side of the Delaware, and so *vice versa:* To conclude this head: we observe that the judges of the courts of Congress would not be independent, as they are not debarred from holding other offices, during the pleasure of the president and senate, and as they may derive their support in part from fees, alterable by the legislature.

The next consideration that the constitution presents, is the undue and dangerous mixture of the powers of government: the same body possessing legislative, executive, and judicial powers. The senate is a constituent branch of the legislature, it has judicial power in judging on impeachments, and in this case unites in some measure the characters of judge and party as all the principal officers are appointed by the president-general with the concurrence of the senate and therefore they derive their offices in part from the senate. This may bias the judgments of the senators, and tend to screen great delinquents from punishment. And the senate has, moreover, various and great executive powers, viz. in concurrence with the president-general, they form treaties with foreign nations, that may control and abrogate the constitutions and laws of the several states. Indeed, there is no power, privilege, or liberty of the state governments, or of the people, but what may be affected by virtue of this power. For all treaties, made by them, are to be the "supreme law of the land: any thing in the constitution or laws of any state, to the contrary notwithstanding."

And this great power may be exercised by the president and ten senators (being two-thirds of fourteen, which is a quorum of that body). What an inducement would this offer to the ministers of foreign powers to compass by bribery *such concessions* as could not otherwise be obtained. It is the unvaried usage of all free states, whenever treaties interfere with the positive laws of the land, to make the intervention of the legislature necessary to give them operation. This became necessary, and was afforded by the parliament of Great Britain, in consequence of the late commercial treaty between that kingdom and France—As the senate judges on impeachments, who is to try the members of the senate for the abuse of this power! And none of the great appointments to office can be made without the consent of the senate.

Such various, extensive, and important powers combined in one body of men, are inconsistent with all freedom; the celebrated Montesquieu tells us, that "when the legislative and executive powers are united in the same person, or in the same body of magistrates, there can be no liberty, because apprehensions may arise, lest the same monarch or *senate* should enact tyrannical laws, to execute them in a tyrannical manner."

"Again, there is no liberty, if the power of judging be not separated from the legislative and executive powers. Were it joined with the legislative, the life and liberty of the subject would be exposed to arbitrary control; for the judge would then be legislator. Were it joined to the executive power, the judge might behave with all the violence of an oppressor. There would be an end of everything, were the same man, or the same body of the nobles, or of the people, to exercise those three powers; that of enacting laws; that of executing the public resolutions; and that of judging the crimes or differences of individuals."

The president-general is dangerously connected with the senate; his coincidence with the views of the ruling junto in that body, is made essential to his weight and importance in the government, which will destroy the independency and purity in the executive department, and having the power of pardoning without the concurrence of a council, he may screen from punishment the most [treasonable] attempts that may be made on the liberties of the people, when instigated by his enadjutors[6] in the senate. Instead of this dangerous and improper mixture of the executive with the legislative and judicial, the supreme executive powers ought to have been placed in the president, with a small independent council, made personally responsible for every appointment to office or other act, by having their opinions recorded; and that without the concurrence of the majority of the quorum of this council, the president should not be capable of taking any step.

The power of direct taxation applies to every individual, as congress, under this government, is expressly vested with the authority of laying a capitation or poll tax upon every person to any amount. This is a tax that, however oppressive in its nature, and unequal in its operation, is certain as to its produce and simple in its collection; it cannot be evaded like the objects of imposts or excise, and will be paid, because all that a man hath will he give for his head. This tax is so congenial to the nature of despotism, that it has ever been a favorite under such governments. Some of those who were in the late general convention from this state, have long labored to introduce a poll tax among us.

The power of direct taxation will further apply to every individual as congress may tax land, cattle, trades, occupations, etc. to any amount, and every object of internal taxation is of that nature that however oppressive, the people will have but this alternative, either to pay the tax, or let their property be taken, for all resistance will be vain. The standing army and select militia would enforce the collection,

For the moderate exercise of this power, there is no control left in the state governments, whose intervention is destroyed. No relief, or redress of grievances can be extended, as heretofore by them. There is not even a declaration of RIGHTS to which the people may appeal

---

[6] [Possibly meaning coconspirators]

for the vindication of their wrongs in the court of justice. They must therefore, implicitly, obey the most arbitrary laws, as the worst of them will be pursuant to the principles and form of the constitution, and that strongest of all checks upon the conduct of administration, *responsibility to the people,* will not exist in this government. The permanency of the appointments of senators and representatives, and the control the congress have over their election, will place them independent of the sentiments and resentment of the people, and the administration having a greater interest in the government than in the community, there will be no consideration to restrain them from oppression and tyranny. In the government of this state, under the old confederation, the members of the legislature are taken from among the people, and their interests and welfare are so inseparably connected with those of their constituents, that they can derive no advantage from oppressive laws and taxes, for they would suffer in common with their fellow citizens; would participate in the burdens they impose on the community, as they must return to the common level, after a short period; and notwithstanding every exertion of influence, every means of corruption, a necessary rotation excludes them from permanency in the legislature.

This large state is to have but ten members in that Congress which is to have the liberty, property, and dearest concerns of every individual in this vast country at absolute command and even these ten persons, who are to be our only guardians; who are to supersede the legislature of Pennsylvania, will not be of the choice of the people, nor amenable to them. From the mode of their election and appointment they will consist of the lordly and high-minded; of men who will have no congenial feelings with the people, but a perfect indifference for, and contempt of them; they will consist of those harpies of power, that prey upon the very vitals; that riot on the miseries of the community. But we will suppose, although in all probability it may never be realized in fact, that our deputies in Congress have the welfare of their constituents at heart, and will exert themselves in their behalf, what security could even this afford; what relief could they extend to their oppressed constituents? To attain this, the majority of the deputies of the twelve other states in Congress must be alike well-disposed; must alike forego the sweets of power, and relinquish the pursuits of ambition which from the nature of things is not to be expected. If the people part with a responsible representation in the legislature, founded upon fair, certain, and frequent elections, they have nothing left they can call their own. Miserable is the lot of that people whose every concern depends on the WILL and PLEASURE of their rulers. Our soldiers will become Janissaries, and our officers of government Bashaws;[7] in short, the system of despotism will soon be completed.

From the foregoing investigation, it appears that the Congress under this constitution will not possess the confidence of the people, which is an essential requisite in a good government; for unless the laws command the confidence and respect of the great body of the people so as to induce them to support them, when called on by the civil magistrate, they must be executed by the aid of a numerous standing army, which would be inconsistent with every idea of liberty; for the same force that may be employed to compel obedience to good laws, might and probably would be used to wrest from the people their constitutional liberties. The framers of this constitution appear to have been aware of this great deficiency; to have been sensible that no dependence could be placed on the people for their support; but on the contrary, that the government must be executed by force. They have therefore made a provision for this purpose in a permanent STANDING ARMY, and a MILITIA that may be subjected to as strict discipline and government.

A standing army in the hands of a government placed so independent of the people, may be made a fatal instrument to overturn the public liberties; it may be employed to enforce the collection of the most oppressive taxes, and to carry into execution the most arbitrary measures. An ambitious man who may have the army at his devotion, may step up into the throne, and seize upon absolute power.

The absolute unqualified command that Congress have over the militia may be made instrumental to the destruction of all liberty, both public and private; whether of a personal, civil, or religious nature.

First, the personal liberty of every man probably from sixteen to sixty years of age, may be destroyed by the power Congress have in organizing and governing of the militia. As militia they may be subjected to fines to any amount, levied in a military manner; they may be subjected to corporal punishments of the most disgraceful and humiliating kind, and to death itself, by the sentence of a court martial: To this our young men will be more immediately subjected, as a select militia, composed of them, will best answer the purposes of government.

Secondly, the rights of conscience may be violated, as there is no exemption of those persons who are conscientiously scrupulous

---

[7] [Janissaries were soldiers and Bashaws provincial governors.]

of bearing arms. These compose a respectable proportion of the community in the state. This is the more remarkable, because even when the distresses of the late war, and the evident disaffection of many citizens of that description, inflamed our passions, and when every person, who was obliged to risk his own life, must have been exasperated against such as on any account kept back from the common danger, yet even then, when outrage and violence might have been expected, the rights of conscience were held sacred.

At this momentous crisis, the framers of our state constitution made the most express and decided declaration and stipulations in favor of the rights of conscience; but now when no necessity exists, those dearest rights of men are left insecure.

Thirdly, the absolute command of Congress over the militia may be destructive of public liberty; for under the guidance of an arbitrary government, they may be made the unwilling instruments of tyranny. The militia of Pennsylvania may be marched to New England or Virginia to quell an insurrection occasioned by the most galling oppression, and aided by the standing army, they will no doubt be successful in subduing their liberty and independency; but in so doing, although the magnanimity of their minds will be extinguished, yet the meaner passions of resentment and revenge will be increased, and these in turn will be the ready and obedient instruments of despotism to enslave the others; and that with an irritated vengeance. Thus, may the militia be made the instruments of crushing the last efforts of expiring liberty, of riveting the chains of despotism on their fellow citizens, and on one another. This power can be exercised not only without violating the constitution but in strict conformity with it; it is calculated for this express purpose, and will doubtless be executed accordingly.

As this government will not enjoy the confidence of the people, but be executed by force, it will be a very expensive and burdensome government. The standing army must be numerous, and as a further support, it will be the policy of this government to multiply officers in every department; judges, collectors, tax gatherers, excise men, and the whole host of revenue officers will swarm over the land, devouring the hard earnings of the industrious. Like the locusts of old, impoverishing and defoliating all before them.

We have not noticed the smaller, nor many of the considerable blemishes, but have confined our objections to the great and essential defects; the main pillars of the constitution; which we have shown to be inconsistent with the liberty and happiness of the people, as its establishment will annihilate the state governments, and produce one consolidated government, that will eventually and speedily issue in the supremacy of despotism.

In this investigation, we have not confined our views to the interests or welfare of this state, in preference to the others. We have overlooked all local circumstances—we have considered this subject on the broad scale of the general good: we have asserted the cause of the present and future ages; the cause of liberty and mankind.

NATHANIEL BREADING, JOHN SMILIE, RICHARD BAIRD, ADAM ORTH, JOHN A. HANNA, JOHN WHITEHILL, JOHN HARRIS, ROBERT WHITEHILL, JOHN REYNOLDS, JONATHAN HOGE, NICHOLAS LUTZ, JOHN LUDWIG, ABRAHAM LINCOLN, JOHN BISHOP, JOSEPH HEISTER, JOSEPH POWEL, JAMES MARTIN, WILLIAM FINDLEY, JOHN BAIRD, JAMES EDGAR, WILLIAM TODD

"CENTINEL," NUMBER I

(ANTI-FEDERALIST NO. 47)

5 October 1787

As the political and propaganda battle over ratification of the new Constitution heated up in the Fall of 1787, Samuel Bryan, a prominent Pennsylvania anti-Federalist (see previous Note), published under the pen name "Centinel" the first of a series of newspaper articles pressing the anti-Federalist case in the Philadelphia Freeman's Journal. *The series of 18 articles ran from October 5, 1787, to April 9, 1788. The first one, reprinted here, presents the case against thinking of the Constitution's elaborate scheme of checks and balances as a workable defense of the rights and freedoms of citizens.*

I

Friends, Countrymen and Fellow Citizens,

Permit one of yourselves to put you in mind of certain *liberties* and *privileges* secured to you by the constitution of this commonwealth, and to beg your serious attention to his uninterested opinion upon the plan of federal government submitted to your consideration, before you surrender these great and valuable privileges up forever. Your present frame of government, secures to you a right to hold yourselves, houses, papers and possessions free from search and seizure, and therefore warrants granted without oaths or affirmations first made, affording sufficient foundation for them, whereby any officer or messenger may be commanded or required to search your houses or seize your persons or property, not particularly described in such warrant, shall not be granted. Your constitution further provides "that in controversies respecting property, and in suits between man and man, the parties have a right *to trial by jury, which ought to be held sacred.*" It also provides and declares, "*that the people have a right of* FREEDOM OF SPEECH, *and of* WRITING *and* PUBLISHING *their sentiments, therefore* THE FREEDOM OF THE PRESS OUGHT NOT TO BE RESTRAINED." The constitution of Pennsylvania is *yet* in existence, *as yet* you have the right to *freedom of speech,* and of *publishing your sentiments.* How long those rights will appertain to you, you yourselves are called upon to say, whether your *houses* shall continue to be your *castles;* whether your *papers,* your *persons* and your *property,* are to be held sacred and free from *general warrants,* you are now to determine. Whether the *trial by jury* is to continue as your birth-right, the freemen of Pennsylvania, nay, of all America, are now called upon to declare.

Without presuming upon my own judgment, I cannot think it an unwarrantable presumption to offer my private opinion, and call upon others for theirs; and if I use my pen with the boldness of a freeman, it is because I know that *the liberty of the press yet remains unviolated,* and *juries yet are judges.*

The late convention have submitted to your consideration a plan of a new federal government.—The subject is highly interesting to your future welfare.—Whether it be calculated to promote the great ends of civil society, viz. the happiness and prosperity of the community; it behoves you well to consider, uninfluenced by the authority of names. Instead of that frenzy of enthusiasm, that has actuated the citizens of Philadelphia, in their approbation of the proposed plan, before it was possible that it could be the result of a rational investigation into its principles; it ought to be dispassionately and deliberately examined, and its own intrinsic merit the only criterion of your patronage. If ever free and unbiased discussion was proper or necessary, it is on such an occasion.—All the blessings of liberty and the dearest privileges of freemen, are now at stake and dependent on your present conduct. Those who are competent to the task of developing the principles of government, ought to be encouraged to come forward, and thereby the better enable the people to make a proper judgment; for the science of government is so abstruse, that few are able to judge for themselves: without such assistance the people are too apt to yield an implicit assent to the opinions of those characters, whose abilities are held in the highest esteem, and to those in whose integrity and patriotism they can confide: not considering that the love of domination is generally in proportion to talents, abilities, and superior acquirements; and that the men of the greatest purity of intention may be made instruments of despotism in the hands of the *artful and designing*. If it were not for the stability and attachment which time and habit gives to forms of government, it would be in the power of the enlightened and aspiring few, if they should combine, at any time to destroy the best establishments, and even make the people the instruments of their own subjugation.

The late revolution having effaced in a great measure all former habits, and the present institutions are so recent, that there exists not that great reluctance to innovation, so remarkable in old communities, and which accords with reason, for the most comprehensive mind cannot foresee the full operation of material changes on civil polity; it is the genius of the common law to resist innovation.

The wealthy and ambitious, who in every community think they have a right to lord it over their fellow creatures, have availed themselves, very successfully, of this favorable disposition; for the people thus unsettled in their sentiments, have been prepared to accede to any extreme of government; all the distresses and difficulties they experience, proceeding from various causes, have been ascribed to the impotency of the present confederation, and thence they have been led to expect full relief from the adoption of the proposed system of government; and in the other event, immediately ruin and annihilation as a nation. These characters flatter themselves that they have lulled all distrust and jealousy of their new plan, by gaining the concurrence of the two men in whom America has the highest confidence, and now triumphantly exult in the completion of their long meditated schemes of power and aggrandisement. I would be very far from insinuating that the two illustrious personages alluded to, have not the welfare of their country at heart; but that the unsuspecting goodness and zeal of the one, has been imposed on, in a subject of which he must be necessarily inexperienced, from his other arduous engagements; and that the weakness and indecision attendant on old age, has been practised on in the other.

I am fearful that the principles of government inculcated in Mr. Adams's treatise, and enforced in the numerous essays and paragraphs in the newspapers, have misled some well designing members of the late Convention.—But it will appear in the sequel, that the construction of the proposed plan of government is infinitely more extravagant.

I have been anxiously expecting that some enlightened patriot would, ere this, have taken up the pen to expose the futility, and counteract the baneful tendency of such principles. Mr. Adams's *sine qua non* of a good government is three balancing powers, whose repelling qualities are to produce an equilibrium of interests, and thereby promote the happiness of the whole community. He asserts that the administrators of every government, will ever be actuated by views of private interest and ambition, to the prejudice of the public good; that therefore the only effectual method to secure the rights of the people and promote their welfare, is to create an opposition of interests between the members of two distinct bodies, in the exercise of the powers of government, and balanced by those of a third. This hypothesis supposes human wisdom competent to the task of instituting three co-equal orders in government, and a corresponding weight in the community to enable them respectively to exercise their several parts, and whose views and interests should be so distinct as to prevent a coalition of any two of them for the destruction of the third. Mr. Adams, although he has traced the constitution of every form of government that ever existed, as far as history affords materials, has not been able to adduce a single instance of such a government; he indeed says that the British constitution is such in theory, but this is rather a confirmation that his principles are chimerical and not to be reduced to practice. If such an organization of power were practicable, how long would it continue? not a day— for there is so great a disparity in the talents, wisdom and industry of mankind, that the scale would presently preponderate to one or the other body, and with every accession of power the means of further increase would be greatly extended. The state of society in England is much more favorable to such a scheme of government than that of America. There they have a powerful hereditary nobility, and real distinctions of rank and interests; but even there, for want of that perfect equallity of power and distinction of interests, in the three orders of government, they exist but in name; the only operative and efficient check, upon the conduct of administration, is the sense of the people at large.

Suppose a government could be formed and supported on such principles, would it answer the great purposes of civil society; if the administrators of every government are actuated by views of private interest and ambition, how is the welfare and happiness of the community to be the result of such jarring adverse interests?

Therefore, as different orders in government will not produce the good of the whole, we must recur to other principles. I believe it will be found that the form of government, which holds those entrusted with power, in the greatest responsibility to their constitutents, the best calculated for freemen. A republican, or free government, can only exist where the body of the people are virtuous, and where property is pretty equally divided; in such a government the people are the sovereign and their sense or opinion is the criterion of every public measure; for when this ceases to be the case, the nature of the government is changed, and an aristocracy, monarchy or despotism will rise on its ruin. The highest responsibility is to be attained, in a simple structure of government, for the great body of the people never steadily attend to the operations of government, and for want of due information are liable to be imposed on.—If you complicate the plan by various orders, the people will be perplexed and divided in their sentiments about the source of abuses or misconduct, some will impute it to the senate, others to the house of representatives, and so on, that the interposition of the people may be rendered imperfect or perhaps wholly abortive. But if, imitating the constitution of Pennsylvania, you vest all the legislative power in one body of men (separating the executive and judicial) elected for a short period, and necessarily excluded by rotation from permanency, and guarded from precipitancy and surprise by delays imposed on its proceedings, you will create the most perfect responsibility for then, whenever the people feel a grievance they cannot mistake the authors, and will apply the remedy with certainty and effect, discarding them at the next election. This tie of responsibility will obviate all the dangers apprehended from a single legislature, and will best secure the rights of the people.

Having premised this much, I shall now proceed to the examination of the proposed plan of government, and I trust, shall make it appear to the meanest capacity, that it has none of the essential requisites of a free government; that it is neither founded on those balancing restraining powers, recommended by Mr. Adams and attempted in the British constitution, or possessed of that responsibility to its constituents, which, in my opinion, is the only effectual security for the liberties and happiness of the people; but on the contrary, that it is a most daring attempt to establish a despotic aristocracy among freemen, that the world has ever witnessed.

I shall previously consider the extent of the powers intended to be vested in Congress, before I examine the construction of the general government.

It will not be controverted that the legislative is the highest delegated power in government, and that all others are subordinate to it. The celebrated *Montesquieu* establishes it as a maxim, that legislation necessarily follows the power of taxation. By sect. 8, of the first article of the proposed plan of government, "the Congress are to have power to lay and collect taxes, duties, imposts and excises, to pay the debts and provide for the common defence and *general welfare* of the United States; but all duties, imposts and excises, shall be uniform throughout the United States." Now what can be more comprehensive than these words; not content by other sections of this plan, to grant all the great executive powers of a confederation, and a STANDING ARMY IN TIME OF PEACE, that grand engine of oppression, and moreover the absolute control over the commerce of the United States and all external objects of revenue, such as unlimited imposts upon imports, etc.—they are to be vested with every species of *internal* taxation;—whatever taxes, duties and excises that they may deem requisite for the *general welfare,* may be imposed on the citizens of these states, levied by the officers of Congress, distributed through every district in America; and the collection would be enforced by the standing army, however grievous or improper they may be. The Congress may construe every purpose for which the state legislatures now lay taxes, to be for the *general welfare,* and thereby seize upon every object of revenue.

The judicial power by 1st sect. of article 3 "shall extend to all cases, in law and equity, arising under this constitution, the laws of the United States, and treaties made or which shall be made under their authority; to all cases affecting ambassadors, other public ministers and consuls; to all cases of admirality and maritime jurisdiction, to controversies to which the United States shall be a party, to controversies between two or more states, between a state and citizens of another state, between citizens of different states, between citizens of the same state claiming lands under grants of different states, and between a state, or the citizens thereof, and foreign states, citizens or subjects."

The judicial power to be vested in one Supreme Court, and in such Inferior Courts as the Congress may from time to time ordain and establish.

The objects of jurisdiction recited above, are so numerous, and the shades of distinction between civil causes are oftentimes so slight, that it is more than probable that the state judicatories would be wholly superceded; for in contests about jurisdiction, the federal court, as the most powerful, would ever prevail. Every person acquainted with the history of the courts in England, knows by what ingenious sophisms they have, at different periods, extended the sphere of their jurisdiction over objects out of the line of their institution, and contrary to their very nature; courts of a criminal jurisdiction obtaining cognizance in civil causes.

To put the omnipotency of Congress over the state government and judicatories out of all doubt, the 6th article ordains that "this constitution and the laws of the United States which shall be made in pursuance thereof, and all treaties made, or which shall be made under the authority of the United States, shall be the *supreme law of the land,* and the judges in every state shall be bound thereby, any thing in the constitution or laws of any state to the contrary notwithstanding."

By these sections the all-prevailing power of taxation, and such extensive legislative and judicial powers are vested in the general government, as must in their operation, necessarily absorb the state legislatures and judicatories; and that such was in the contemplation of the framers of it, will appear from the provision made for such event, in another part of it (but that, fearful of alarming the people by so great an innovation, they have suffered the forms of the separate governments to remain, as a blind). By sect. 4th of the 1st article, "the times, places and manner of holding elections for senators and representatives, shall be prescribed in each state by the legislature thereof; *but the Congress may at any time, by law, make or alter such regulations, except as to the place of chusing senators.*" The plain construction of which is, that when the state legislatures drop out of sight, from the necessary operation of this government, then Congress are to provide for the election and appointment of representatives and senators.

If the foregoing be a just comment—if the United States are to be melted down into one empire, it becomes you to consider, whether such a government, however constructed, would be eligible in so extended a territory; and whether it would be practicable, consistent with freedom? It is the opinion of the greatest writers, that a very extensive country cannot be governed on democratical principles, on any other plan, than a confederation of a number of small republics, possessing all the powers of internal government, but united in the management of their foreign and general concerns.

It would not be difficult to prove, that any thing short of despotism, could not bind so great a country under one government; and that whatever plan you might, at the first setting out, establish, it would issue in a despotism.

If one general government could be instituted and maintained on principles of freedom, it would not be so competent to attend to the various local concerns and wants, of every particular district, as well as the peculiar governments, who are nearer the scene, and possessed of superior means of information; besides, if the business of the *whole* union is to be managed by one government, there would not be time. Do we not already see, that the inhabitants in a number of larger states, who are remote from the seat of government, are loudly complaining of the inconveniencies and disadvantages they are subjected to on this account, and that, to enjoy the comforts of local government, they are separating into smaller divisions.

Having taken a review of the powers, I shall now examine the construction of the proposed general government.

Art. I. Sect. I. "All legislative powers herein granted shall be vested in a Congress of the United States, which shall consist of a senate and house of representatives." By another section, the president (the principal executive officer) has a conditional control over their proceedings.

Sect. 2. "The house of representatives shall be composed of members chosen every second year, by the people of the several states. The number of representatives shall not exceed one for every 30,000 inhabitants."

The senate, the other constituent branch of the legislature, is formed by the legislature of each state appointing two senators, for the term of six years.

The executive power by Art. 2, Sect. 1. is to be vested in a president of the United States of America, elected for four years: Sect. 2. gives him "power, by and with the consent of the senate to make treaties, provided two thirds of the senators present concur; and he shall nominate, and by and with the advice and consent of the senate, shall appoint ambassadors, other public ministers and consuls, judges of the Supreme Court, and all other officers of the United States, whose appointments are not herein otherwise provided for, and which shall be established by law," etc. And by another section he has the absolute power of granting reprieves and pardons for treason and all other high crimes and misdemeanors, except in case of impeachment.

The foregoing are the outlines of the plan.

Thus we see, the house of representatives, are on the part of the people to balance the senate, who I suppose will be composed of the *better sort,* the *well born,* etc. The number of the representatives (being only one for every 30,000 inhabitants) appears to be too few, either to communicate the requisite information, of the wants, local circumstances and sentiments of so extensive an empire, or to prevent corruption and undue influence, in the exercise of such great powers; the term for which they are to be chosen, too long to preserve a due dependence and accountability to their constituents; and the mode and places of their election not sufficiently ascertained, for as Congress have the control over both, they may govern the choice, by ordering the *representatives* of a *whole* state, to be *elected* in *one* place, and that too may be the most *inconvenient*.

The senate, the great efficient body in this plan of government, is constituted on the most unequal principles. The smallest state in the union has equal weight with the great states of Virginia, Massachusetts, or Pennsylvania.—The Senate, besides its legislative functions, has a very considerable share in the Executive; none of the principal appointments to office can be made without its advice and consent. The term and mode of its appointment, will lead to permanency; the members are chosen for six years, the mode is under the control of Congress, and as there is no exclusion by rotation, they may be continued for life, which, from their extensive means of influence, would follow of course. The President, who would be a mere pageant of state, unless he coincides with the views of the Senate, would either become the head of the aristocratic junto in that body, or its minion; besides, their influence being the most predominant, could the best secure his re-election to office. And from his power of granting pardons, he might skreen from punishment the most treasonable attempts on the liberties of the people, when instigated by the Senate.

From this investigation into the organization of this government, it appears that it is devoid of all responsibility or accountability to the great body of the people, and that so far from being a regular balanced government, it would be in practice a *permanent* ARISTOCRACY.

The framers of it, actuated by the true spirit of such a government, which ever abominates and suppresses all free enquiry and discussion, have made no provision for the *liberty of the press,* that grand *palladium of freedom,* and *scourge of tyrants;* but observed a total silence on that head. It is the opinion of some great writers, that if the liberty of the press, by an institution of religion, or otherwise, could be rendered *sacred,* even in *Turkey,* that despotism would fly before it. And it is worthy of remark, that there is no declaration of personal rights, premised in most free constitutions; and that trial by *jury* in *civil* cases is taken away; for what other construction can be put on the following, viz. Article III. Sect. 2d. "In all cases affecting ambassadors, other public ministers and consuls, and those in which a State shall be party, the

Supreme Court shall have *original* jurisdiction. In all the other cases above mentioned, the Supreme Court shall have *appellate* jurisdiction, both as to *law and fact*"? It would be a novelty in jurisprudence, as well as evidently improper to allow an appeal from the verdict of a jury, on the matter of fact; therefore, it implies and allows of a dismission of the jury in civil cases, and especially when it is considered, that jury trial in criminal cases is expressly stipulated for, but not in civil cases.

But our situation is represented to be so *critically* dreadful, that, however reprehensible and exceptionable the proposed plan of government may be, there is no alternative, between the adoption of it and absolute ruin.—My fellow citizens, things are not at that crisis, it is the argument of tyrants; the present distracted state of Europe secures us from injury on that quarter, and as to domestic dissentions, we have not so much to fear from them, as to precipitate us into this form of government, without it is a safe and a proper one. For remember, of all *possible* evils, that of *despotism* is the *worst* and the most to be *dreaded*.

Besides, it cannot be supposed, that the first essay on so difficult a subject, is so well digested, as it ought to be,—if the proposed plan, after a mature deliberation, should meet the approbation of the respective States, the matter will end; but if it should be found to be fraught with dangers and inconveniencies, a future general Convention being in possession of the objections, will be the better enabled to plan a suitable government.

> *Who's here so base, that would a bondman be?*
> *If any, speak; for him have I offended.*
> *Who's here so vile, that will not love his country?*
> *If any, speak; for him have I offended.*
> [*Julius Caesar*, Act 3, Scene 2]

Centinel.

"FEDERAL FARMER," LETTERS I AND II

8 October 1787 / 9 October 1787

A lengthy and thoughtful presentation of the anti-Federalist case against the new Constitution was issued in a series of "Letters from the Federal Farmer," and first published in the Poughkeepsie (NY) County Journal between November, 1787 and January, 1788. The five original "Federal Farmer" letters, of which we reprint the first two, were also widely circulated in pamphlet form.

An additional series of later "Federal Farmer" letters added more fuel to the fire. (The pamphlet publication carried the ponderous, but not untypical for the period title of "Observations Leading to a Fair Examination of the System of Government Proposed by the Late Convention; and to Several Essential and Necessary Alterations to It. In a Number of Letters From the Federal Farmer to the Republican.") In the past, it was generally believed that the "Federal Farmer" was likely Virginia's Richard Henry Lee, but scholarly opinion on this still unresolved question has recently pointed more strongly toward the New York anti-Federalist Melancton Smith.

I

October 8, 1787

Dear Sir,

My letters to you last winter, on the subject of a well balanced national government for the United States, were the result of free enquiry; when I passed from that subject to enquiries relative to our commerce, revenues, past administration, etc. I anticipated the anxieties I feel, on carefully examining the plan of government proposed by the convention. It appears to be a plan retaining some federal features; but to be the first important step, and to aim strongly to one consolidated government of the United States. It leaves the powers of government, and the representation of the people, so unnaturally divided between the general and state governments, that the operations of our system must be very uncertain. My uniform federal attachments, and the interest I have in the protection of property, and a steady execution of the laws, will convince you, that, if I am under any biass at all, it is in favor of any general system which shall promise those advantages. The instability of our laws increases my wishes for firm and steady government; but then, I can consent to no government, which, in my opinion, is not calculated equally to preserve the rights of all orders of men in the community. My object has been to join with those who have endeavoured to supply the defects in the forms of our governments by a steady and proper administration of them. Though I have long apprehended that fraudalent debtors, and embarrassed men, on the one hand, and men, on the other, unfriendly to republican equality, would produce an uneasiness among the people, and prepare the way, not for cool and deliberate reforms in the governments, but for changes calculated to promote the interests of particular orders of men. Acquit me, sir, of any agency in the formation of the new system; I shall be satisfied with seeing, if it shall be adopted, a prudent administration. Indeed I am so much convinced of the truth of Pope's maxim, that "That which is best administered is best," that I am much inclined to subscribe to it from experience. I am not disposed to unreasonably contend about forms. I know our situation is critical, and it behoves us to make the best of it. A federal government of some sort is necessary. We have suffered the present to languish; and whether the confederation was capable or not originally of answering any valuable purposes, it is now but of little importance. I will pass by the men, and states, who have been particularly instrumental in preparing the way for a change, and, perhaps, for governments not very favourable to the people at large. A constitution is now presented which we may reject, or which we may accept, with or without amendments; and to which point we ought to direct our exertions, is the question. To determine this question, with propriety, we must attentively examine the system itself, and the probable consequences of either step. This I shall endeavour to do, so far as I am able, with candor and fairness;

and leave you to decide upon the propriety of my opinions, the weight of my reasons, and how far my conclusions are well drawn. Whatever may be the conduct of others, on the present occasion, I do not mean, hastily and positively to decide on the merits of the constitution proposed. I shall be open to conviction, and always disposed to adopt that which, all things considered, shall appear to me to be most for the happiness of the community. It must be granted, that if men hastily and blindly adopt a system of government, they will as hastily and as blindly be led to alter or abolish it; and changes must ensue, one after another, till the peaceable and better part of the community will grow weary with changes, tumults and disorders, and be disposed to accept any government, however despotic, that shall promise stability and firmness.

The first principal question that occurs, is, Whether, considering our situation, we ought to precipitate the adoption of the proposed constitution? If we remain cool and temperate, we are in no immediate danger of any commotions; we are in a state of perfect peace, and in no danger of invasions; the state governments are in the full exercise of their powers; and our governments answer all present exigencies, except the regulation of trade, securing credit, in some cases, and providing for the interest, in some instances, of the public debts; and whether we adopt a change, three or nine months hence, can make but little odds with the private circumstances of individuals; their happiness and prosperity, after all, depend principally upon their own exertions. We are hardly recovered from a long and distressing war: The farmers, fishmen etc. have not yet fully repaired the waste made by it. Industry and frugality are again assuming their proper station. Private debts are lessened, and public debts incurred by the war have been, by various ways, diminished; and the public lands have now become a productive source for diminishing them much more. I know uneasy men, who wish very much to precipitate, do not admit all these facts; but they are facts well known to all men who are thoroughly informed in the affairs of this country. It must, however, be admitted, that our federal system is defective, and that some of the state governments are not well administered; but, then, we impute to the defects in our governments many evils and embarrassments which are most clearly the result of the late war. We must allow men to conduct on the present occasion, as on all similar ones. They will urge a thousand pretences to answer their purposes on both sides. When we want a man to change his condition, we describe it as miserable, wretched, and despised; and draw a pleasing picture of that which we would have him assume. And when we wish the contrary, we reverse our descriptions. Whenever a clamor is raised, and idle men get to work, it is highly necessary to examine facts carefully, and without unreasonably suspecting men of falsehood, to examine, and enquire attentively, under what impressions they act. It is too often the case in political concerns, that men state facts not as they are, but as they wish them to be; and almost every man, by calling to mind past scenes, will find this to be true.

Nothing but the passions of ambitious, impatient, or disorderly men, I conceive, will plunge us into commotions, if time should be taken fully to examine and consider the system proposed. Men who feel easy in their circumstances, and such as are not sanguine in their expectations relative to the consequences of the proposed change, will remain quiet under the existing governments. Many commercial and monied men, who are uneasy, not without just cause, ought to be respected; and, by no means, unreasonably disappointed in their expectations and hopes; but as to those who expect employments under the new constitution; as to those weak and ardent men who always expect to be gainers by revolutions, and whose lot it generally is to get out of one difficulty into another, they are very little to be regarded: and as to those who designedly avail themselves of this weakness and ardor, they are to be despised. It is natural for men, who wish to hasten the adoption of a measure, to tell us, now is the crisis—now is the critical moment which must be seized, or all will be lost: and to shut the door against free enquiry, whenever conscious the thing presented has defects in it, which time and investigation will probably discover. This has been the custom of tyrants and their dependants in all ages. If it is true, what has been so often said, that the people of this country cannot change their condition for the worse, I presume it still behoves them to endeavour deliberately to change it for the better. The fickle and ardent, in any community, are the proper tools for establishing despotic government. But it is deliberate and thinking men, who must establish and secure governments on free principles. Before they decide on the plan proposed, they will enquire whether it will probably be a blessing or a curse to this people.

The present moment discovers a new face in our affairs. Our object has been all along, to reform our federal system, and to strengthen our governments—to establish peace, order and justice in the community—but a new object now presents. The plan of government now proposed is evidently calculated totally to change, in time, our condition as a people. Instead of being thirteen republics, under a federal head, it is clearly designed to make us one consolidated government. Of this, I think, I shall fully convince you, in my following letters on this subject. This consolidation of the states has been the object of several men in this country for some time past. Whether such a change can ever be effected in any manner; whether it can be effected without convulsions and civil wars; whether such a change will not totally destroy the liberties of this country—time only can determine.

To have a just idea of the government before us, and to shew that a consolidated one is the object in view, it is necessary not only to examine the plan, but also its history, and the politics of its particular friends.

The confederation was formed when great confidence was placed in the voluntary exertions of individuals, and of the respective states; and the framers of it, to guard against usurpation, so limited and checked the powers, that, in many respects, they are inadequate to the exigencies of the union. We find, therefore, members of congress urging alterations in the federal system almost as soon as it was adopted. It was early proposed to vest congress with powers to levy an impost, to regulate trade, etc., but such was known to be the caution of the states in parting with power, that the vestment, even of these, was proposed to be under several checks and limitations. During the war, the general confusion, and the introduction of paper money, infused in the minds of people vague ideas respecting government and credit. We expected too much from the return of peace, and of course we have been disappointed. Our governments have been new and unsettled; and several legislatures, by making tender, suspension, and paper money laws, have given just cause of uneasiness to creditors. By these and other causes, several orders of men in the community have been prepared, by degrees, for a change of government; and this very abuse of power in the legislatures, which, in some cases, has been charged upon the democratic part of the community, has furnished aristocratical men with those very weapons, and those very means, with which, in great measure, they are rapidly effecting their favourite object. And should an oppressive government be the consequence of the proposed change, posterity may reproach not only a few overbearing unprincipled men, but those parties in the states which have misused their powers.

The conduct of several legislatures, touching paper money, and tender laws, has prepared many honest men for changes in government, which otherwise they would not have thought of—when by the evils, on the one hand, and by the secret instigations of artful men, on the other, the minds of men were become sufficiently uneasy, a bold step was taken, which is usually followed by a revolution, or a civil war. A general convention for mere commercial purposes was moved for—the authors of this measure saw that the people's attention was turned solely to the amendment of the federal system; and that, had the idea of a total change been started, probably no state would have appointed members to the convention. The idea of destroying, ultimately, the state government, and forming one consolidated system, could not have been admitted—a convention, therefore, merely for vesting in congress power to regulate trade was proposed. This was pleasing to the commercial towns; and the landed people had little or no concern about it. September, 1786, a few men from the middle states met at Annapolis, and hastily proposed a convention to be held in May, 1787, for the purpose, generally, of amending the confederation—this was done before the delegates of Massachusetts, and of the other states arrived—still not a word was said about destroying the old constitution, and making a new one.— The states still unsuspecting, and not aware that they were passing the Rubicon, appointed members to the new convention, for the sole and express purpose of revising and amending the confederation— and, probably, not one man in ten thousand in the United States, till within these ten or twelve days, had an idea that the old ship was to be destroyed, and he put to the alternative of embarking in the new ship presented, or of being left in danger of sinking.—The States, I believe, universally supposed the convention would report alterations in the confederation, which would pass an examination in congress, and after being agreed to there, would be confirmed by all the legislatures, or be rejected. Virginia made a very respectable appointment, and placed at the head of it the first man in America: In this appointment there was a mixture of political characters; but Pennsylvania appointed principally those men who are esteemed aristocratical. Here the favourite moment for changing the government was evidently discerned by a few men, who seized it with address. Ten other states appointed, and though they chose men principally connected with commerce and the judicial department yet they appointed many good republican characters—had they all attended we should now see, I am persuaded a better system presented. The non-attendace of eight or nine men, who were appointed members of the convention, I shall ever consider as a very unfortunate event to the United States.—Had they attended, I am pretty clear, that the result of the convention would not have had that strong tendency to aristocracy now discernable in every part of the plan. There would not have been so great an accumulation of powers, especially as to the internal police of the country, in a few hands, as the constitution reported proposes to vest in them—the young visionary men, and the consolidating aristocracy, would have been more restrained than they have been. Eleven states met in the convention, and after four months' close attention presented the new constitution, to be adopted or rejected by the people. The uneasy and fickle part of the community may be prepared to receive any form of government; but, I presume, the enlightened and substantial part will give any constitution presented for their adoption, a candid and thorough examination; and silence those designing or empty men, who weakly and rashly attempt to precipitate the adoption of a system of so much importance.—We shall view the convention with proper respect—and, at the same time, that we reflect there were men of abilities and integrity in it, we must recollect how disproportionably the democratic and aristocratic parts of the community were represented.—Perhaps the judicious friends and opposers of the new constitution will agree, that it is best to let it rest solely on its own merits, or be condemned for its own defects.

In the first place, I shall premise, that the plan proposed is a plan of accommodation—and that it is in this way only, and by giving up a part of our opinions, that we can ever expect to obtain a government founded in freedom and compact. This circumstance candid men will always keep in view, in the discussion of this subject.

The plan proposed appears to be partly federal, but principally however, calculated ultimately to make the states one consolidated government.

The first interesting question, therefore suggested, is, how far the states can be consolidated into one entire government on free principles. In considering this question extensive objects are to be taken into view, and important changes in the forms of government to be carefully attended to in all their consequences. The happiness of the people at large must be the great object with every honest statesman, and he will direct every movement to this point. If we are so situated as a people, as not to be able to enjoy equal happiness and advantages under one government, the consolidation of the states cannot be admitted.

There are three different forms of free government under which the United States may exist as one nation; and now is, perhaps, the time to determine to which we will direct our views. 1. Distinct republics connected under a federal head. In this case the respective state governments must be the principal guardians of the people's rights, and exclusively regulate their internal police; in them must rest the balance of government. The congress of the states, or federal head, must consist of delegates amenable to, and removeable by the respective states: This congress must have general directing powers; powers to require men and monies of the states; to make treaties, peace and war; to direct the operations of armies, etc. Under this federal modification of government, the powers of congress would be rather advisary or recommendatory than coercive. 2. We may do away the several state governments, and form or consolidate all the states into one entire government, with one executive, one judiciary, and one legislature, consisting of senators and representatives collected from all parts of the union: In this case there would be a compleat consolidation of the states. 3. We may consolidate the states as to certain national objects, and leave them severally distinct independent republics, as to internal police generally. Let the general government consist of an executive, a judiciary, and balanced legislature, and its powers extend exclusively to all foreign concerns, causes arising on the seas to commerce, imports, armies, navies, Indian affairs, peace and war, and to a few internal concerns of the community; to the coin, post-offices, weights and measures, a general plan for the militia, to naturalization, *and, perhaps to bankruptcies,* leaving the internal police of the community, in other respects, exclusively to the state governments; as the administration of justice in all causes arising internally, the laying and collecting of internal taxes, and the forming of the militia according to a general plan prescribed. In this case there would be a compleat consolidation, *quoad* certain objects only.

Touching the first, or federal plan, I do not think much can be said in its favor: The sovereignty of the nation, without coercive and efficient powers to collect the strength of it, cannot always be depended on to answer the purposes of government; and in a congress of representatives of sovereign states, there must necessarily be an unreasonable mixture of powers in the same hands.

As to the second, or compleat consolidating plan, it deserves to be carefully considered at this time, by every American: If it be impracticable, it is a fatal error to model our governments, directing our views ultimately to it.

The third plan, or partial consolidation, is, in my opinion, the only one that can secure the freedom and happiness of this people. I once had some general ideas that the second plan was practicable, but from long attention, and the proceedings of the convention, I am fully satisfied, that this third plan is the only one we can with safety and propriety proceed upon. Making this the standard to point out, with candor and fairness, the parts of the new constitution which appear to be improper, is my object. The convention appears to have proposed the partial consolidation evidently with a view to collect all powers ultimately, in the United States into one entire government; and from its views in this respect, and from the tenacity of the small states to have an equal vote in the senate, probably originated the greatest defects in the proposed plan.

Independent of the opinions of many great authors, that a free elective government cannot be extended over large territories, a few reflections must evince, that one government and general legislation alone, never can extend equal benefits to all parts of the United States: Different laws, customs, and opinions exist in the different states, which by a uniform system of laws would be unreasonably invaded. The United States contain about a million of square miles, and in half a century will, probably, contain ten millions of people; and from the center to the extremes is about 800 miles.

Before we do away the state governments, or adopt measures that will tend to abolish them, and to consolidate the states into one entire government, several principles should be considered and facts ascertained:—These, and my examination into the essential parts of the proposed plan, I shall pursue in my next.

II

October 9, 1787

Dear Sir,

The essential parts of a free and good government are a full and equal representation of the people in the legislature, and the jury trial of the vicinage in the administration of justice—a full and equal representation, is that which possesses the same interests, feelings, opinions, and views the people themselves would were they all assembled—a fair representation, therefore, should be so regulated, that every order of men in the community, according to the common course of elections, can have a share in it—in order to allow professional men, merchants, traders, farmers, mechanics, etc. to bring a just proportion of their best informed men respectively into the legislature, the representation must be considerably numerous.—We have about 200 state senators in the United States, and a less number than that of federal representatives cannot, clearly, be a full representation of this people, in the affairs of internal taxation and police, were there but one legislature for the whole union. The representation cannot be equal, or the situation of the people proper for one government only—if the extreme parts of the society cannot be represented as fully as the central.—It is apparently impracticable that this should be the case in this extensive country—it would be impossible to collect a representation of the parts of the country five, six, and seven hundred miles from the seat of government.

Under one general government alone, there could be but one judiciary, one supreme and a proper number of inferior courts. I think it would be totally impracticable in this case to preserve a due administration of justice, and the real benefits of the jury trial of the vicinage—there are now supreme courts in each state in the union; and a great number of county and other courts subordinate to each supreme court—most of these supreme and inferior courts are itinerant, and hold their sessions in different parts every year of their respective states, counties and districts—with all these moving courts, our citizens, from the vast extent of the country must travel very considerable distances from home to find the place where justice is administered. I am not for bringing justice so near to individuals as to afford them any temptation to engage in law suits; though I think it one of the greatest benefits in a good government, that each citizen should find a court of justice within a reasonable distance, perhaps, within a day's travel of his home; so that, without great inconveniences and enormous expences, he may have the advantages of his witnesses and jury—it would be impracticable to derive these advantages from one judiciary—the one supreme court at most could only set in the centre of the union, and move once a year into the centre of the eastern and southern extremes of it—and, in this case, each citizen, on an average, would travel 150 or 200 miles to find this court—that, however, inferior courts might be properly placed in the different counties, and districts of the union, the appellate jurisdiction would be intolerable and expensive.

If it were possible to consolidate the states, and preserve the features of a free government, still it is evident that the middle states, the parts of the union, about the seat of government, would enjoy great advantages, while the remote states would experience the many inconveniences of remote provinces. Wealth, offices, and the benefits of government would collect in the centre: and the extreme states and their principal towns, become much less important.

There are other considerations which tend to prove that the idea of one consolidated whole, on free principles, is ill-founded—the laws of a free government rest on the confidence of the people, and operate gently—and never can extend their influence very far—if they are executed on free principles, about the centre, where the benefits of the government induce the people to support it voluntarily; yet they must be executed on the principles of fear and force in the extremes.—This has been the case with every extensive republic of which we have any accurate account.

There are certain unalienable and fundamental rights, which in forming the social compact, ought to be explicitly ascertained and fixed—a free and enlightened people, in forming this compact, will not resign all their rights to those who govern, and they will fix limits to their legislators and rulers, which will soon be plainly seen by those who are governed, as well as by those who govern; and the latter will know they cannot be passed unperceived by the former, and without giving a general alarm.—These rights should be made the basis of every constitution: and if a people be so situated, or have such different opinions that they cannot agree in ascertaining and fixing them, it is a very strong argument against their attempting to form one entire society, to live under one system of laws only.—I confess, I never thought the people of these states differed essentially in these respects; they having derived all these rights from one common source, the British systems; and having in the formation of their state constitutions, discovered that their ideas relative to these rights are very similar. However, it is now said that the states differ so essentially in these respects, and even in the important article of the trial by jury, that when assembled in convention, they can agree to no words by which to establish that trial, or by which to ascertain and establish many other of these rights, as fundamental articles in the social compact. If so, we proceed to consolidate the states on no solid basis whatever.

But I do not pay much regard to the reasons given for not bottoming the new constitution on a better bill of rights. I still believe a complete federal bill of rights to be very practicable. Nevertheless I acknowledge the proceedings of the convention furnish my mind with many new and strong reasons, against a complete consolidation of the states. They tend to convince me, that it cannot be carried with propriety very far—that the convention have gone much farther in one respect than they found it practicable to go in another; that is, they propose to lodge in the general government very extensive powers—*powers* nearly, if not altogether, complete and unlimited, over the purse and the sword. But, in its organization, they furnish the strongest proof that the proper limbs, or parts of a government, to support and execute those powers on proper principles (or in which they can be safely lodged) cannot be formed. These powers must be lodged somewhere in every society; but then they should be lodged where the strength and guardians of the people are collected. They can be wielded, or safely used, in a free country only by an able executive and judiciary, a respectable senate, and a secure, full, and equal representation of the people. I think the principles I have premised or brought into view, are well founded—I think they will not be denied by any fair reasoner. It is in connection with these, and other solid principles, we are to examine the constitution. It is not a few democratic phrases, or a few well formed features, that will prove its merits; or a few small omissions that will produce its rejection among men of sense; they will enquire what are the essential powers in a community, and what are nominal ones; where and how the essential powers shall be lodged to secure government, and to secure true liberty.

In examining the proposed constitution carefully, we must clearly perceive an unnatural separation of these powers from the substantial representation of the people. The state governments will exist, with all their governors, senators, representatives, officers and expences; in these will be nineteen-twentieths of the representatives of the people; they will have a near connection, and their members an immediate intercourse with the people; and the probability is, that the state governments will possess the confidence of the people, and be considered generally as their immediate guardians.

The general government will consist of a new species of executive, a small senate, and a very small house of representatives. As many citizens will be more than three hundred miles from the seat of this government as will be nearer to it, its judges and officers cannot be very numerous, without making our governments very expensive. Thus will stand the state and the general governments, should the constitution be adopted without any alterations in their organization; but as to powers, the general government will possess all essential ones, at least on paper, and those of the states a mere shadow of power. And therefore, unless the people shall make some great exertions to restore to the state governments their powers in matters of internal police; as the powers to lay and collect, exclusively, internal taxes, to govern the militia, and to hold the decisions of their own judicial courts upon their own laws final, the balance cannot possibly continue long; but the state governments must be annihilated, or continue to exist for no purpose.

It is however to be observed, that many of the essential powers given the national government are not exclusively given; and the general government may have prudence enough to forbear the exercise of those which may still be exercised by the respective states. But this cannot justify the impropriety of giving powers, the exercise of which prudent men will not attempt, and imprudent men will, or probably can, exercise only in a manner destructive of free government. The general government, organized as it is, may be adequate to many valuable objects, and be able to carry its laws into execution on proper principles in several cases; but I think its warmest friends will not contend, that it can carry all the powers proposed to be lodged in it into effect, without calling to its aid a military force, which must very soon destroy all elective governments in the country, produce anarchy, or establish despotism. Though we cannot have now a complete idea of what will be the operations of the proposed system, we may, allowing things to have their common course, have a very tolerable one. The powers lodged in the general government, if exercised by it, must intimately effect the internal police of the states, as well as external concerns; and there is no reason to expect the numerous state governments, and their connections, will be very friendly to the execution of federal laws in those internal affairs, which hitherto have been under their own immediate management. There is more reason to believe, that the general government, far removed from the people, and none of its members elected oftener than once in two years, will be forgot or neglected, and its laws in many cases disregarded, unless a multitude of officers and military force be continually kept in view, and employed to enforce the execution of the laws, and to make the government feared and respected. No position can be truer than this, that in this country either neglected laws, or a military execution of them, must lead to a revolution, and to the destruction of freedom. Neglected laws must first lead to anarchy and confusion; and a military execution of laws is only a shorter way to the same point—despotic government.

"BRUTUS," ESSAYS

Published in the New York Journal *between October 1787 and April 1788, during the same exact time period when the famous series of Federalist essays by Hamilton, Madison, and Jay were also appearing the nation's newspapers, the "Brutus" series, named for the Roman republication who killed the usurper-tyrant Caesar, went to considerable lengths on the side of the anti-Federalists. These essays weighed in on such matters as the danger of a large central government, the dangers in the granting of the power to tax, to raise and maintain armies, to set the tenure of judges, and others. It is likely that "Brutus" was Robert Yates, a New York judge, delegate to the Philadelphia Convention, and an ally of New York's Governor George Clinton, also an anti-Federalist on many issues.*

Reprinted here are "Brutus" essays I, II, VI, IX, X, XI, XII, XV, and XVI.

I
18 OCTOBER 1787

To the Citizens of the State of New York:

When the public is called to investigate and decide upon a question in which not only the present members of the community are deeply interested, but upon which the happiness and misery of generations yet unborn is in great measure suspended, the benevolent mind cannot help feeling itself peculiarly interested in the result.

In this situation, I trust the feeble efforts of an individual, to lead the minds of the people to a wise and prudent determination, cannot fail of being acceptable to the candid and dispassionate part of the community. Encouraged by this consideration, I have been induced to offer my thoughts upon the present important crisis of our public affairs.

Perhaps this country never saw so critical a period in their political concerns. We have felt the feebleness of the ties by which these United States are held together, and the want of sufficient energy in our present confederation, to manage, in some instances, our general concerns. Various expedients have been proposed to remedy these evils, but none have succeeded. At length a Convention of the states has been assembled, they have formed a constitution which will now, probably, be submitted to the people to ratify or reject, who are the fountain of all power, to whom alone it of right belongs to make or unmake constitutions, or forms of government, at their pleasure. The most important question that was ever proposed to your decision, or to the decision of any people under heaven, is before you, and you are to decide upon it by men of your own election, chosen specially for this purpose, if the constitution, offered to your acceptance, be a wise one, calculated to preserve the invaluable blessings of liberty, to secure the inestimable rights of mankind, and promote human happiness, then, if you accept it, you will lay a lasting foundation of happiness for millions yet unborn; generations to come will rise up and call you blessed. You may rejoice in the prospects of this vast extended continent becoming filled with freemen, who will assert the dignity of human nature. You may solace yourselves with the idea, that society, in this favoured land, will fast advance to the highest point of perfection; the human mind will expand in knowledge and virtue, and the golden age be, in some measure, realised. But if, on the other hand, this form of government contains principles that will lead to the subversion of liberty—if it tends to establish a despotism, or, what is worse, a tyrannic aristocracy; then, if you adopt it, this only remaining assylum for liberty will be shut up, and posterity will execrate your memory.

Momentous then is the question you have to determine, and you are called upon by every motive which should influence a noble and virtuous mind, to examine it well, and to make up a wise judgment. It is insisted, indeed, that this constitution must be received, be it ever so imperfect. If it has its defects, it is said, they can be best amended when they are experienced. But remember, when the people once part with power, they can seldom or never resume it again but by force. Many instances can be produced in which the people have voluntarily increased the powers of their rulers; but few, if any, in which rulers have willingly abridged their authority. This is a sufficient reason to induce you to be careful, in the first instance, how you deposit the powers of government.

With these few introductory remarks, I shall proceed to a consideration of this constitution:

The first question that presents itself on the subject is, whether a confederated government be the best for the United States or not? Or in other words, whether the thirteen United States should be reduced to one great republic, governed by one legislature, and under the direction of one executive and judicial; or whether they should continue thirteen confederated republics, under the direction and control of a supreme federal head for certain defined national purposes only?

This enquiry is important, because, although the government reported by the convention does not go to a perfect and entire consolidation, yet it approaches so near to it, that it must, if executed, certainly and infallibly terminate in it.

This government is to possess absolute and uncontrolable power, legislative, executive and judicial, with respect to every object to which it extends, for by the last clause of section 8th, article 1st, it is declared "that the Congress shall have power to make all laws which shall be necessary and proper for carrying into execution the foregoing powers, and all other powers vested by this constitution, in the government of the United States; or in any department or office thereof." And by the 6th article, it is declared "that this constitution, and the laws of the United States, which shall be made in pursuance thereof, and the treaties made, or which shall be made, under the authority of the United States, shall be the supreme law of the land; and the judges in every state shall be bound thereby, any thing in the constitution, or law of any state to the contrary notwithstanding." It appears from these articles that there is no need of any intervention of the state governments, between the Congress and the people, to execute any one power vested in the general government, and that the constitution and laws of every state are nullified and declared void, so far as they are or shall be inconsistent with this constitution, or the laws made in pursuance of it, or with treaties made under the authority of the United States.—The government then, so far as it extends, is a complete one, and not a confederation. It is as much one complete government as that of New York or Massachusetts, has as absolute and perfect powers to make and execute all laws, to appoint officers, institute courts, declare offences, and annex penalties, with respect to every object to which it extends, as any other in the world. So far therefore as its powers reach, all ideas of confederation are given up and lost. It is true this government is limited to certain objects, or to speak more properly, some small degree of power is still left to the states, but a little attention to the powers vested in the general government, will convince every candid man, that if it is capable of being executed, all that is reserved for the individual states must very soon be annihilated, except so far as they are barely necessary to the organization of the general government. The powers of the general legislature extend to every case that is of the least importance—there is nothing valuable to human nature, nothing dear to free men, but what is within its power. It has authority to make laws which will affect the lives, the liberty, and property of every man in the United States; nor can the constitution or laws of any state, in any way prevent or impede the full and complete execution of every power given. The legislative power is competent to lay taxes, duties, imposts, and excises—there is no limitation to this power, unless it be said that the clause which directs the use to which those taxes, and duties shall be applied, may be said to be a limitation: but this is no restriction of the power at all, for by this clause they are to be applied to pay the debts and provide for the common defence and general welfare of the United States; but the legislature have authority to contract debts at their discretion; they are the sole judges of what is necessary to provide for the common defence, and they only are to determine what is for the general welfare; this power therefore is neither more nor less, than a power to lay and collect taxes, imposts, and excises, at their pleasure; not only [is] the power to lay taxes unlimited, as to the amount they may require, but it is perfect and absolute to raise them in any mode they please. No state legislature, or any power in the state governments, have any more to do in carrying this into effect, than the authority of one state has to do with that of another. In the business therefore of laying and collecting taxes, the idea of confederation is totally lost, and that of one entire republic is embraced. It is proper here to remark, that the authority to lay and collect taxes is the most important of any power that can be granted; it connects with it almost all other powers, or at least will in process of time draw all other after it; it is the great means of protection, security, and defence, in a good government, and the great engine of oppression and tyranny in a bad one. This cannot fail of being the case, if we consider the contracted limits which are set by this constitution, to the late [state?] governments, on this article of raising money. No state can emit paper money—lay any duties, or imposts, on imports, or exports, but by consent of the Congress; and then the net produce shall be for the benefit of the United States: the only mean therefore left, for any state to support its government and discharge its debts, is by direct taxation; and the United States have also power to lay and collect taxes, in any way they please. Every one who has thought on the subject, must be convinced that but small sums of money can be collected in any country, by direct taxes; when the federal government begins to exercise the right of taxation in all its parts, the legislatures of the several states will find it impossible to raise monies to support their governments. Without money they cannot be supported, and they must dwindle away, and, as before observed, their powers absorbed in that of the general government.

It might be here shown, that the power in the federal legislative, to raise and support armies at pleasure, as well in peace as in war, and their control over the militia, tend, not only to a consolidation of the government, but the destruction of liberty—I shall not, however, dwell upon these, as a few observations upon the judicial power of this government, in addition to the preceding, will fully evince the truth of the position.

The judicial power of the United States is to be vested in a supreme court, and in such inferior courts as Congress may from time to time ordain and establish. The powers of these courts are very extensive; their jurisdiction comprehends all civil causes, except such as arise between citizens of the same state; and it extends to all cases in law and equity arising under the constitution. One inferior court must be established, I presume, in each state, at least, with the necessary executive officers appendant thereto. It is easy to see, that in the common course of things, these courts will eclipse the dignity, and take away from the respectability, of the state courts. These courts will be, in themselves, totally independent of the states, deriving their authority from the United States, and receiving from them fixed salaries; and in the course of human events it is to be expected, that they will swallow up all the powers of the courts in the respective states.

How far the clause in the 8th section of the 1st article may operate to do away all idea of confederated states, and to effect an entire consolidation of the whole into one general government, it is impossible to say. The powers given by this article are very general and comprehensive, and it may receive a construction to justify the passing almost any law. A power to make all laws, which shall be *necessary and proper,* for carrying into execution, all powers vested by the constitution in the government of the United States, or any department or officer thereof, is a power very comprehensive and definite [indefinite?], and may, for ought I know, be exercised in a such manner as entirely to abolish the state legislature. Suppose the legislature of a state should pass a law to raise money to support their government and pay the state debt, may the Congress repeal this law, because it may prevent the collection of a tax which they may think proper and necessary to lay, to provide for the general welfare of the United States? For all laws made, in pursuance of this constitution, are the supreme law of the land, and the judges in every state shall be bound thereby, any thing in the constitution or laws of the different states to the contrary notwithstanding.—By such a law, the government of a particular state might be overturned at one stroke, and thereby be deprived of every means of its support.

It is not meant, by stating this case, to insinuate that the constitution would warrant a law of this kind; or unnecessarily to alarm the fears of the people, by suggesting, that the federal legislature would be more likely to pass the limits assigned them by the constitution, than that of an individual state, further than they are less responsible to the people. But what is meant is, that the legislature of the United States are vested with the great and uncontrolable powers, of laying and collecting taxes, duties, imposts, and excises; of regulating trade, raising and supporting armies, organizing, arming, and disciplining the militia, instituting courts, and other general powers. And are by this clause invested with the power of making all laws, *proper and necessary,* for carrying all these into execution; and they may so exercise this power as entirely to annihilate all the state governments, and reduce this country to one single government. And if they may do it, it is pretty certain they will; for it will be found that the power retained by individual states, small as it is, will be a clog upon the wheels of the government of the United States; the latter therefore will be naturally inclined to remove it out of the way. Besides, it is a truth confirmed by the unerring experience of ages, that every man, and every body of men, invested with power, are ever disposed to increase it, and to acquire a superiority over every thing that stands in their way. This disposition, which is implanted in human nature, will operate in the federal legislature to lessen and ultimately to subvert the state authority, and having such advantages, will most certainly succeed, if the federal government succeeds at all. It must be very evident then, that what this constitution wants of being a complete consolidation of the several parts of the union into one complete government, possessed of a perfect legislative, judicial, and executive powers, to all intents and purposes, it will necessarily acquire in its exercise and operation.

Let us now proceed to enquire, as I at first proposed, whether it be best the thirteen United States should be reduced to one great republic, or not? It is here taken for granted that all agree in this, that whatever government we adopt, it ought to be a free one; that it should be so framed as to secure the liberty of the citizens of America, and such an one as to admit of a full, fair, and equal representation of the people. The question then will be, whether a government thus constituted, and founded on such principles, is practicable, and can be exercised over the whole United States, reduced into one state?

If respect is to be paid to the opinion of the greatest and wisest men who have ever thought or wrote on the science of government, we shall be constrained to conclude, that a free republic cannot succeed over a country of such immense extent, containing such a number of inhabitants, and these encreasing in such rapid progression as that of the whole United States. Among the many illustrious authorities which might be produced to this point, I shall content myself with quoting only two. The one is the Baron de Montesquieu, *Spirit of Laws,* chap. xvi. vol. 1 [book VIII]. "It is natural to a republic to have only a small territory, otherwise it cannot long subsist. In a large republic there are men of larger fortunes, and consequently of less moderation; there are trusts too great to be placed in any single subject; he has interest of his own; he soon begins to think that he may be happy, great and glorious, by oppressing his fellow citizens; and that he may raise himself to grandeur on the ruins of his country. In a large republic, the public good is sacrificed to a thousand views; it is subordinate to exceptions, and depends on accidents. In a small one, the interest of the public is easier perceived, better understood, and more within the reach of every citizen; abuses are of less extent, and of course are less protected." Of the same opinion is the Marquis Beccaria.

History furnishes no example of a free republic, any thing like the extent of the United States. The Grecian republics were of small extent; so also was that of the Romans. Both of these, it is true, in process of time, extended their conquests over large territories of country; and the consequence was, that their governments were changed from that of free governments to those of the most tyrannical that ever existed in the world.

Not only the opinion of the greatest men, and the experience of mankind, are against the idea of an extensive republic, but a variety of reasons may be drawn from the reason and nature of things, against it, in every government, the will of the sovereign is the law. In despotic governments, the supreme authority being lodged in one, his will is law, and can be as easily expressed to a large extensive territory as to a small one. In a pure democracy the people are the sovereign, and their will is declared by themselves; for this purpose they must all come together to deliberate, and decide. This kind of government cannot be exercised, therefore, over a country of any considerable extent; it must be confined to a single city, or at least limited to such bounds as that the people can conveniently assemble, be able to debate, understand the subject submitted to them, and declare their opinion concerning it.

In a free republic, although all laws are derived from the consent of the people, yet the people do not declare their consent by themselves in person, but by representatives, chosen by them, who are supposed to know the minds of their constituents, and to be possessed of integrity to declare this mind.

In every free government, the people must give their assent to the laws by which they are governed. This is the true criterion between a free government and an arbitrary one. The former are ruled by the will of the whole, expressed in any manner they may agree upon; the latter by the will of one, or a few. If the people are to give their assent to the laws, by persons chosen and appointed by them, the manner of the choice and the number chosen, must be such, as to possess, be disposed, and consequently qualified to declare the sentiments of the people; for if they do not know, or are not disposed to speak the sentiments of the people, the people do not govern, but the sovereignty is in a few. Now, in a large extended country, it is impossible to have a representation, possessing the sentiments, and of integrity, to declare the minds of the people, without having it so numerous and unwieldly, as to be subject in great measure to the inconveniency of a democratic government.

The territory of the United States is of vast extent; it now contains near three millions of souls, and is capable of containing much more than ten times that number. Is it practicable for a country, so large and so numerous as they will soon become, to elect a representation, that will speak their sentiments, without their becoming so numerous as to be incapable of transacting public business? It certainly is not.

In a republic, the manners, sentiments, and interests of the people should be similar. If this be not the case, there will be a constant clashing of opinions; and the representatives of one part will be continually striving against those of the other. This will retard the operations of government, and prevent such conclusions as will promote the public good. If we apply this remark to the condition of the United States, we shall be convinced that it forbids that we should be one government. The United States includes a variety of climates. The productions of the different parts of the union are very variant, and their interests, of consequence, diverse. Their manners and habits differ as much as their climates and productions; and their sentiments are by no means coincident. The laws and customs of the several states are, in many respects, very diverse, and in some opposite; each would be in favor of its own interests and customs, and, of consequence, a legislature, formed of representatives from the respective parts, would not only be too numerous to act with any care or decision, but would be composed of such heterogenous and discordant principles, as would constantly be contending with each other.

The laws cannot be executed in a republic, of an extent equal to that of the United States, with promptitude.

The magistrates in every government must be supported in the execution of the laws, either by an armed force, maintained at the public expence for that purpose; or by the people turning out to aid the magistrate upon his command, in case of resistance.

In despotic governments, as well as in all the monarchies of Europe, standing armies are kept up to execute the commands of the prince or the magistrate, and are employed for this purpose when occasion requires: But they have always proved the destruction of liberty, and are abhorrent to the spirit of a free republic. In England, where they depend upon the parliament for their annual support, they have always been complained of as oppressive and unconstitutional, and are seldom employed in executing of the laws; never except on extraordinary occasions, and then under the direction of a civil magistrate.

A free republic will never keep a standing army to execute its laws. It must depend upon the support of its citizens. But when a government is to receive its support from the aid of the citizens, it must be so constructed as to have the confidence, respect, and affection of the

people. Men who, upon the call of the magistrate, offer themselves
to execute the laws, are influenced to do it either by affection to
the government, or from fear; where a standing army is at hand to
punish offenders, every man is actuated by the latter principle, and
therefore, when the magistrate calls, will obey; but, where this is not
the case, the government must rest for its support upon the confidence
and respect which the people have for their government and laws.
The body of the people being attached, the government will always
be sufficient to support and execute its laws, and to operate upon
the fears of any faction which may be opposed to it, not only to
prevent an opposition to the execution of the laws themselves, but
also to compel the most of them to aid the magistrate; but the people
will not be likely to have such confidence in their rulers, in a republic
so extensive as the United States, as necessary for these purposes. The
confidence which the people have in their rulers, in a free republic,
arises from their knowing them, from their being responsible to them
for their conduct, and from the power they have of displacing them
when they misbehave; but in a republic of the extent of this continent,
the people in general would be acquainted with very few of their
rulers; the people at large would know little of their proceedings,
and it would be extremely difficult to change them. The people in
Georgia and New Hampshire would not know one another's mind,
and therefore could not act in concert to enable them to effect a
general change of representatives. The different parts of so extensive
a country could not possibly be made acquainted with the conduct
of their representatives, nor be informed of the reasons upon which
measures were founded. The consequence will be, they will have no
confidence in their legislature, suspect them of ambitious views, be
jealous of every measure they adopt, and will not support the laws they
pass. Hence the government will be nerveless and inefficient, and no
way will be left to render it otherwise, but by establishing an armed
force to execute the laws at the point of bayonet—a government of
all others the most to be dreaded.

In a republic of such vast extent as the United States, the legislature
cannot attend to the various concerns and wants of its different parts.
It cannot be sufficiently numerous to be acquainted with the local
condition and wants of the different districts, and if it could, it is
impossible it should have sufficient time to attend to and provide for
all the variety of cases of this nature, that would be continually arising.

In so extensive a republic, the great officers of government would
soon become above the control of the people, and abuse their power

to the purpose of aggrandizing themselves, and oppressing them. The trust committed to the executive offices, in a country of the extent of the United States, must be various and of magnitude. The command of all the troops and navy of the republic, the appointment of officers, the power of pardoning offences, the collecting of all the public revenues, and the power of expending them, with a number of other powers, must be lodged and exercised in every state, in the hands of a few. When these are attended with great honor and emolument, as they always will be in large states, so as greatly to interest men to pursue them, and to be proper objects for ambitious and designing men, such men will be ever restless in their pursuit after them. They will use the power, when they have acquired it, to the purposes of gratifying their own interest and ambition, and it is scarcely possible, in a very large republic, to call them to account for their misconduct, or to prevent their abuse of power.

These are some of the reasons by which it appears, that a free republic cannot long subsist over a country of the great extent of these states. If then this new constitution is calculated to consolidate the thirteen states into one, as it evidently is, it ought not to be adopted.

Though I am of opinion, that it is a sufficient objection to this government to reject it, that it creates the whole union into one government, under the form of a republic, yet if this objection was obviated, there are exceptions to it, which are so material and fundamental, that they ought to determine every man, who is a friend to the liberty and happiness of mankind, not to adopt it. I beg the candid and dispassionate attention of my countrymen while I state these objections—they are such as have obtruded themselves upon my mind upon a careful attention to the matter, and such as I sincerely believe are well founded. There are many objections, of small moment, of which I shall take no notice—perfection is not to be expected in any thing that is the production of man—and if I did not in my conscience believe that this scheme was defective in the fundamental principles—in the foundation upon which a free and equal government must rest—I would hold my peace.

Brutus

II
1 NOVEMBER 1787

To the Citizens of the State of New York:

I flatter myself that my last address established this position, that to reduce the Thirteen States into one government, would prove the destruction of your liberties.

But lest this truth should be doubted by some, I will now proceed to consider its merits.

Though it should be admitted, that the argument[s] against reducing all the states into one consolidated government, are not sufficient fully to establish this point; yet they will, at least, justify this conclusion, that in forming a constitution for such a country, great care should be taken to limit and definite its powers, adjust its parts, and guard against an abuse of authority. How far attention has been paid to these objects, shall be the subject of future enquiry. When a building is to be erected which is intended to stand for ages, the foundation should be firmly laid. The constitution proposed to your acceptance, is designed not for yourselves alone, but for generations yet unborn. The principles, therefore, upon which the social compact is founded, ought to have been clearly and precisely stated, and the most express and full declaration of rights to have been made—But on this subject there is almost an entire silence.

If we may collect the sentiments of the people of America, from their own most solemn declarations, they hold this truth as self evident, that all men are by nature free. No one man, therefore, or any class of men, have a right, by the law of nature, or of God, to assume or exercise authority over their fellows. The origin of society then is to be sought, not in any natural right which one man has to exercise authority over another, but in the united consent of those who associate. The mutual wants of men, at first dictated the propriety of forming societies; and when they were established, protection and defence pointed out the necessity of instituting government. In a state of nature every individual pursues his own interest; in this pursuit it frequently happened, that the possessions or enjoyments of one were sacrificed to the views and designs of another; thus the weak were a prey to the strong, the simple and unwary were subject to impositions from those who were more crafty and designing. In this state of things, every individual was insecure; common interest therefore directed, that government should be established, in which the force of the whole community should be collected, and under such directions, as to protect and defend every one who composed it. The common good, therefore, is the end of civil government, and common consent, the foundation on which it is established. To effect this end, it was necessary that a certain portion of natural liberty should be surrendered, in order, that what remained should be preserved: how great a proportion of natural freedom is necessary to be yielded by individuals, when they submit to government, I shall not now enquire. So much, however, must be given up, as will be sufficient to enable those, to whom the administration of the government is committed, to establish laws for the promoting the happiness of the community, and to carry those laws into effect. But it is not necessary, for this purpose, that individuals should relinquish all their natural rights. Some are of such a nature that they cannot be surrendered. Of this kind are the rights of conscience, the right of enjoying and defending life, etc. Others are not necessary to be resigned, in order to attain the end for which government is instituted, these therefore ought not to be given up. To surrender them, would counteract the very end of government, to wit, the common good. From these observations it appears, that in forming a government on its true principles, the foundation should be laid in the manner I before stated, by expressly reserving to the people such of their essential natural rights, as are not necessary to be parted with. The same reasons which at first induced mankind to associate and institute government, will operate to influence them to observe this precaution. If they had been disposed to conform themselves to the rule of immutable righteousness, government would not have been requisite. It was because one part exercised fraud, oppression, and violence on the other, that men came together, and agreed that certain rules should be formed, to regulate the conduct of all, and the power of the whole community lodged in the hands of rulers to enforce an obedience to them. But rulers have the same propensities as other men; they are as likely to use the power with which they are vested for private purposes, and to the injury and oppression of those over whom they are placed, as individuals in a state of nature are to injure and oppress one another. It is therefore as proper that bounds should be set to their authority, as that government should have at first been instituted to restrain private injuries.

This principle, which seems so evidently founded in the reason and nature of things, is confirmed by universal experience. Those who have governed, have been found in all ages ever active to enlarge their powers and abridge the public liberty. This has induced the people in all countries, where any sense of freedom remained, to fix barriers against the encroachments of their rulers. The country from which we have derived our origin, is an eminent example of this. Their magna charta and bill of rights have long been the boast, as well as the security, of that nation. I need say no more, I presume, to an American, than, that this principle is a fundamental one, in all the constitutions of our own states; there is not one of them but what is either founded on a declaration or bill of rights, or has certain express reservation of rights interwoven in the body of them. From this it appears, that at a time when the pulse of liberty beat high and when an appeal was made to the people to form constitutions for the government of themselves, it was their universal sense, that such declarations should make a part of their frames of government. It is therefore the more astonishing, that this grand security, to the rights of the people, is not to be found in this constitution.

It has been said, in answer to this objection, that such declaration[s] of rights, however requisite they might be in the constitutions of the states, are not necessary in the general constitution, because, "in the former case, every thing which is not reserved is given, but in the latter the reverse of the proposition prevails, and every thing which is not given is reserved." It requires but little attention to discover, that this mode of reasoning is rather specious than solid. The powers, rights, and authority, granted to the general government by this constitution, are as complete, with respect to every object to which they extend, as that of any state government—It reaches to every thing which concerns human happiness—Life, liberty, and property, are under its controul. There is the same reason, therefore, that the exercise of power, in this case, should be restrained within proper limits, as in that of the state governments. To set this matter in a clear light, permit me to instance some of the articles of the bills of rights of the individual states, and apply them to the case in question.

For the security of life, in criminal prosecutions, the bills of rights of most of the states have declared, that no man shall be held to answer for a crime until he is made fully acquainted with the charge brought against him; he shall not be compelled to accuse, or furnish evidence against himself—The witnesses against him shall be brought face to face, and he shall be fully heard by himself or counsel. That it is essential to the security of life and liberty, that trial of facts be in the vicinity where they happen. Are not provisions of this kind as necessary in the general government, as in that of a particular state? The powers vested in the new Congress extend in many cases to life; they are authorised to provide for the punishment of a variety of capital crimes, and no restraint is laid upon them in its exercise, save only, that "the trial of all crimes, except in cases of impeachment, shall be by jury; and such trial shall be in the state where the said crimes shall have been committed." No man is secure of a trial in the county where he is charged to have committed a crime; he may be brought from Niagara to New-York, or carried from Kentucky to Richmond for trial for an offence, supposed to be committed. What security is there, that a man shall be furnished with a full and plain description of the charges against him? That he shall be allowed to produce all proof he can in his favor? That he shall see the witnesses against him face to face, or that he shall be fully heard in his own defence by himself or counsel?

For the security of liberty it has been declared, "that excessive bail should not be required, nor excessive fines imposed, nor cruel or unusual punishments inflicted—That all warrants, without oath or affirmation, to search suspected places, or seize any person, his papers or property, are grievous and oppressive."

These provisions are as necessary under the general government as under that of the individual states; for the power of the former is as complete to the purpose of requiring bail, imposing fines, inflicting punishments, granting search warrants, and seizing persons, papers, or property, in certain cases, as the other.

For the purpose of securing the property of the citizens, it is declared by all the states, "that in all controversies at law, respecting property, the ancient mode of trial by jury is one of the best securities of the rights of the people, and ought to remain sacred and inviolable."

Does not the same necessity exist of reserving this right, under this national compact, as in that of these states? Yet nothing is said respecting it. In the bills of rights of the states it is declared, that a well regulated militia is the proper and natural defence of a free government—That as standing armies in time of peace are dangerous, they are not to be kept up, and that the military should be kept under strict subordination to, and controuled by the civil power.

The same security is as necessary in this constitution, and much more so; for the general government will have the sole power to raise and to pay armies, and are under no controul in the exercise of it; yet nothing of this is to be found in this new system.

I might proceed to instance a number of other rights, which were as necessary to be reserved, such as, that elections should be free, that the liberty of the press should be held sacred; but the instances adduced, are sufficient to prove, that this argument is without foundation.— Besides, it is evident, that the reason here assigned was not the true one, why the framers of this constitution omitted a bill of rights; if it had been, they would not have made certain reservations, while they totally omitted others of more importance. We find they have, in the 9th section of the 1st article, declared, that the writ of habeas corpus shall not be suspended, unless in cases of rebellion—that no bill of attainder, or expost facto law, shall be passed—that no title of nobility shall be granted by the United States, &c. If every thing which is not given is reserved, what propriety is there in these exceptions? Does this constitution any where grant the power of suspending the habeas corpus, to make expost facto laws, pass bills of attainder, or grant titles of nobility? It certainly does not in express terms. The only answer that can be given is, that these are implied in the general powers granted. With equal truth it may be said, that all the powers, which the bills of right, guard against the abuse of, are contained or implied in the general ones granted by this constitution.

So far it is from being true, that a bill of rights is less necessary in the general constitution than in those of the states, the contrary is evidently the fact.—This system, if it is possible for the people of America to accede to it, will be an original compact: and being the last, will, in the nature of things, vacate every former agreement inconsistent with it. For it being a plan of government received and ratified by the whole people, all other forms, which are in existence at the time of its adoption, must yield to it. This is expressed in positive and unequivocal terms, in the 6th article, "That this constitution and the laws of the United States, which shall be made in pursuance thereof, and all treaties made, or which shall be made, under the authority of the United States, shall be the supreme law of the land; and the judges in every state shall be bound thereby, any thing in the *constitution,* or laws of any state, *to the contrary* notwithstanding.

"The senators and representatives before-mentioned, and the members of the several state legislatures, and all executive and judicial officers, both of the United States, and of the several states, shall be bound, by oath or affirmation, to support this constitution."

It is therefore not only necessarily implied thereby, but positively expressed, that the different state constitutions are repealed and entirely done away, so far as they are inconsistent with this, with the laws which shall be made in pursuance thereof, or with treaties made, or which shall be made, under the authority of the United States; of what avail will the constitutions of the respective states be to preserve the rights of its citizens? should they be plead, the answer would be the constitution of the United States, and the laws made in pursuance thereof, is the supreme law, and all legislatures and judicial officers, whether of the general or state governments, are bound by oath to support it. No priviledge, reserved by the bills of rights, or secured by the state government, can limit the power granted by this, or restrain any laws made in pursuance of it. It stands therefore on its own bottom, and must receive a construction by itself without any reference to any other—And hence it was of the highest importance, that the most precise and express declarations and reservations of rights should have been made.

This will appear the more necessary, when it is considered, that not only the constitution and laws made in pursuance thereof, but all treaties made, or which shall be made, under the authority of the United States, are the supreme law of the land, and supersede the constitutions of all the states. The power to make treaties, is vested in the president, by and with the advice and consent of two thirds of the senate. I do not find any limitation, or restriction, to the exercise of this power. The most important article in any constitution may therefore be repealed, even without a legislative act. Ought not a government, vested with such extensive and indefinite authority, to have been restricted by a declaration of rights? It certainly ought.

So clear a point is this, that I cannot help suspecting, that persons who attempt to persuade people, that such reservations were less necessary under this constitution than under those of the states, are wilfully endeavouring to deceive, and to lead you into an absolute state of vassalage.

Brutus

VI
27 December 1787

To the Citizens of the State of New York:

It is an important question, whether the general government of the United States should be so framed, as to absorb and swallow up the state governments? or whether on the contrary, the former ought not to be confined to certain defined national objects, while the latter should retain all the powers which concern the internal police of the state?

I have, in my former papers, offered a variety of arguments to prove, that a simple free government could not be exercised over this whole continent, and that therefore we must either give up our liberties and submit to an arbitrary one, or frame a constitution on the plan of confederation. Further reasons might be urged to prove this point—but it seems unnecessary, because the principal advocates of the new constitution admit of the position. The question therefore between us, this being admitted, is, whether or not this system is so formed as either directly to annihilate the state governments, or that in its operation it will certainly effect it. If this is answered in the affirmative, then the system ought not to be adopted, without such amendments as will avoid this consequence. If on the contrary it can be seen, that the state governments are secured in their rights to manage the internal police of the respective states, we must confine ourselves in our enquiries to the organization of the government and the guards and provisions it contains to prevent a misuse or abuse of power. To determine this question, it is requisite, that we fully investigate the nature, and the extent of the powers intended to be granted by this constitution to the rulers.

In my last number I called your attention to this subject, and proved, as I think, uncontrovertibly, that the powers given the legislature under the 8th section of the 1st article, had no other limitation than the discretion of the Congress. It was shown, that even if the most favorable construction was given to this paragraph, that the advocates for the new constitution could wish, it will convey a power to lay and collect taxes, imposts, duties, and excises, according to the discretion of the legislature, and to make all laws which they shall judge proper and necessary to carry this power into execution. This I showed would totally destroy all the power of the state governments. To confirm this, it is worth while to trace the operation of the government in some particular instances.

The general government is to be vested with authority to levy and collect taxes, duties, and excises; the separate states have also power to impose taxes, duties, and excises, except that they cannot lay duties on exports and imports without the consent of Congress. Here then the two governments have concurrent jurisdiction: both may lay impositions of this kind. But then the general government have supperadded to this power, authority to make all laws which shall be necessary and proper for carrying the foregoing power into execution. Suppose then that both governments should lay taxes, duties, and excises, and it should fall so heavy on the people that they would be unable, or be so burdensome that they would refuse to pay them both—would it not be necessary that the general legislature should suspend the collection of the state tax? It certainly would. For, if the people could not, or would not pay both, they must be discharged from the tax to the state, or the tax to the general government could not be collected.—The conclusion therefore is inevitable, that the respective state governments will not have the power to raise one shilling in any way, but by the permission of the Congress. I presume no one will pretend, that the states can exercise legislative authority, or administer justice among their citizens for any length of time, without being able to raise a sufficiency to pay those who administer their governments.

If this be true, and if the states can raise money only by permission of the general government, it follows that the state governments will be dependent on the will of the general government for their existence.

What will render this power in Congress effectual and sure in its operation is, that the government will have complete judicial and executive authority to carry all their laws into effect, which will be paramount to the judicial and executive authority of the individual states: in vain therefore will be all interference of the legislatures, courts, or magistrates of any of the states on the subject; for they will be subordinate to the general government, and engaged by oath to support it, and will be constitutionally bound to submit to their decisions.

The general legislature will be empowered to lay any tax they chuse, to annex any penalties they please to the breach of their revenue laws; and to appoint as many officers as they may think proper to collect the taxes. They will have authority to farm the revenues and to vest the farmer general, with his subalterns, with plenary powers to collect them, in any way which to them may appear eligible. And the courts of law, which they will be authorized to institute, will have cognizance of every case arising under the revenue laws, the conduct of all the officers employed in collecting them; and the officers of these courts will execute their judgments. There is no way, therefore, of avoiding the destruction of the state governments, whenever the Congress please to do it, unless the people rise up, and with a strong hand, resist and prevent the execution of constitutional laws. The fear of this, will, it is presumed, restrain the general government, for some time, within proper bounds; but it will not be many years before they will have a revenue, and force, at their command, which will place them above any apprehensions on the score.

How far the power to lay and collect duties and excises, may operate to dissolve the state governments, and oppress the people, it is impossible to say. It would assist us much in forming a just opinion on this head, to consider the various objects to which this kind of taxes extend, in European nations, and the infinity of laws they have passed respecting them. Perhaps, if leisure will permit, this may be essayed in some future paper.

It was observed in my last number, that the power to lay and collect duties and excises, would invest the Congress with authority to impose a duty and excise on every necessary and convenience of life. As the principal object of the government, in laying a duty or excise, will be, to raise money, it is obvious, that they will fix on such articles as are of the most general use and consumption; because, unless great quantities of the article, on which the duty is laid, is used, the revenue cannot be considerable. We may therefore presume, that the articles which will be the object of this species of taxes will be either the real necessaries of life; or if not these, such as from custom and habit are esteemed so. I will single out a few of the productions of our own country, which may, and probably will, be of the number.

Cider is an article that most probably will be one of those on which an excise will be laid, because it is one, which this country produces in great abundance, which is in very general use, is consumed in great quantities, and which may be said too not to be a real necessary of life. An excise on this would raise a large sum of money in the United States. How would the power, to lay and collect an excise on cider, and to pass all laws proper and necessary to carry it into execution, operate in its exercise? It might be necessary, in order to collect the excise on cider, to grant to one man, in each county, an exclusive right of building and keeping cider mills, and oblige him to give bounds and security for payment of the excise; or, if this was not done, it might be necessary to license the mills, which are to make this liquor, and to take from them security, to account for the excise; or, if otherwise, a great number of officers must be employed, to take account of the cider made, and to collect the duties on it.

Porter, ale, and all kinds of malt liquors, are the articles that would probably be subject also to an excise. It would be necessary, in order to collect such an excise, to regulate the manufactory of these, that the quantity made might be ascertained or otherwise security could not be had for the payment of the excise. Every brewery must then be licensed, and officers appointed, to take account of its product, and to secure the payment of the duty, or excise, before it is sold. Many other articles might be named, which would be objects of this species of taxation, but I refrain from enumerating them. It will probably be said, by those who advocate this system, that the observations already made on this head, are calculated only to inflame the minds of the people, with the apprehension of dangers merely imaginary. That there is not the least reason to apprehend, the general legislature will exercise their power in this manner. To this I would only say, that these kinds of taxes exist in Great Britain, and are severely felt. The excise on cider and perry, was imposed in that nation a few years ago, and it is in the memory of every one, who read the history of the transaction, what great tumults it occasioned.

This power, exercised without limitation, will introduce itself into every corner of the city, and country.—It will wait upon the ladies as their toilett, and will not leave them in any of their domestic concerns; it will accompany them to the ball, the play, and the assembly; it will go with them when they visit, and will, on all occasions, sit beside them in their carriages, nor will it desert them even at church; it will enter the house of every gentleman, watch over his cellar, wait upon his cook in the kitchen, follow the servants into the parlour, preside over the table, and note down all he eats or drinks; it will attend him to his bedchamber, and watch him while he sleeps; it will take cognizance of the professional man in his office, or his study; it will watch the merchant in the counting-house, or in his store; it will follow the mechanic to his shop, and in his work, and will haunt him in his family, and in his bed; it will be a constant companion of the industrious farmer in all his labour, it will be with him in the house, and in the field, observe the toil of his hands, and the sweat of his brow; it will penetrate into the most obscure cottage; and finally, it will light upon the head of every person in the United States. To all these different classes of people, and in all these circumstances, in which it will attend them, the language in which it will address them, will be GIVE! GIVE!

A power that has such latitude, which reaches every person in the community in every conceivable circumstance, and lays hold of every species of property they possess, and which has no bounds set to it, but the discretion of those who exercise it, I say, such a power must necessarily, from its very nature, swallow up all the power of the state governments.

I shall add but one other observation on this head, which is this—it appears to me a solecism, for two men, or bodies of men, to have unlimited power respecting the same object. It contradicts the scripture maxim, which saith "no man can serve two masters." The one power or the other must prevail, or else they will destroy each other, and neither of them effect their purpose. It may be compared to two mechanic powers, acting upon the same body in opposite directions; the consequence would be, if the powers were equal, the body would remain in a state of rest, or if the force of the one was superior to that of the other, the stronger would prevail, and overcome the resistance of the weaker.

But it is said, by some of the advocates of this system, "That the idea that Congress can levy taxes at pleasure, is false, and the suggestion wholly unsupported: that the preamble to the constitution is declaratory of the purposes of the union, and the assumption of any power not necessary to establish justice, etc. to provide for the common defence, etc. will be unconstitutional. Besides, in the very clause which gives the power of levying duties and taxes, the purposes to which the money shall be appropriated, are specified, viz., to pay the debts, and provide for the common defence and general welfare." I would ask those, who reason thus, to define what ideas are included under the terms, to provide for the common defence and general welfare? Are these terms definite, and will they be understood in the same manner, and to apply to the same cases by every one? No one will pretend they will. It will then be matter of opinion, what tends to the general welfare; and the Congress will be the only judges in the matter. To provide for the general welfare, is an abstract proposition, which mankind differ in the explanation of, as much as they do on any political or moral proposition that can be proposed; the most opposite measures may be pursued by different parties, and both may profess, that they have in view the general welfare; and both sides may be honest in their professions, or both may have sinister views. Those who advocate this new constitution declare, they are influenced by a regard to the general welfare; those who oppose it, declare they are moved by the same principle; and I have no doubt but a number on both sides are honest in their professions; and yet nothing is more certain than this, that to adopt this constitution, and not to adopt it, cannot both of them be promotive of the general welfare.

It is as absurd to say, that the power of Congress is limited by these general expressions, "to provide for the common safety, and general welfare," as it would be to say, that it would be limited, had the constitution said they should have power to lay taxes, etc. at will and pleasure. Were this authority given, it might be said, that under it the legislature could not do injustice, or pursue any measures, but such as were calculated to promote the public good, and happiness. For every man, rulers as well as others, are bound by the immutable laws of God and reason, always to will what is right. It is certainly right and fit, that the governors of every people should provide for the common defence and general welfare; every government, therefore, in the world, even the greatest despot, is limited in the exercise of his power. But however just this reasoning may be, it would be found, in practice, a most pitiful restriction. The government would always say, their measures were designed and calculated to promote the public good; and there being no judge between them and the people, the rulers themselves must, and would always, judge for themselves.

There are others of the favourers of this system, who admit, that the power of the Congress under it, with respect to revenue, will exist without limitation, and contend, that so it ought to be.

It is said, "The power to raise armies, to build and equip fleets, and to provide for their support, ought to exist without limitation, because it is impossible to foresee, or to define, the extent and variety of national exigencies, or the correspondent extent and variety of the means which may be necessary to satisfy them.["]

This, it is said, "is one of those truths which, to correct and unprejudiced minds, carries its own evidence along with it. It rests upon axioms as simple as they are universal: the means ought to be proportioned to the end; the person, from whose agency the attainment of any end is expected, ought to possess the means by which it is to be attained."

This same writer insinuates, that the opponents to the plan promulgated by the convention, manifests a want of candor, in objecting to the extent of the powers proposed to be vested in this government; because he asserts, with an air of confidence, that the powers ought to be unlimited as to the object to which they extend; and that this position, if not self-evident, is at least clearly demonstrated by the foregoing mode of reasoning. But with submission to this author's better judgment, I humbly conceive his reasoning will appear, upon examination, more specious than solid. The means, says the gentleman, ought to be proportioned to the end: admit the proposition to be true it is then necessary to enquire, what is the end of the government of the United States, in order to draw any just conclusions from it. Is this end simply to preserve the general government, and to provide for the common defence and general welfare of the union only? certainly not: for beside this, the state government are to be supported, and provision made for the managing such of their internal concerns as are allotted to them. It is admitted, "that the circumstances of our country are such, as to demand a compound, instead of a simple, a confederate, instead of a sole government," that the objects of each ought to be pointed out, and that each ought to possess ample authority to execute the powers committed to them. The government then, being complex in its nature, the end it has in view is so also; and it is as necessary, that the state governments should possess the means to attain the ends expected from them, as for the general government. Neither the general government, nor the state governments, ought to be vested with all the powers proper to be exercised for promoting the ends of government. The powers are divided between them— certain ends are to be attained by the one, and other certain ends by the other; and these, taken together, include all the ends of good government. This being the case, the conclusion follows, that each should be furnished with the means, to attain the ends, to which they are designed.

To apply this reasoning to the case of revenue; the general government is charged with the care of providing for the payment of the debts of the United States; supporting the general government, and providing for the defence of the union. To obtain these ends, they should be furnished with means. But does it thence follow, that they should command all the revenues of the United States! Most certainly it does not. For if so, it will follow, that no means will be left to attain other ends, as necessary to the happiness of the country, as those committed to their care. The individual states have debts to discharge; their legislatures and executives are to be supported, and provision is to be made for the administration of justice in the respective states. For these objects the general government has no authority to provide; nor is it proper it should. It is clear then, that the states should have the command of such revenues, as to answer the ends they have to obtain. To say, "that the circumstances that endanger the safety of nations are infinite," and from hence to infer, that all the sources of revenue in the states should be yielded to the general government, is not conclusive reasoning: for the Congress are authorized only to control in general concerns, and not regulate local and internal ones; and these are as essentially requisite to be provided for as those. The peace and happiness of a community is as intimately connected with the prudent direction of their domestic affairs, and the due administration of justice among themselves, as with a competent provision for their defence against foreign invaders, and indeed more so.

Upon the whole, I conceive, that there cannot be a clearer position than this, that the state governments ought to have an uncontrollable power to raise a revenue, adequate to the exigencies of their governments; and, I presume, no such power is left them by this constitution.

Brutus

IX
17 JANUARY 1788

To the Citizens of the State of New York:

The design of civil government is to protect the rights and promote the happiness of the people.

For this end, rulers are invested with powers. But we cannot from hence justly infer that these powers should be unlimited. There are certain rights which mankind possess, over which government ought not to have any controul, because it is not necessary they should, in order to attain the end of its institution. There are certain things which rulers should be absolutely prohibited from doing, because, if they should do them, they would work an injury, not a benefit to the people. Upon the same principles of reasoning, if the exercise of a power, is found generally or in most cases to operate to the injury of the community, the legislature should be restricted in the exercise of that power, so as to guard, as much as possible, against the danger. These principles seem to be the evident dictates of common sense, and what ought to give sanction to them in the minds of every American, they are the great principles of the late revolution, and those which governed the framers of all our state constitutions. Hence we find, that all the state constitutions, contain either formal bills of rights, which set bounds to the powers of the legislature, or have restrictions for the same purpose in the body of the constitutions.

Some of our new political Doctors, indeed, reject the idea of the necessity, or propriety of such restrictions in any elective government, but especially in the general one.

But it is evident, that the framers of this new system were of a contrary opinion, because they have prohibited the general government, the exercise of some powers, and restricted them in that of others.

I shall adduce two instances, which will serve to illustrate my meaning, as well as to confirm the truth of the preceeding remark.

In the 9th section, it is declared, "no bill of attainder shall be passed." This clause takes from the legislature all power to declare a particular person guilty of a crime by law. It is proper the legislature should be deprived of the exercise of this power, because it seldom is exercised to the benefit of the community, but generally to its injury.

In the same section it is provided, that "the privilege of the writ of habeas corpus shall not be suspended, unless when in cases of rebellion and invasion, the public safety may require it." This clause limits the power of the legislature to deprive a citizen of the right of habeas corpus, to particular cases viz. those of rebellion and invasion; the reason is plain, because in no other cases can this power be exercised for the general good.

Let us apply these remarks to the case of standing armies in times of peace. If they generally prove the destruction of the happiness and liberty of the people, the legislature ought not to have power to keep them up, or if they had, this power should be so restricted, as to secure the people against the danger arising from the exercise of it.

That standing armies are dangerous to the liberties of a people was proved in my last number—If it was necessary, the truth of the position might be confirmed by the history of almost every nation in the world. A cloud of the most illustrious patriots of every age and country, where freedom has been enjoyed, might be adduced as witnesses in support of the sentiment. But I presume it would be useless, to enter into a laboured argument, to prove to the people of America, a position, which has so long and so generally been received by them as a kind of axiom.

Some of the advocates for this new system controvert this sentiment, as they do almost every other that has been maintained by the best writers on free government.—Others, though they will not expressly deny, that standing armies in times of peace are dangerous, yet join with these in maintaining, that it is proper the general government should be vested with the power to do it. I shall now proceed to examine the arguments they adduce in support of their opinions.

A writer, in favor of this system, treats this objection as a ridiculous one. He supposes it would be as proper to provide against the introduction of Turkish janizaries, or against making the Alcoran a rule of faith.

From the positive, and dogmatic manner, in which this author delivers his opinions, and answers objections made to his sentiments—one would conclude, that he was some pedantic pedagogue who had been accustomed to deliver his dogmas to pupils, who always placed implicit faith in what he delivered.

But, why is this provision so ridiculous? because, says this author, it is unnecessary. But, why is it unnecessary? "because, the principles and habits, as well as the power of the Americans are directly opposed to standing armies; and there is as little necessity to guard against them by positive constitutions, as to prohibit the establishment of the Mahometan religion." It is admitted then, that a standing army in time of peace, is an evil. I ask then, why should this government be authorised to do evil? If the principles and habits of the people of this country are opposed to standing armies in time of peace, if they do not contribute to the public good, but would endanger the public liberty and happiness, why should the government be vested with the power? No reason can be given, why rulers should be authorised to do, what, if done, would oppose the principles and habits of the people, and endanger the public safety, but there is every reason in the world, that they should be prohibited from the exercise of such a power. But this author supposes, that no danger is to be apprehended from the exercise of this power, because, if armies are kept up, it will be by the people themselves, and therefore, to provide against it, would be as absurd as for a man to "pass a law in his family, that no troops should be quartered in his family by his consent." This reasoning supposes, that the general government is to be exercised by the people of America themselves—But such an idea is groundless and absurd. There is surely a distinction between the people and their rulers, even when the latter are representatives of the former.—They certainly are not identically the same, and it cannot be disputed, but it may and often does happen, that they do not possess the same sentiments or pursue the same interests. I think I have shewn, that as this government is constituted, there is little reason to expect, that the interest of the people and their rulers will be the same.

Besides, if the habits and sentiments of the people of America are to be relied upon, as the sole security against the encroachment of their rulers, all restrictions in constitutions are unnecessary; nothing more is requisite, than to declare who shall be authorized to exercise the powers of government, and about this we need not be very careful—for the habits and principles of the people will oppose every abuse of power. This I suppose to be the sentiments of this author, as it seems to be of many of the advocates of this new system. An opinion like this, is as directly opposed to the principles and habits of the people of America, as it is to the sentiments of every writer of reputation on the science of government, and repugnant to the principles of reason and common sense.

The idea that there is no danger of the establishment of a standing army, under the new constitution, is without foundation.

It is a well known fact, that a number of those who had an agency in producing this system, and many of those who it is probable will have a principal share in the administration of the government under it, if it is adopted, are avowedly in favour of standing armies. It is a language common among them, "That no people can be kept in order, unless the government have an army to awe them into obedience; it is necessary to support the dignity of government, to have a military establishment." And there will not be wanting a variety of plausible reason to justify the raising one, drawn from the danger we are in from the Indians on our frontiers, or from the European provinces in our neighbourhood. If to this we add, that an army will afford a decent support, and agreeable employment to the young men of many families, who are too indolent to follow occupations that will require care and industry, and too poor to live without doing any business[,] we can have little reason to doubt, but that we shall have a large standing army, as soon as this government can find money to pay them, and perhaps sooner.

A writer, who is the boast of the advocates of this new constitution, has taken great pains to shew, that this power was proper and necessary to be vested in the general government.

He sets out with calling in question the candour and integrity of those who advance the objection, and with insinuating, that it is their intention to mislead the people, by alarming their passions, rather than to convince them by arguments addressed to their understandings.

The man who reproves another for a fault, should be careful that he himself be not guilty of it. How far this writer has manifested a spirit of candour, and has pursued fair reasoning on this subject, the impartial public will judge, when his arguments pass before them in review.

He first attempts to shew, that this objection is futile and disingenuous, because the power to keep up standing armies, in time of peace, is vested, under the present government, in the legislature of every state in the union, except two. Now this is so far from being true, that it is expressly declared, by the present articles of confederation, that no body of forces "shall be kept up by any state, in time of peace, except such number only, as in the judgment of the United States in Congress assembled, shall be deemed requisite to garrison the forts necessary for the defence of such state." Now, was it candid and ingenuous to endeavour to persuade the public, that the general government had no other power than your own legislature have on this head; when the truth is, your legislature have no authority to raise and keep up any forces?

He next tells us, that the power given by this constitution, on this head, is similar to that which Congress possess under the present confederation. As little ingenuity is manifested in this representation as in that of the former.

I shall not undertake to enquire whether or not Congress are vested with a power to keep up a standing army in time of peace; it has been a subject, warmly debated in Congress, more than once, since the peace; and one of the most respectable states in the union, were so fully convinced that they had no such power, that they expressly instructed their delegates to enter a solemn protest against it on the journals of Congress, should they attempt to exercise it.

But should it be admitted that they have the power, there is such a striking dissimilarity between the restrictions under which the present Congress can exercise it, and that of the proposed government, that the comparison will serve rather to shew the impropriety of vesting the proposed government with the power, than of justifying it.

It is acknowledged by this writer, that the powers of Congress, under the present confederation, amount to little more than that of recommending. If they determine to raise troops, they are obliged to effect it through the authority of the state legislatures. This will, in the first instance, be a most powerful restraint upon them, against ordering troops to be raised. But if they should vote an army, contrary to the opinion and wishes of the people, the legislatures of the respective states would not raise them. Besides, the present Congress hold their places at the will and pleasure of the legislatures of the states who send them, and no troops can be raised, but by the assent of nine states out of the thirteen. Compare the power proposed to be lodged in the legislature on this head, under this constitution, with that vested in the present Congress, and every person of the least discernment, whose understanding is not totally blinded by prejudice, will perceive, that they bear no analogy to each other. Under the present confederation, the representatives of nine states, out of thirteen, must assent to the raising of troops, or they cannot be levied: under the proposed constitution, a less number than the representatives of two states, in the house of representatives, and the representatives of three states and an half in the senate, with the assent of the president, may raise any number of troops they please. The present Congress are restrained from an undue exercise of this power, from this consideration, they know [that] the state legislatures, through whose authority it must be carried into effect, would not comply with the requisition for the purpose, if it was evidently opposed to the public good: the proposed constitution authorizes the legislature to carry their determinations into execution, without the intervention of any other body between them and the people. The Congress under the present form are amenable to, and removable by, the legislatures of the respective states, and are chosen for one year only: the proposed constitution does not make the members of the legislature accountable to, or removeable by the state legislatures at all; and they are chosen, the one house for six, and the other for two years; and cannot be removed until their time of service is expired, let them conduct [themselves] ever so badly.—The public will judge, from the above comparison, how just a claim this writer has to that candour he affects to possess. In the mean time, to convince him, and the advocates for this system, that I possess some share of candor, I pledge myself to give up all opposition to it, on the head of standing armies, if the power to raise them be restricted as it is in the present confederation; and I believe I may safely answer, not only for myself, but for all who make the objection, that they will be satisfied with less.

Brutus

X
24 January 1788

To the Citizens of the State of New York:

The liberties of a people are in danger from a large standing army, not only because the rulers may employ them for the purposes of supporting themselves in any usurpations of power, which they may see proper to exercise, but there is great hazard, that an army will subvert the forms of the government, under whose authority they are raised, and establish one according to the pleasure of their leader.

We are informed, in the faithful pages of history, of such events frequently happening.—Two instances have been mentioned in a former paper. They are so remarkable, that they are worthy of the most careful attention of every lover of freedom.—They are taken from the history of the two most powerful nations that have ever existed in the world; and who are the most renowned, for the freedom they enjoyed, and the excellency of their constitutions:—I mean Rome and Britain.

In the first, the liberties of the commonwealth was destroyed, and the constitution overturned, by an army, lead by Julius Caesar, who was appointed to the command, by the constitutional authority of that commonwealth. He changed it from a free republic, whose fame had sounded, and is still celebrated by all the world, into that of the most absolute despotism. A standing army effected this change, and a standing army supported it through a succession of ages, which are marked in the annals of history, with the most horrid cruelties, bloodshed, and carnage;—the most devilish, beastly, and unnatural vices, that ever punished or disgraced human nature.

The same army, that in Britain, vindicated the liberties of that people from the encroachments and despotism of a tyrant king, assisted Cromwell, their General, in wresting from the people, that liberty they had so dearly earned.

You may be told, these instances will not apply to our case:—But those who would persuade you to believe this, either mean to deceive you, or have not themselves considered the subject.

I firmly believe, no country in the world had ever a more patriotic army, than the one which so ably served this country, in the late war.

But had the General who commanded them, been possessed of the spirit of a Julius Caesar or a Cromwell, the liberties of this country, had in all probability, terminated with the war; or had they been maintained, might have cost more blood and treasure, than was expended in the conflict with Great Britain. When an anonimous writer addressed the officers of the army at the close of the war, advising them not to part with their arms, until justice was done them—the effect it had is well known. It affected them like an electric shock. He wrote like Caesar; and had the commander in chief, and a few more officers of rank, countenanced the measure, the desperate resolution had been taken, to refuse to disband. What the consequences of such a determination would have been, heaven only knows.— The army were in the full vigor of health and spirits, in the habit of discipline, and possessed of all our military stores and apparatus. They would have acquired great accessions of strength from the country.—Those who were disgusted at our republican forms of government (for such there then were, of high rank among us) would have lent them all their aid.—We should in all probability have seen a constitution and laws, dictated to us, at the head of an army, and at the point of a bayonet, and the liberties for which we had so severely struggled, snatched from us in a moment. It remains a secret, yet to be revealed, whether this measure was not suggested, or at least countenanced, by some, who have had great influence in producing the present system.—Fortunately indeed for this country, it had at the head of the army, a patriot as well as a general; and many of our principal officers, had not abandoned the characters of citizens, by assuming that of soldiers, and therefore, the scheme proved abortive. But are we to expect, that this will always be the case? Are we so much better than the people of other ages and of other countries, that the same allurements of power and greatness, which led them aside from their duty, will have no influence upon men in our country? Such an idea, is wild and extravagant.—Had we indulged such a delusion, enough has appeared in a little time past, to convince the most credulous, that the passion for pomp, power and greatness, works as powerfully in the hearts of many of our better sort, as it ever did in any country under heaven.—Were the same opportunity again to offer, we should very probably be grossly disappointed, if we made dependence, that all who then rejected the overture, would do it again.

From these remarks, it appears, that the evil to be feared from a large standing army in time of peace, does not arise solely from the apprehension, that the rulers may employ them for the purpose of promoting their own ambitious views, but that equal, and perhaps greater danger, is to be apprehended from their overturning the constitutional powers of the government, and assuming the power to dictate any form they please.

The advocates for power, in support of this right in the proposed government, urge that a restraint upon the discretion of the legislature, in respect to military establishments in time of peace, would be improper to be imposed, because they say, it will be necessary to maintain small garrisons on the frontiers, to guard against the depredations of the Indians, and to be prepared to repel any encroachments or invasions that may be made by Spain or Britain.

The amount of this argument stripped of the abundant verbiages with which the author has dressed it, is this:

It will probably be necessary to keep up a small body of troops to garrison a few posts, which it will be necessary to maintain, in order to guard against the sudden encroachments of the Indians, or of the Spaniards and British; and therefore, the general government ought to be invested with power to raise and keep up a standing army in time of peace, without restraint; at their discretion.

I confess, I cannot perceive that the conclusion follows from the premises. Logicians say, it is no good reasoning to infer a general conclusion from particular premises; though I am not much of a Logician, it seems to me, this argument is very like that species of reasoning.

When the patriots in the parliament in Great Britain, contended with such force of argument, and all the powers of eloquence, against keeping up standing armies in time of peace, it is obvious, they never entertained an idea, that small garrisons on their frontiers, or in the neighbourhood of powers, from whom they were in danger of encroachments, or guards, to take care of public arsenals would thereby be prohibited.

The advocates for this power farther urge that it is necessary, because it may, and probably will happen, that circumstances will render it requisite to raise an army to be prepared to repel attacks of an enemy, before a formal declaration of war, which in modern times has fallen into disuse. If the constitution prohibited the raising an army, until a war actually commenced, it would deprive the government of the power of providing for the defence of the country, until the enemy were within our territory. If the restriction is not to extend to the raising armies in case of emergency, but only to the keeping them up, this would leave the matter to the discretion of the legislature; and they might, under the pretence that there was danger of an invasion, keep up the army as long as they judged proper—and hence it is inferred, that the legislature should have authority to raise and keep up an army without any restriction. But from these premises nothing more will follow than this, that the legislature should not be so restrained, as to put it out of their power to raise an army, when such exigencies as are instanced shall arise. But it does not thence follow, that the government should be empowered to raise and maintain standing armies at their discretion as well in peace as in war. If indeed, it is impossible to vest the general government with the power of raising troops to garrison the frontier posts, to guard arsenals, or to be prepared to repel an attack, when we saw a power preparing to make one, without giving them a general and indefinite authority, to raise and keep up armies, without any restriction or qualification, then this reasoning might have weight; but this has not been proved nor can it be.

It is admitted that to prohibit the general government, from keeping up standing armies, while yet they were authorised to raise them in case of exigency, would be an insufficient guard against the danger. A discretion of such latitude would give room to elude the force of the provision.

It is also admitted that an absolute prohibition against raising troops, except in case of actual war, would be improper; because it will be requisite to raise and support a small number of troops to garrison the important frontier posts, and to guard arsenals; and it may happen, that the danger of an attack from a foreign power may be so imminent, as to render it highly proper we should raise an army, in order to be prepared to resist them. But to raise and keep up forces for such purposes and on such occasions, is not included in the idea, of keeping up standing armies in time of peace.

It is a thing very practicable to give the government sufficient authority to provide for these cases, and at the same time to provide a reasonable and competent security against the evil of a standing army—a clause to the following purpose would answer the end:

As standing armies in time of peace are dangerous to liberty, and have often been the means of overturning the best constitutions of government, no standing army, or troops of any description whatsoever, shall be raised or kept up by the legislature, except so many as shall be necessary for guards to the arsenals of the United States, or for garrisons to such posts on the frontiers, as it shall be deemed absolutely necessary to hold, to secure the inhabitants, and facilitate the trade with the Indians: unless when the United States are threatened with an attack or invasion from some foreign power, in which case the legislature shall be authorised to raise an army to be prepared to repel the attack; provided that no troops whatsoever shall be raised in time of peace, without the assent of two thirds of the members, composing both houses of the legislature.

A clause similar to this would afford sufficient latitude to the legislature to raise troops in all cases that were really necessary, and at the same time competent security against the establishment of that dangerous engine of despotism, a standing army.

The same writer who advances the arguments I have noticed, makes a number of other observations with a view to prove that the power to raise and keep up armies, ought to be discretionary in the general legislature; some of them are curious; he instances the raising of troops in Massachusetts and Pennsylvania, to show the necessity of keeping a standing army in time of peace; the least reflection must convince every candid mind that both these cases are totally foreign to his purpose—Massachusetts raised a body of troops for six months, at the expiration of which they were to disband of course; this looks very little like a standing army. But beside, was that commonwealth in a state of peace at that time? So far from it that they were in the most violent commotions and contents, and their legislature had formally declared that an unnatural rebellion existed within the state. The situation of Pennsylvania was similar; a number of armed men had levied war against the authority of the state, and openly avowed their intention of withdrawing their allegiance from it. To what purpose examples are brought, of states raising troops for short periods in times of war or insurrections, on a question concerning the propriety of keeping up standing armies in times of peace, the public must judge.

It is farther said, that no danger can arise from this power being lodged in the hands of the general government, because the legislatures will be a check upon them, to prevent their abusing it.

This is offered, as what force there is in it will hereafter receive a more particular examination. At present, I shall only remark, that it is difficult to conceive how the state legislatures can, in any case, hold a check over the general legislature, in a constitutional way. The latter has, in every instance to which their powers extend, complete control over the former. The state legislatures can, in no case, by law, resolution, or otherwise, of right, prevent or impede the general government, from enacting any law, or executing it, which this constitution authorizes them to enact or execute. If then the state legislatures check the general legislatures [*sic*], it must be by exciting the people to resist constitutional laws. In this way every individual, or every body of men, may check any government, in proportion to the influence they may have over the body of the people. But such kinds of checks as these, though they sometimes correct the abuses of government, oftner destroy all government.

It is further said, that no danger is to be apprehended from the exercise of this power, because it is lodged in the hands of representatives of the people; if they abuse it, it is in the power of the people to remove them, and chuse others who will pursue their interests. Not to repeat what has been said before, that it is unwise in any people, to authorize their rulers to do, what, if done, would prove injurious—I have, in some former numbers, shown, that the representation in the proposed government will be a mere shadow without the substance. I am so confident that I am well founded in this opinion, that I am persuaded, if it was to be adopted or rejected, upon a fair discussion of its merits, without taking into contemplation circumstances extraneous to it, as reasons for its adoption, nineteen twentieths of the sensible men in the union would reject it on this account alone: unless its powers were confined to much fewer objects than it embraces.

Brutus

XI
31 JANUARY 1788

To the Citizens of the State of New York:

The nature and extent of the judicial power of the United States, proposed to be granted by this constitution, claims our particular attention.

Much has been said and written upon the subject of this new system on both sides, but I have not met with any writer, who has discussed the judicial powers with any degree of accuracy. And yet it is obvious, that we can form but very imperfect ideas of the manner in which this government will work, or the effect it will have in changing the internal police and mode of distributing justice at present subsisting in the respective states, without a thorough investigation of the powers of the judiciary and of the manner in which they will operate. This government is a complete system, not only for making, but for executing laws. And the courts of law, which will be constituted by it, are not only to decide upon the constitution and the laws made in pursuance of it, but by officers subordinate to them to execute, all their decisions. The real effect of this system of government, will therefore be brought home to the feelings of the people, through the medium of the judicial power. It is, moreover, of great importance, to examine with care the nature and extent of the judicial power, because those who are to be vested with it, are to be placed in a situation altogether unprecedented in a free country. They are to be rendered totally independent, both of the people and the legislature, both with respect to their offices and salaries. No errors they may commit can be corrected by any power above them, if any such power there be, nor can they be removed from office for making ever so many erroneous adjudications.

The only causes for which they can be displaced, is, conviction of treason, bribery, and high crimes and misdemeanors.

This part of the plan is so modelled, as to authorise the courts, not only to carry into execution the powers expressly given, but where these are wanting or ambiguously expressed, to supply what is wanting by their own decisions.

That we may be enabled to form a just opinion on this subject, I shall, in considering it,

1st. Examine the nature and extent of the judicial powers—and,

2d. Enquire, whether the courts who are to exercise them, are so constituted as to afford reasonable ground of confidence, that they will exercise them for the general good.

With a regard to the nature and extent of the judicial powers, I have to regret my want or capacity to give that full and minute explanation of them that the subject merits. To be able to do this, a man should be possessed of a degree of law knowledge far beyond what I pretend to. A number of hard words and technical phrases are used in this part of the system, about the meaning of which gentlemen learned in the law differ.

Its advocates know how to avail themselves of these phrases. In a number of instances, where objections are made to the powers given to the judicial, they give such an explanation to the technical terms as to avoid them.

Though I am not competent, to give a perfect explanation of the powers granted to this department of the government, I shall yet attempt to trace some of the leading features of it, from which I presume it will appear, that they will operate to a total subversion of the state judiciaries, if not, to the legislative authority of the states.

In article 3d, sect. 2d, it is said, "The judicial power shall extend to all cases in law and equity arising under this constitution, the laws of the United States, and treaties made, or which shall be made, under their authority etc."

The first article to which this power extends, is, all cases in law and equity arising under this constitution.

What latitude of construction this clause should receive, it is not easy to say. At first view, one would suppose, that it meant no more than this, that the courts under the general government should exercise, not only the powers of courts of law, but also that of courts of equity, in the manner in which those powers are usually exercised in the different states. But this cannot be the meaning, because the next clause authorises the courts to take cognizance of all cases in law and equity arising under the laws of the United States; this last article, I conceive, conveys as much power to the general judicial as any of the state courts possess.

The cases arising under the constitution must be different from those arising under the laws, or else the two clauses mean exactly the same thing.

The cases arising under the constitution must include such, as bring into question its meaning, and will require an explanation of the nature and extent of the powers of the different departments under it.

This article, therefore, vests the judicial with a power to resolve all questions that may arise on any case on the construction of the constitution, either in law or in equity.

1st. They are authorised to determine all questions that may arise upon the meaning of the constitution in law. This article vests the courts with authority to give the constitution a legal construction, or to explain it according to the rules laid down for construing a law.—These rules give a certain degree of latitude of explanation. According to this mode of construction, the courts are to give such meaning to the constitution as comports best with the common, and generally received acceptation of the words in which it is expressed, regarding their ordinary and popular use, rather than their grammatical propriety. Where words are dubious, they will be explained by the context. The end of the clause will be attended to, and the words will be understood, as having a view to it; and the words will not be so understood as to bear no meaning or a very absurd one.

2d. The judicial are not only to decide questions arising upon the meaning of the constitution in law, but also in equity.

By this they are empowered, to explain the constitution according to the reasoning spirit of it, without being confined to the words or letter.

"From this method of interpreting laws," says Blackstone, "by the reason of them, arises what we call equity"; which is thus defined by Grotius, "the correction of that, wherein the law, by reason of its universality, is deficient"; for since in laws, all cases cannot be foreseen, or expressed, it is necessary, that when the decrees of the laws cannot be applied to particular cases, there should some where be a power vested of defining those circumstances, which had they been foreseen the legislator would have expressed; and these are the cases, which according to Grotius, "lex non exacte definit, sed arbitrio boni viri permittet."

The same learned author observes, "That equity, thus depending essentially upon each individual case, there can be no established rules and fixed principles of equity laid down, without destroying its very essence, and reducing it to a positive law."

From these remarks, the authority and business of the courts of law, under this clause, may be understood.

They will give the sense of every article of the constitution, that may from time to time come before them. And in their decisions they will not confine themselves to any fixed or established rules, but will determine, according to what appears to them, the reason and spirit of the constitution. The opinions of the supreme court, whatever they may be, will have the force of law; because there is no power provided in the constitution, that can correct their errors, or control their adjudications. From this court there is no appeal. And I conceive the legislature themselves, cannot set aside a judgment of this court, because they are authorised by the constitution to decide in the last resort. The legislature must be controled by the constitution, and not the constitution by them. They have therefore no more right to set aside any judgment pronounced upon the construction of the constitution, than they have to take from the president, the chief command of the army and navy, and commit it to some other person. The reason is plain; the judicial and executive derive their authority from the same source, that the legislature do theirs; and therefore in all cases, where the constitution does not make the one responsible to, or controlable by the other, they are altogether independent of each other.

The judicial power will operate to effect, in the most certain, but yet silent and imperceptible manner, what is evidently the tendency of the constitution—I mean, an entire subversion of the legislative, executive and judicial powers of the individual states. Every adjudication of the supreme court, on any question that may arise upon the nature and extent of the general government, will affect the limits of the state jurisdiction. In proportion as the former enlarge the exercise of their powers, will that of the latter be restricted.

That the judicial power of the United States, will lean strongly in favour of the general government, and will give such an explanation to the constitution, as will favour an extension of its jurisdiction, is very evident from a variety of considerations.

1st. The constitution itself strongly countenances such a mode of construction. Most of the articles in this system, which convey powers of any considerable importance, are conceived in general and indefinite terms, which are either equivocal, ambiguous, or which require long definitions to unfold the extent of their meaning. The two most important powers committed to any government, those of raising money, and of raising and keeping up troops, have already been considered, and shown to be unlimited by any thing but the discretion of the legislature. The clause which vests the power to pass all laws which are proper and necessary, to carry the powers given into execution, it has been shown, leaves the legislature at liberty, to do every thing, which in their judgment is best. It is said, I know, that this clause confers no power on the legislature, which they could not have had without it—though I believe this is not the fact, yet, admitting it to be, it implies that the constitution is not to receive an explanation strictly, according to its letter; but more power is implied than is expressed. And this clause, if it is to be considered, as explanatory of the extent of the powers given, rather than giving a new power, is to be understood as declaring, that in construing any of the articles conveying power, the spirit, intent and design of the clause, should be attended to, as well as the words in their common acceptation.

This constitution gives sufficient colour for adopting an equitable construction, if we consider the great end and design it professedly has in view—these appear from its preamble to be, "to form a more perfect union, establish justice, insure domestic tranquility, provide for the common defence, promote the general welfare, and secure the blessings of liberty to ourselves and posterity." The design of this system is here expressed, and it is proper to give such a meaning to the various parts, as will best promote the accomplishment of the end; this idea suggests itself naturally upon reading the preamble, and will countenance the court in giving the several articles such a sense, as will the most effectually promote the ends the constitution had in view—how this manner of explaining the constitution will operate in practice, shall be the subject of future enquiry.

2d. Not only will the constitution justify the courts in inclining to this mode of explaining it, but they will be interested in using this latitude of interpretation. Every body of men invested with office are tenacious of power; they feel interested, and hence it has become a kind of maxim, to hand down their offices, with all its rights and privileges, unimpared to their successors; the same principle will influence them to extend their power, and increase their rights; this of itself will operate strongly upon the courts to give such a meaning to the constitution in all cases where it can possibly be done, as will enlarge the sphere of their own authority. Every extension of the power of the general legislature, as well as of the judicial powers, will increase the powers of the courts; and the dignity and importance of the judges, will be in proportion to the extent and magnitude of the powers they exercise. I add, it is highly probable the emolument of the judges will be increased, with the increase of the business they will have to transact and its importance. From these considerations the judges will be interested to extend the powers of the courts, and to construe the constitution as much as possible, in such a way as to favour it; and that they will do it, appears probable.

3d. Because they will have precedent to plead, to justify them in it. It is well known, that the courts in England, have by their own authority, extended their jurisdiction far beyond the limits set them in their original institution, and by the laws of the land.

The court of exchequer is a remarkable instance of this. It was originally intended principally to recover the king's debts, and to order the revenues of the crown. It had a common law jurisdiction, which was established merely for the benefit of the king's accomptants. We learn from Blackstone, that the proceedings in this court are grounded on a writ called quo minus, in which the plaintiff suggests, that he is the king's farmer or debtor, and that the defendant hath done him the damage complained of, by which he is less able to pay the king. These suits, by the statute of Rutland, are expressly directed to be confined to such matters as specially concern the king, or his ministers in the exchequer. And by the *articuli super cartas,* it is enacted, that no common pleas be thenceforth held in the exchequer contrary to the form of the great charter: but now any person may sue in the exchequer. The surmise of being debtor to the king being matter of form, and mere words of course; and the court is open to all the nation.

When the courts will have a precedent before them of a court which extended its jurisdiction in opposition to an act of the legislature, is it not to be expected that they will extend theirs, especially when there is nothing in the constitution expressly against it? and they are authorised to construe its meaning, and are not under any control?

This power in the judicial, will enable them to mould the government, into almost any shape they please.—The manner in which this may be effected we will hereafter examine.

Brutus

XII
7 FEBRUARY 1788

To the Citizens of the State of New York:

In my last, I showed, that the judicial power of the United States under the first clause of the second section of article eight, would be authorized to explain the constitution, not only according to its letter, but according to its spirit and intention; and having this power, they would strongly incline to give it such a construction as to extend the powers of the general government, as much as possible, to the diminution, and finally to the destruction, of that of the respective states.

I shall now proceed to show how this power will operate in its exercise to effect these purposes. In order to perceive the extent of its influence, I shall consider,

First. How it will tend to extend the legislative authority.

Second. In what manner it will increase the jurisdiction of the courts, and

Third. The way in which it will diminish, and destroy, both the legislative and judicial authority of the United States.

First. Let us enquire how the judicial power will effect an extension of the legislative authority.

Perhaps the judicial power will not be able, by direct and positive decrees, ever to direct the legislature, because it is not easy to conceive how a question can be brought before them in a course of legal discussion, in which they can give a decision, declaring, that the legislature have certain powers which they have not exercised, and which, in consequence of the determination of the judges, they will be bound to exercise. But it is easy to see, that in their adjudications they may establish certain principles, which being received by the legislature, will enlarge the sphere of their power beyond all bounds.

It is to be observed, that the supreme court has the power, in the last resort, to determine all questions that may arise in the course of legal discussion, on the meaning and construction of the constitution. This power they will hold under the constitution, and independent of the legislature. The latter can no more deprive the former of this right, than either of them, or both of them together, can take from the president, with the advice of the senate, the power of making treaties, or appointing ambassadors.

In determining these questions, the court must and will assume certain principles, from which they will reason, in forming their decisions. These principles, whatever they may be, when they become fixed, by a course of decisions, will be adopted by the legislature, and will be the rule by which they will explain their own powers. This appears evident from this consideration, that if the legislature pass laws, which, in the judgment of the court, they are not authorised to do by the constitution, the court will not take notice of them; for it will not be denied, that the constitution is the highest or supreme law. And the courts are vested with the supreme and uncontrollable power, to determine, in all cases that come before them, what the constitution means; they cannot, therefore, execute a law, which, in their judgment, opposes the constitution, unless we can suppose they can make a superior law give way to an inferior. The legislature, therefore, will not go over the limits by which the courts may adjudge they are confined. And there is little room to doubt but that they will come up to those bounds, as often as occasion and opportunity may offer, and they may judge it proper to do it. For as on the one hand, they will not readily pass laws which they know the courts will not execute, so on the other, we may be sure they will not scruple to pass such as they know will give effect, as often as they may judge it proper.

From these observations it appears, that the judgment of the judicial, on the constitution, will become the rule to guide the legislature in their construction of their powers.

What the principles are, which the courts will adopt, it is impossible for us to say; but taking up the powers as I have explained them in my last number, which they will possess under this clause, it is not difficult to see, that they may, and probably will, be very liberal ones.

We have seen, that they will be authorized to give the constitution a construction according to its spirit and reason, and not to confine themselves to its letter.

To discover the spirit of the constitution, it is of the first importance to attend to the principal ends and designs it has in view. These are expressed in the preamble, in the following words, viz, "We, the people of the United States, in order to form a more perfect union, establish justice, insure domestic tranquility, provide for the common defence, promote the general welfare, and secure the blessings of liberty to ourselves and our posterity, do ordain and establish this constitution," etc. If the end of the government is to be learned from these words, which are clearly designed to declare it, it is obvious it has in view every object which is embraced by any government. The preservation of internal peace—the due administration of justice—and to provide for the defence of the community, seems to include all the objects of government; but if they do not, they are certainly comprehended in the words, "to provide for the general welfare." If it be further considered, that this constitution, if it is ratified, will not be a compact entered into by states, in their corporate capacities, but an agreement of the people of the United States, as one great body politic, no doubt can remain, but that the great end of the constitution, if it is to be collected from the preamble, in which its end is declared, is to constitute a government which is to extend to every case for which any government is instituted, whether external or internal. The courts, therefore, will establish this as a principle in expounding the constitution, and will give every part of it such an explanation, as will give latitude to every department under it, to take cognizance of every matter, not only that affects the general and national concerns of the union, but also of such as relate to the administration of private justice, and to regulating the internal and local affairs of the different parts.

Such a rule of exposition is not only consistent with the general spirit of the preamble, but it will stand confirmed by considering more minutely the different clauses of it.

The first object declared to be in view is "To form a perfect union." It is to be observed, it is not an union of states or bodies corporate; had this been the case the existence of the state governments, might have been secured. But it is a union of the people of the United States considered as one body, who are to ratify this constitution, if it is adopted. Now to make a union of this kind perfect, it is necessary to abolish all inferior governments, and to give the general one compleat legislative, executive and judicial powers to every purpose. The courts therefore will establish it as a rule in explaining the constitution to give it such a construction as will best tend to perfect the union or take from the state governments every power of either making or executing laws. The second object is "to establish justice." This must include not only the idea of instituting the rule of justice, or of making laws which shall be the measure or rule of right, but also of providing for the application of this rule or of administering justice under it. And under this the courts will in their decisions extend the power of the governments to all cases they possibly can, or otherwise they will be restricted in doing what appears to be the intent of the constitution they should do, to wit, pass laws and provide for the execution of them, for the general distribution of justice between man and man. Another end declared is "to insure domestic tranquility." This comprehends a provision against all private breaches of the peace, as well as against all public commotions or general insurrections; and to attain the object of this clause fully, the government must exercise the power of passing laws on these subjects, as well as of appointing magistrates with authority to execute them. And the courts will adopt these ideas in their expositions. I might proceed to the other clause, in the preamble, and it would appear by a consideration of all of them separately, as it does by taking them together, that if the spirit of this system is to be known from its declared end and design in the preamble, its spirit is to subvert and abolish all the powers of the state government, and to embrace every object to which any government extends.

As it sets out in the preamble with this declared intention, so it proceeds in the different parts with the same idea. Any person, who will peruse the 8th section with attention, in which most of the powers are enumerated, will perceive that they either expressly or by implication extend to almost every thing about which any legislative power can be employed. But if this equitable mode of construction is applied to this part of the constitution, nothing can stand before it.

This will certainly give the first clause in that article a construction which I confess I think the most natural and grammatical one, to authorise the Congress to do any thing which in their judgment will tend to provide for the general welfare, and this amounts to the same thing as general and unlimited powers of legislation in all cases.

XII (PART II)
14 FEBRUARY 1788

To the Citizens of the State of New York:

This same manner of explaining the constitution, will fix a meaning, and a very important one too, to the 18th clause of the same section, which authorises the Congress to make all laws which shall be proper and necessary for carrying into effect the foregoing powers, etc. A voluminous writer in favor of this system, has taken great pains to convince the public, that this clause means nothing; for that the same powers expressed in this, are implied in other parts of the constitution. Perhaps it is so, but still this will undoubtedly be an excellent auxilliary to assist the courts to discover the spirit and reason of the constitution, and when applied to any and every of the other clauses granting power, will operate powerfully in extracting the spirit from them.

I might instance a number of clauses in the constitution, which, if explained in an *equitable* manner, would extend the powers of the government to every case, and reduce the state legislatures to nothing; but, I should draw out my remarks to an undue length, and I presume enough has been said to show, that the courts have sufficient ground in the exercise of this power, to determine, that the legislature have no bounds set to them by this constitution, by any supposed right the legislatures of the respective states may have, to regulate any of their local concerns.

I proceed, 2d, to inquire, in what manner this power will increase the jurisdiction of the courts.

I would here observe, that the judicial power extends, expressly, to all civil cases that may arise save such as arise between citizens of the same state, with this exception to those of that description, that the judicial of the United States have cognizance of cases between citizens of the same state, claiming lands under grants of different states. Nothing more, therefore, is necessary to give the courts of law, under this constitution, complete jurisdiction of all civil causes, but to comprehend cases between citizens of the same state not included in the foregoing exception.

I presume there will be no difficulty in accomplishing this. Nothing more is necessary than to set forth, in the process, that the party who brings the suit is a citizen of a different state from the one against whom the suit is brought, and there can be little doubt but that the court will take cognizance of the matter, and if they do, who is to restrain them? Indeed, I will freely confess, that it is my decided opinion, that the courts ought to take cognizance of such causes, under the powers of the constitution. For one of the great ends of the constitution is, "to establish justice." This supposes that this cannot be done under the existing governments of the states; and there is certainly as good reason why individuals, living in the same state, should have justice, as those who live in different states. Moreover, the constitution expressly declares, that "the citizens of each state shall be entitled to all the privileges and immunities of citizens in the several states." It will therefore be no fiction, for a citizen of one state to set forth, in a suit, that he is a citizen of another; for he that is entitled to all the privileges and immunities of a country, is a citizen of that country. And in truth, the citizen of one state will, under this constitution, be a citizen of every state.

But supposing that the party, who alledges that he is a citizen of another state, has recourse to fiction in bringing in his suit, it is well known, that the courts have high authority to plead, to justify them in suffering actions to be brought before them by such fictions. In my last number I stated, that the court of exchequer tried all causes in virtue of such a fiction. The court of king's bench, in England, extended their jurisdiction in the same way. Originally, this court held pleas, in civil cases, only of trespasses and other injuries alleged to be committed *vi et armis*. They might likewise, says Blackstone, upon the division of the *aula regia,* have originally held pleas of any other civil action whatsoever (except in real actions which are now very seldom in use) provided the defendant was an officer of the court, or in the custody of the marshall or prison-keeper of this court, for breach of the peace, etc. In process of time, by a fiction, this court began to hold pleas of any personal action whatsoever; it being surmised, that the defendant has been arrested for a supposed trespass that "he has never committed, and being thus in the custody of the marshall of the court, the plaintiff is at liberty to proceed against him, for any other personal injury; which surmise of being in the marshall's custody, the defendant is not at liberty to dispute." By a much less fiction, may the pleas of the courts of the United States extend to cases between citizens of the same state. I shall add no more on this head, but proceed briefly to remark, in what way this power will diminish and destroy both the legislative and judicial authority of the states.

It is obvious that these courts will have authority to decide upon the validity of the laws of any of the states, in all cases where they come in question before them. Where the constitution gives the general government exclusive jurisdiction, they will adjudge all laws made by the states, in such cases, void *ab initio*. Where the constitution gives them concurrent jurisdiction, the laws of the United States must prevail, because they are the supreme law. In such cases, therefore, the laws of the state legislatures must be repealed, restricted, or so construed, as to give full effect to the laws of the union on the same subject. From these remarks it is easy to see, that in proportion as the general government acquires power and jurisdiction, by the liberal construction which the judges may give the constitution, will those of the states lose its rights, until they become so trifling and unimportant, as not to be worth having. I am much mistaken, if this system will not operate to effect this with as much celerity, as those who have the administration of it will think prudent to suffer it. The remaining objections to the judicial power shall be considered in a future paper.

Brutus

XV
20 March 1788

To the Citizens of the State of New York:

I said in my last number, that the supreme court under this constitution would be exalted above all other power in the government, and subject to no control. The business of this paper will be to illustrate this, and to show the danger that will result from it. I question whether the world ever saw, in any period of it, a court of justice invested with such immense powers, and yet placed in a situation so little responsible. Certain it is, that in England, and in the several states, where we have been taught to believe, the courts of law are put upon the most prudent establishment, they are on a very different footing.

The judges in England, it is true, hold their offices during their good behaviour, but then their determinations are subject to correction by the house of lords; and their power is by no means so extensive as that of the proposed supreme court of the union.—I believe they in no instance assume the authority to set aside an act of parliament under the idea that it is inconsistent with their constitution. They consider themselves bound to decide according to the existing laws of the land, and never undertake to control them by adjudging that they are inconsistent with the constitution—much less are they vested with the power of giving an *equitable* construction to the constitution.

The judges in England are under the control of the legislature, for they are bound to determine according to the laws passed by them. But the judges under this constitution will control the legislature, for the supreme court are authorised in the last resort, to determine what is the extent of the powers of the Congress; they are to give the constitution an explanation, and there is no power above them to set aside their judgment. The framers of this constitution appear to have followed that of the British, in rendering the judges independent, by granting them their offices during good behaviour, without following the constitution of England, in instituting a tribunal in which their errors may be corrected; and without averting to this, that the judicial under this system have a power which is above the legislative, and which indeed transcends any power before given to a judicial by any free government under heaven.

I do not object to the judges holding their commissions during good behaviour. I suppose it a proper provision provided they were made properly responsible. But I say, this system has followed the English government in this, while it has departed from almost every other principle of their jurisprudence, under the idea, of rendering the judges independent; which, in the British constitution, means no more than that they hold their places during good behaviour, and have fixed salaries, they have made the judges *independent,* in the fullest sense of the word. There is no power above them, to control any of their decisions. There is no authority that can remove them, and they cannot be controlled by the laws of the legislature. In short, they are independent of the people, of the legislature, and of every power under heaven. Men placed in this situation will generally soon feel themselves independent of heaven itself. Before I proceed to illustrate the truth of these assertions, I beg liberty to make one remark—Though in my opinion the judges ought to hold their offices during good behaviour, yet I think it is clear, that the reasons in favour of this establishment of the judges in England, do by no means apply to this country.

The great reason assigned, why the judges in Britain ought to be commissioned during good behaviour, is this, that they may be placed in a situation, not to be influenced by the crown, to give such decisions, as would tend to increase its powers and prerogatives. While the judges held their places at the will and pleasure of the king, on whom they depended not only for their offices, but also for their salaries, they were subject to every undue influence. If the crown wished to carry a favorite point, to accomplish which the aid of the courts of law was necessary, the pleasure of the king would be signified to the judges. And it required the spirit of a martyr, for the judges to determine contrary to the king's will.—They were absolutely dependent upon him both for their offices and livings. The king, holding his office during life, and transmitting it to his posterity as an inheritance, has much stronger inducements to increase the prerogatives of his office than those who hold their offices for stated periods, or even for life. Hence the English nation gained a great point, in favour of liberty. When they obtained the appointment of the judges, during good behaviour, they got from the crown a concession, which deprived it of one of the most powerful engines with which it might enlarge the boundaries of the royal prerogative and encroach on the liberties of the people. But these reasons do not apply to this country, we have no hereditary monarch; those who appoint the judges do not hold their offices for life, nor do they descend to their children. The same arguments, therefore, which will conclude in favor of the tenor of the judge's offices for good behaviour, lose a considerable part of their weight when applied to the state and condition of America. But much less can it be shown, that the nature of our government requires that the courts should be placed beyond all account more independent, so much so as to be above control.

I have said that the judges under this system will be *independent* in the strict sense of the word: To prove this I will show—that there is no power above them that can control their decisions, or correct their errors. There is no authority that can remove them from office for any errors or want of capacity, or lower their salaries, and in many cases their power is superior to that of the legislature.

1st. There is no power above them that can correct their errors or control their decisions.—The adjudications of this court are final and irreversible, for there is no court above them to which appeals can lie, either in error or on the merits.—In this respect it differs from the courts in England, for there the house of lords is the highest court, to whom appeals, in error, are carried from the highest of the courts of law.

2d. They cannot be removed from office or suffer a diminution of their salaries, for any error in judgment or want of capacity.

It is expressly declared by the constitution, "That they shall at stated times receive a compensation for their services which shall not be diminished during their continuance in office."

The only clause in the constitution which provides for the removal of the judges from office, is that which declares, that "the president, vice-president, and all civil officers of the United States, shall be removed from office, on impeachment for, and conviction of treason, bribery, or other high crimes and misdemeanors." By this paragraph, civil officers, in which the judges are included, are removable only for crimes. Treason and bribery are named, and the rest are included under the general terms of high crimes and misdemeanors.—Errors in judgment, or want of capacity to discharge the duties of the office, can never be supposed to be included in these words, *high crimes and misdemeanors*. A man may mistake a case in giving judgment, or manifest that he is incompetent to the discharge of the duties of a judge, and yet give no evidence of corruption or want of integrity. To support the charge, it will be necessary to give in evidence some facts that will show, that the judges commited the error from wicked and corrupt motives.

3d. The power of this court is in many cases superior to that of the legislature. I have showed, in a former paper, that this court will be authorised to decide upon the meaning of the constitution, and that, not only according to the natural and ob[vious] meaning of the words, but also according to the spirit and intention of it. In the exercise of this power they will not be subordinate to, but above the legislature. For all the departments of this government will receive their powers, so far as they are expressed in the constitution, from the people immediately, who are the source of power. The legislature can only exercise such powers as are given them by the constitution, they cannot assume any of the rights annexed to the judicial, for this plain reason, that the same authority which vested the legislature with their powers, vested the judicial with theirs—both are derived from the same source, both therefore are equally valid, and the judicial hold their powers independently of the legislature, as the legislature do of the judicial.—The supreme court then have a right, independent of the legislature, to give a construction to the constitution and every part of it, and there is no power provided in this system to correct their construction or do it away. If, therefore, the legislature pass any laws, inconsistent with the sense the judges put upon the constitution, they will declare it void; and therefore in this respect their power is superior to that of the legislature. In England the judges are not only subject to have their decisions set aside by the house of lords, for error, but in cases where they give an explanation to the laws or constitution of the country, contrary to the sense of the parliament, though the parliament will not set aside the judgment of the court, yet, they have authority, by a new law, to explain a former one, and by this means to prevent a reception of such decisions. But no such power is in the legislature. The judges are supreme—and no law, explanatory of the constitution, will be binding on them.

From the preceding remarks, which have been made on the judicial powers proposed in this system, the policy of it may be fully developed.

I have, in the course of my observation on this constitution, affirmed and endeavored to shew, that it was calculated to abolish entirely the state governments, and to melt down the states into one entire government, for every purpose as well internal and local, as external and national. In this opinion the opposers of the system have generally agreed—and this has been uniformly denied by its advocates in public. Some individuals, indeed, among them, will confess, that it has this tendency, and scruple not to say, it is what they wish; and I will venture to predict, without the spirit of prophecy, that if it is adopted without amendments, or some such precautions as will ensure amendments immediately after its adoption, that the same gentlemen who have employed their talents and abilities with such success to influence the public mind to adopt this plan, will employ the same to persuade the people, that it will be for their good to abolish the state governments as useless and burdensome.

Perhaps nothing could have been better conceived to facilitate the abolition of the state governments than the constitution of the judicial. They will be able to extend the limits of the general government gradually, and by insensible degrees, and to accommodate themselves to the temper of the people. Their decisions on the meaning of the constitution will commonly take place in cases which arise between individuals, with which the public will not be generally acquainted; one adjudication will form a precedent to the next, and this to a following one. These cases will immediately affect individuals only; so that a series of determinations will probably take place before even the people will be informed of them. In the mean time all the art and address of those who wish for the change will be employed to make converts to their opinion. The people will be told, that their state officers, and state legislatures are a burden and expence without affording any solid advantage, for that all the laws passed by them, might be equally well made by the general legislature. If to those who will be interested in the change, be added, those who will be under their influence, and such who will submit to almost any change of government, which they can be persuaded to believe will ease them of taxes, it is easy to see, the party who will favor the abolition of the state governments would be far from being inconsiderable.—In this situation, the general legislature, might pass one law after another, extending the general and abridging the state jurisdictions, and to sanction their proceedings would have a course of decisions of the judicial to whom the constitution has committed the power of explaining the constitution.—If the states remonstrated, the constitutional mode of deciding upon the validity of the law, is with the supreme court, and neither people, nor state legislatures, nor the general legislature can remove them or reverse their decrees.

Had the construction of the constitution been left with the legislature, they would have explained it at their peril; if they exceed their powers, or sought to find, in the spirit of the constitution, more than was expressed in the letter, the people from whom they derived their power could remove them, and do themselves right; and indeed I can see no other remedy that the people can have against their rulers for encroachments of this nature. A constitution is a compact of a people with their rulers; if the rulers break the compact, the people have a right and ought to remove them and do themselves justice; but in order to enable them to do this with the greater facility, those whom the people choose at stated periods, should have the power in the last resort to determine the sense of the compact; if they determine contrary to the understanding of the people, an appeal will lie to the people at the period when the rulers are to be elected, and they will have it in their power to remedy the evil; but when this power is lodged in the hands of men independent of the people, and of their representatives, and who are not, constitutionally, accountable for their opinions, no way is left to control them but *with a high hand and an outstretched arm.*

Brutus

XVI
10 April 1788

To the Citizens of the State of New York:

When great and extraordinary powers are vested in any man, or body of men, which in their exercise, may operate to the oppression of the people, it is of high importance that powerful checks should be formed to prevent the abuse of it.

Perhaps no restraints are more forcible, than such as arise from responsibility to some superior power.—Hence it is that the true policy of a republican government is, to frame it in such manner, that all persons who are concerned in the government, are made accountable to some superior for their conduct in office.—This responsibility should ultimately rest with the People. To have a government well administered in all its parts, it is requisite the different departments of it should be separated and lodged as much as may be in different hands. The legislative power should be in one body, the executive in another, and the judicial in one different from either—but still each of these bodies should be accountable for their conduct. Hence it is impracticable, perhaps, to maintain a perfect distinction between these several departments—for it is difficult, if not impossible, to call to account the several officers in government, without in some degree mixing the legislative and judicial. The legislature in a free republic are chosen by the people at stated periods, and their responsibility consists, in their being amenable to the people. When the term, for which they are chosen, shall expire, who will then have opportunity to displace them if they disapprove of their conduct—but it would be improper that the judicial should be elective, because their business requires that they should possess a degree of law knowledge, which is acquired only by a regular education, and besides it is fit that they should be placed, in a certain degree in an independent situation, that they may maintain firmness and steadiness in their decisions. As the people therefore ought not to elect the judges, they cannot be amenable to them immediately, some other mode of amenability must therefore be devised for these, as well as for all other officers which do not spring from the immediate choice of the people: this is to be effected by making one court subordinate to another, and by giving them cognizance of the behaviour of all officers; but on this plan we at last arrive at some supreme, over whom there is no power to control but the people themselves. This supreme controlling power should be in the choice of the people, or else you establish an authority independent, and not amenable at all, which is repugnant to the principles of a free government. Agreeable to these principles I suppose the supreme judicial ought to be liable to be called to account, for any misconduct, by some body of men, who depend upon the people for their places; and so also should all other great officers in the state, who are not made amenable to some superior officers. This policy seems in some measure to have been in view of the framers of the new system, and to have given rise to the institution of a court of impeachments.—How far this Court will be properly qualified to execute the trust which will be reposed in them, will be the business of a future paper to investigate. To prepare the way to do this, it shall be the business of this, to make some remarks upon the constitution and powers of the senate, with whom the power of trying impeachments is lodged.

The following things may be observed with respect to the constitution of the senate.

1st. They are to be elected by the legislatures of the states and not by the people, and each state is to be represented by an equal number.

2d. They are to serve for six years, except that one third of those first chosen are to go out of office at the expiration of two years, one third at the expiration of four years, and one third at the expiration of six years, after which this rotation is to be preserved, but still every member will serve for the term of six years.

3d. If vacancies happen by resignation or otherwise, during the recess of the legislature of any state, the executive is authorised to make temporary appointments until the next meeting of the legislature.

4. No person can be a senator who has not arrived to the age of thirty years, been nine years a citizen of the United States, and who is not at the time he is elected an inhabitant of the state for which he is elected.

The apportionment of members of senate among the states is not according to numbers, or the importance of the states; but is equal. This, on the plan of a consolidated government, is unequal and improper; but is proper on the system of confederation—on this principle I approve of it. It is indeed the only feature of any importance in the constitution of a confederated government. It was obtained after a vigorous struggle of that part of the Convention who were in favor of preserving the state governments. It is to be regretted, that they were not able to have infused other principles into the plan, to have secured the government of the respective states, and to have marked with sufficient precision the line between them and the general government.

The term for which the senate are to be chosen, is in my judgment too long, and no provision being made for a rotation will, I conceive, be of dangerous consequence.

It is difficult to fix the precise period for which the senate should be chosen. It is a matter of opinion, and our sentiments on the matter must be formed, by attending to certain principles. Some of the duties which are to be performed by the senate, seem evidently to point out the propriety of their term of service being extended beyond the period of that of the assembly. Besides as they are designed to represent the aristocracy of the country, it seems fit they should possess more stability, and so continue a longer period than that branch who represent the democracy. The business of making treaties and some other which it will be proper to commit to the senate, requires that they should have experience, and therefore that they should remain some time in office to acquire it.—But still it is of equal importance that they should not be so long in office as to be likely to forget the hand that formed them, or be insensible of their interests. Men long in office are very apt to feel themselves independent and to form and pursue interests separate from those who appointed them. And this is more likely to be the case with the senate, as they will for the most part of the time be absent from the state they represent, and associate with such company as will possess very little of the feelings of the middling class of people. For it is to be remembered that there is to be a *federal city,* and the inhabitants of it will be the great and the mighty of the earth. For these reasons I would shorten the term of their service to four years. Six years is a long period for a man to be absent from his home, it would have a tendency to wean him from his constituents.

A rotation in the senate, would also in my opinion be of great use. It is probable that senators once chosen for a state will, as the system now stands, continue in office for life. The office will be honorable if not lucrative. The persons who occupy it will probably wish to continue in it, and therefore use all their influence and that of their friends to continue in office.—Their friends will be numerous and powerful, for they will have it in their power to confer great favors; besides it will before long be considered as disgraceful not to be re-elected. It will therefore be considered as a matter of delicacy to the character of the senator not to return him again.—Every body acquainted with public affairs knows how difficult it is to remove from office a person who is [has?] long been in it. It is seldom done except in cases of gross misconduct. It is rare that want of competent ability procures it. To prevent this inconvenience I conceive it would be wise to determine, that a senator should not be eligible after he had served for the period assigned by the constitution for a certain number of years; perhaps three would be sufficient. A farther benefit would be derived from such an arrangement; it would give opportunity to bring forward a greater number of men to serve their country, and would return those, who had served, to their state, and afford them the advantage of becoming better acquainted with the condition and politics of their constituents. It farther appears to me proper, that the legislatures should retain the right which they now hold under the confederation, of recalling their members. It seems an evident dictate of reason, that when a person authorises another to do a piece of business for him, he should retain the power to displace him, when he does not conduct according to his pleasure. This power in the state legislatures, under confederation, has not been exercised to the injury of the government, nor do I see any danger of its being so exercised under the new system. It may operate much to the public benefit.

These brief remarks are all I shall make on the organization of the senate. The powers with which they are invested will require a more minute investigation.

This body will possess a strange mixture of legislative, executive and judicial powers, which in my opinion will in some cases clash with each other.

1. They are one branch of the legislature, and in this respect will possess equal powers in all cases with the house of representatives; for I consider the clause which gives the house of representatives the right of originating bills for raising a revenue as merely nominal, seeing the senate be authorised to propose or concur with amendments.

2. They are a branch of the executive in the appointment of ambassadors and public ministers, and in the appointment of all other officers, not otherwise provided for; whether the forming of treaties, in which they are joined with the president, appertains to the legislative or the executive part of the government, or to neither, is not material.

3. They are part of the judicial, for they form the court of impeachments.

It has been a long established maxim, that the legislative, executive and judicial departments in government should be kept distinct. It is said, I know, that this cannot be done. And therefore that this maxim is not just, or at least that it should only extend to certain leading features in a government. I admit that this distinction cannot be perfectly preserved. In a due ballanced government, it is perhaps absolutely necessary to give the executive qualified legislative powers, and the legislative or a branch of them judicial powers in the last resort. It may possibly also, in some special cases, be advisable to associate the legislature, or a branch of it, with the executive, in the exercise of acts of great national importance. But still the maxim is a good one, and a separation of these powers should be sought as far as is practicable. I can scarcely imagine that any of the advocates of the system will pretend, that it was necessary to accumulate all these powers in the senate. . . .

Brutus

LETTERS OF "CATO"

First published in the New York Journal *during the ratification winter of 1787–88, the "Cato" letters, recalling the then well-known name of another Roman hero opposed to tyranny, were long believed to have been written anonymously by New York's Governor George Clinton. The evidence for that attribution, however, is no longer considered valid, and so Cato's identity remains unknown. Concerned with the various issues that animated the anti-Federalist cause, Cato also argues that the protections in the new Constitution are not strong enough to protect ordinary citizens from the greed and avarice of the powerful few.*

IV
8 NOVEMBER 1787

To the Citizens of the State of New York:

Admitting, however, that the vast extent of America, together with the various other reasons which I offered you in my last number, against the practicability of the just exercise of the new government are insufficient to convince you; still it is an undeniable truth, that its several parts are either possessed of principles, which you have heretofore considered as ruinous, and that others are omitted which you have established as fundamental to your political security, and must in their operation, I will venture to assert—fetter your tongues and minds, enchain your bodies, and ultimately extinguish all that is great and noble in man.

In pursuance of my plan, I shall begin with observations on the executive branch of this new system; and though it is not the first in order, as arranged therein, yet being the *chief* is perhaps entitled by the rules of rank to the first consideration. The executive power as described in the second article, consists of a president and vice president, who are to hold their offices *during* the term of four years; the same article has marked the manner and time of their election, and established the qualifications of the president; it also provides against the removal, death, or inability of the president and vice president—regulates the salary of the president, delineates his duties and powers; and lastly, declares the causes for which the president and vice president shall be removed from office.

Notwithstanding the great learning and abilities of the gentlemen who composed the convention, it may be here remarked with deference, that the construction of the first paragraph of the first section of the second article, is vague and inexplicit, and leaves the mind in doubt, as to the election of a president and vice president, after the expiration of the election for the first term of four years—in every other case, the election of these great officers is expressly provided for; but there is no explicit provision for their election in case of the expiration of their offices, subsequent to the election which is to set this political machine in motion—no certain and express terms as in your state constitution, that *stately* once in every four years, and as often as these offices shall become vacant, by expiration or otherwise, as is therein expressed, an election shall be held as follows, etc.—this inexplicitness perhaps may lead to an establishment for life.

It is remarked by Montesquieu, in treating of republics, that *in all magistracies, the greatness of the power must be compensated by the brevity of the duration; and that a longer time than a year, would be dangerous.* It is therefore obvious to the least intelligent mind, to account why, great power in the hands of a magistrate, and that power connected, with a considerable duration, may be dangerous to the liberties of a republic—the deposit of vast trusts in the hands of a single magistrate, enables him in their exercise, to create a numerous train of dependents—this tempts his *ambition,* which in a republican magistrate is also remarked, *to be pernicious* and the duration of his office for any considerable time favors his views, gives him the means and time to perfect and execute his designs—*he therefore fancies that he may be great and glorious by oppressing his fellow citizens, and raising himself to permanent grandeur on the ruins of his country.*—And here it may be necessary to compare the vast and important powers of the president, together with his continuance in office with the foregoing doctrine—his eminent magisterial situation will attach many adherents to him, and he will be surrounded by expectants and courtiers—his power of nomination and influence on all appointments—the strong posts in each state comprised within his superintendence, and garrisoned by troops under his direction—his control over the army, militia, and navy—the unrestrained power of granting pardons for treason, which may be used to screen from punishment, those whom he had secretly instigated to commit the crime, and thereby prevent a discovery of his own guilt—his duration in office for four years: these, and various other principles evidently prove the truth of the position—that if the president is possessed of ambition, he has power and time sufficient to ruin his country.

Though the president, during the sitting of the legislature, is assisted by the senate, yet he is without a constitutional council in their recess—he will therefore be unsupported by proper information and advice, and will generally be directed by minions and favorites, or a council of state will grow out of the principal officers of the great departments, the most dangerous council in a free country.

The ten miles square, which is to become the seat of government, will of course be the place of residence for the president and the great officers of state—the same observations of a great man will apply to the court of a president possessing the powers of a monarch, that is observed of that of a monarch—*ambition with idleness—baseness with pride—the thirst of riches without labor—aversion to truth—flattery—treason—perfidy—violation of engagements—contempt of civil duties—hope from the magistrates' weakness; but above all, the perpetual ridicule of virtue*—these, he remarks, are the characteristics by which the courts in all ages have been distinguished.

The language and the manners of this court will be what distinguishes them from the rest of the community, not what assimilates them to it, and in being remarked for a behavior that shows they are not *meanly born,* and in adulation to people of fortune and power.

The establishment of a vice president is as unnecessary as it is dangerous. This officer, for want of other employment, is made president of the senate, thereby blending the executive and legislative powers, besides always giving to some one state, from which he is to come, an unjust preeminence.

It is a maxim in republics, that the representative of the people should be of their immediate choice; but by the manner in which the president is chosen he arrives to this office at the fourth or fifth hand, nor does the highest votes, in the way he is elected, determine the choice—for it is only necessary that he should be taken from the highest of five, who may have a plurality of votes.

Compare your past opinions and sentiments with the present proposed establishment, and you will find, that if you adopt it, that it will lead you into a system which you heretofore reprobated as odious. Every American Whig, not long since, bore his emphatic testimony against a monarchical government, though limited, because of the dangerous inequality that it created among citizens as relative to their rights and property; and wherein does this president, invested with his powers and prerogatives, essentially differ from the king of Great Britain (save as to name, the creation of nobility, and some immaterial incidents, the offspring of absurdity and locality) the direct prerogatives of the president, as springing from his political character, are among the following:—It is necessary, in order to distinguish him from the rest of the community, and enable him to keep, and maintain his court, that the compensation for his services; or in other words, his revenue should be such as to enable him to appear with the splendor of a prince; he has the power of receiving ambassadors from, and a great influence on their appointments to foreign courts; as also to make treaties, leagues, and alliances with foreign states, assisted by the senate, which when made, become the supreme law of the land: he is a constituent part of the legislative power; for every bill which shall pass the house of representatives and senate, is to be presented to him for approbation; if he approves of it, he is to sign it, if he disapproves, he is to return it with objections, which in many cases will amount to a complete negative; and in this view he will have a great share in the power of making peace, coining money, etc. and all the various objects of legislation, expressed or implied in this Constitution: for though it may be asserted that the king of Great Britain has the express power of making peace or war, yet he never thinks it prudent so to do without the advice of his parliament from whom he is to derive his support, and therefore these powers, in both president and king, are substantially the same: he is the generalissimo of the nation, and of course, has the command and control of the army, navy, and militia; he is the general conservator of the peace of the union—he may pardon all offenses, except in cases of impeachment, and the principal fountain of all offices and employments. Will not the exercise of these powers therefore tend either to the establishment of a vile and arbitrary aristocracy, or monarchy? The safety of the people in a republic depends on the share or proportion they have in the government; but experience ought to teach you, that when a man is at the head of an elective government invested with great powers, and interested in his reelection, in what circle appointments will be made; by which means *an imperfect aristocracy* bordering on monarchy may be established.

You must, however, my countrymen, beware, that the advocates of this new system do not deceive you, by a fallacious resemblance between it and your own state government, which you so much prize; and if you examine, you will perceive that the chief magistrate of this state, is your immediate choice, controlled and checked by a just and full representation of the people, divested of the prerogative of influencing war and peace, making treaties, receiving and sending embassies, and commanding standing armies and navies, which belong to the power of the confederation, and will be convinced that this government is no more like a true picture of your own, than an Angel of darkness resembles an Angel of light.

Cato

V
22 November 1787

To the Citizens of the State of New York:

In my last number I endeavored to prove that the language of the article relative to the establishment of the executive of this new government was vague and inexplicit, that the great powers of the president, connected with his duration in office would lead to oppression and ruin. That he would be governed by favorites and flatterers, or that a dangerous council would be collected from the great officers of state;—that the ten miles square, if the remarks of one of the wisest men, drawn from the experience of mankind, may be credited, would be the asylum of the base, idle, avaricious and ambitious, and that the court would possess a language and manners different from yours; that a vice president is as unnecessary, as he is dangerous in his influence—that the president cannot represent you because he is not of your own immediate choice, that if you adopt this government, you will incline to an arbitrary and odious aristocracy or monarchy—that the president possessed of the power, given him by this frame of government differs but very immaterially from the establishment of monarchy in Great Britain, and I warned you to beware of the fallacious resemblance that is held out to you by the advocates of this new system between it and your own state governments.

And here I cannot help remarking, that inexplicitness seems to pervade this whole political fabric: certainty in political compacts, which Mr. Coke calls *the mother and nurse of repose and quietness,* the want of which induced men to engage in political society, has ever been held by a wise and free people as essential to their security; as, on the one hand it fixes barriers which the ambitious and tyrannically disposed magistrate dare not overleap, and on the other, becomes a wall of safety to the community—otherwise stipulations between the governors and governed are nugatory; and you might as well deposit the important powers of legislation and execution in one or a few and permit them to govern according to their disposition and will; but the world is too full of examples, which prove that *to live by one man's will became the cause of all men's misery.* Before the existence of express political compacts it was reasonably implied that the magistrate should govern with wisdom and justice, but mere implication was too feeble to restrain the unbridled ambition of a bad man, or afford security against negligence, cruelty, or any other defect of mind. It is alledged that the opinions and manners of the people of America, are capable to resist and prevent an extension of prerogative or oppression; but you must recollect that opinion and manners are mutable, and may not always be a permanent obstruction against the encroachments of government; that the progress of a commercial society begets luxury, the parent of inequality, the foe to virtue, and the enemy to restraint; and that ambition and voluptuousness aided by flattery, will teach magistrates, where limits are not explicitly fixed to have separate and distinct interests from the people, besides it will not be denied that government assimilates the manners and opinions of the community to it. Therefore, a general presumption that rulers will govern well is not a sufficient security.—You are then under a sacred obligation to provide for the safety of your posterity, and would you now basely desert their interests, when by a small share of prudence you may transmit to them a beautiful political patrimony, that will prevent the necessity of their travelling through seas of blood to obtain that, which your wisdom might have secured:—It is a duty you owe likewise to your own reputation, for you have a great name to lose; you are characterised as cautious, prudent and jealous in politics; whence is it therefore, that you are about to precipitate yourselves into a sea of uncertainty, and adopt a system so vague, and which has discarded so many of your valuable rights:—Is it because you do not believe that an American can be a tyrant? If this be the case you rest on a weak basis; Americans are like other men in similar situations, when the manners and opinions of the community are changed by the causes I mentioned before, and your political compact inexplicit, your posterity will find that great power connected with ambition, luxury, and flattery, will as readily produce a Caesar, Caligula, Nero, and Domitian in America, as the same causes did in the Roman empire.

But the next thing to be considered in conformity to my plan, is the first article of this new government, which comprises the erection of the house of representatives and senate, and prescribes their various powers and objects of legislation. The most general objections to the first article, are that biennial elections for representatives are a departure from the safe democratical principles of annual ones—that the number of representatives are too few; that the apportionment and principles of increase are unjust; that no attention has been paid to either the numbers or property in each state in forming the senate; that the mode in which they are appointed and their duration, will lead to the establishment of an aristocracy; that the senate and president are improperly connected, both as to appointments, and the making of treaties, which are to become the supreme law of the land; that the judicial in some measure, to wit, as to the trial of impeachments, is placed in the senate, a branch of the legislative, and some times a branch of the executive: that Congress have the improper power of making or altering the regulations prescribed by the different legislatures, respecting the time, place, and manner of holding elections for representatives, and the time and manner of choosing senators; that standing armies may be established, and appropriation of money made for their support for two years; that the militia of the most remote state may be marched into those states situated at the opposite extreme of this continent; that the slave trade is, to all intents and purposes permanently established; and a slavish capitation, or poll-tax, may at any time be levied—these are some of the many evils that will attend the adoption of this government.

But with respect to the first objection, it may be remarked that a well digested democracy has this advantage over all others, to wit, that it affords to many the opportunity to be advanced to the supreme command, and the honors they thereby enjoy fill them with a desire of rendering themselves worthy of them; hence this desire becomes part of their education, is matured in manhood, and produces an ardent affection for their country, and it is the opinion of the great Sidney, and Montesquieu that this is in a great measure produced by annual election of magistrates.

If annual elections were to exist in this government, and learning and information to become more prevalent, you never will want men to execute whatever you could design.—Sidney observes "that a well governed state is as fruitful to all good purposes as the seven headed serpent is said to have been in evil; when one head is cut off, many rise up in the place of it." He remarks further, that "it was also thought, that free cities by frequent elections of magistrates became nurseries of great and able men, every man endeavoring to excel others, that he might be advanced to the honor he had no other title to, than what might arise from his merit, or reputation," but the framers of this *perfect government,* as it is called, have departed from this democratical principle, and established bi-ennial elections for the house of representatives, who are to be chosen by the people, and sextennial for the senate, who are to be chosen by the legislatures of the different states, and have given to the executive the unprecedented power of making temporary senators, in case of vacancies, by resignation or otherwise; and so far forth establishing a precedent for virtual representation (though in fact, their original appointment is virtual) thereby influencing the choice of the legislatures, or if they should not be so complaisant as to conform to his appointment—offence will be given to the executive and the temporary members will appear ridiculous by rejection; this temporary member, during his time of appointment, will of course act by a power derived from the executive, and for, and under his immediate influence.

It is a very important objection to this government, that the representation consists of so few; too few to resist the influence of corruption, and the temptation to treachery, against which all governments ought to take precautions—how guarded you have been on this head, in your own state constitution, and yet the number of senators and representatives proposed for this vast continent, does not equal those of your own state; how great the disparity, if you compare them with the aggregate numbers in the United States. The history of representation in England, from which we have taken our model of legislation, is briefly this: before the institution of legislating by deputies, the whole free part of the community usually met for that purpose; when this became impossible, by the increase of numbers the community was divided into districts, from each of which was sent such a number of deputies as was a complete representation of the various numbers and orders of citizens within them; but can it be asserted with truth, that six men can be a complete and full representation of the numbers and various orders of the people in this state? Another thing [that] may be suggested against the small number of representatives is, that but few of you will have the chance of sharing even in this branch of the legislature; and that the choice will be confined to a very few; the more complete it is, the better will your interests be preserved, and the greater the opportunity you will have to participate in government, one of the principal securities of a free people; but this subject has been so ably and fully treated by a writer under the signature of Brutus, that I shall content myself with referring you to him thereon, reserving further observations on the other objections I have mentioned, for my future numbers.

Cato

VII
3 JANUARY 1788

To the Citizens of the State of New York:

That the senate and president are further improperly connected, will appear, if it is considered, that their dependence on each other will prevent either from being a check upon the other; they must act in concert, and whether the power and influence of the one or the other is to prevail, will depend on the character and abilities of the men who hold those offices at the time. The senate is vested with such a proportion of the executive, that it would be found necessary that they should be constantly sitting. This circumstance did not escape the convention, and they have provided for the event, in the 2d article, which declares, that the executive may, on extraordinary occasions, *convene both houses or either of them.* No occasion can exist for calling the assembly without the senate; the words *or either of them,* must have been intended to apply only to the senate. Their wages are already provided for; and it will be therefore readily observed, that the partition between a perpetuation of their sessions and a perpetuation of their offices, in the progress of the government, will be found to be but thin and feeble. Besides, the senate, who have the sole power to try all impeachments, in case of the impeachment of the president, are to determine, as judges, the propriety of the advice they gave him, as senators. Can the senate in this, therefore, be an impartial judicature? And will they not rather serve as a screen to great public defaulters?

Among the many evils that are incorporated in this new system of government, is that of congress having the power of making or altering the regulations prescribed by the different legislatures, respecting the time, place, and manner of holding elections for representatives, and the time, and manner of choosing senators. If it is enquired, in what manner this regulation may be exercised to your injury—the answer is easy.

By the first article the house of representatives shall consist of members, chosen every second year by the people of the several states, who are qualified to vote for members of their several state assemblies; it can therefore readily be believed, that the different state legislatures, provided such can exist after the adoption of this government, will continue those easy and convenient modes for the election of representatives for the national legislature, that are in use, for the election of members of assembly for their own states; but the congress have, by the constitution, a power to make other regulations, or alter those in practice, prescribed by your own state legislature; hence, instead of having the places of elections in the precincts, and brought home almost to your own doors, congress may establish a place, or places, at either the extremes, center, or outer parts of the states; at a time and season too, when it may be very inconvenient to attend; and by these means destroy the rights of election; but in opposition to this reasoning, it is asserted, that it is a necessary power because the states might omit making rules for the purpose, and thereby defeat the existence of that branch of the government; this is what logicians call *argumentum absurdum,* for the different states, if they will have any security at all in this government, will find it in the house of representatives, and they, therefore, would not be very ready to eradicate a principle in which it dwells, or involve their country in an instantaneous revolution. Besides, if this was the apprehension of the framers, and the ground of that provision, why did not they extend this controlling power to the other duties of the several state legislatures. To exemplify this the states are to appoint senators and electors for choosing of a president; but the time is to be under the direction of congress. Now, suppose they were to omit the appointment of senators and electors, though congress was to appoint the time, which might [as] well be apprehended as the omission of regulations for the election of members of the house of representatives, provided they had that power; or suppose they were not to meet at all: of course, the government cannot proceed in its exercise. And from this motive, or apprehension, congress ought to have taken these duties entirely in their own hands, and, by a decisive declaration, annihilated them, which they in fact have done by leaving them without the means of support, or at least resting on their bounty. To this, the advocates for this system oppose the common, empty declamation, that there is no danger that congress will abuse this power; but such language, as relative to so important a subject, is mere vapour, and sound without sense. Is it not in their power, however, to make such regulations as may be inconvenient to you? It must be admitted, because the words are unlimited in their sense. It is a good rule, in the construction of a contract, to support, that what may be done will be; therefore, in considering this subject, you are to suppose, that in the exercise of this government, a regulation of congress will be made, for holding an election for the whole state at Poughkeepsie, at New York, or, perhaps, at Fort Stanwix: who will then be the actual electors for the house of representatives? Very few more than those who may live in the vicinity of these places. Could any others afford the expense and time of attending? And would not the government by this means have it in their power to put whom they pleased in the house of representatives? You ought certainly to have as much or more distrust with respect to the exercise of these powers by congress, than congress ought to have with respect to the exercise of those duties which ought to be entrusted to the several states, because over them congress can have a legislative controlling power.

Hitherto we have tied up our rulers in the exercise of their duties by positive restrictions—if the cord has been drawn too tight, loosen it to the necessary extent, but do not entirely unbind them.—I am no enemy to placing a reasonable confidence in them; but such an unbounded one as the advocates and framers of this new system advise you to, would be dangerous to your liberties; it has been the ruin of other governments, and will be yours, if you adopt with all its latitudinal powers—unlimited confidence in governors as well as individuals is frequently the parent of deception [despotism?].—What facilitated the corrupt designs of Philip of Macedon, and caused the ruin of Athens, but the unbounded confidence in their statesmen and rulers? Such improper confidence Demosthenes was so well convinced had ruined his country, that in his second Philippic oration he remarks—"that there is one common bulwark with which men of prudence are naturally provided, the guard and security of all people, particularly of free states, against the assaults of tyrants—What is this? Distrust. Of this be mindful; to this adhere; preserve this carefully, and no calamity can affect you."—Montesquieu observes, that "the course of government is attended with an insensible descent to evil, and there is no reascending to good without very great efforts." The plain inference from this doctrine is, that rulers in all governments will erect an interest separate from the ruled, which will have a tendency to enslave them. There is therefore no other way of interrupting this insensible descent and warding off the evil as long as possible, than by establishing principles of distrust in your constituents, and cultivating the sentiment among yourselves. But let me enquire of you, my countrymen, whether the freedom and independence of elections is a point of magnitude? If it is, what kind of a spirit of amity, deference and concession, is that which has put in the power of congress at one stroke to prevent your interference in government, and do away your liberties forever? Does either the situation or circumstances of things warrant it?

Cato

SPEECHES OF PATRICK HENRY

5 & 7 June 1788

The Virginia Ratifying Convention convened in Richmond on June 2, 1788, and on June 25 became the tenth state to ratify. On July 5 and 7, Patrick Henry delivered two speeches from which these excerpts illustrate the anti-Federalist case against the new Constitution. The vote in Virginia was one of the closer state votes for the new Constitution; ratification passed there by a vote of 89 to 79.

5 June 1788

Mr. Chairman . . . I rose yesterday to ask a question, which arose in my own mind. When I asked the question, I thought the meaning of my interrogation was obvious: The fate of this question and America may depend on this: Have they said, we the States? Have they made a proposal of a compact between States? If they had, this would be a confederation: It is otherwise most clearly a consolidated government. The question turns, Sir, on that poor little thing—the expression, *We, the people,* instead of the States of America. I need not take much pains to show, that the principles of this system, are extremely pernicious, impolitic, and dangerous. Is this a Monarchy, like England—a compact between Prince and people; with checks on the former, to secure the liberty of the latter? Is this a Confederacy, like Holland—an association of a number of independent States, each of which retain its individual sovereignty? It is not a democracy, wherein the people retain all their rights securely. Had these principles been adhered to, we should not have been brought to this alarming transition, from a Confederacy to a consolidated Government. We have no detail of those great considerations which, in my opinion, ought to have abounded before we should recur to a government of this kind. Here is a revolution as radical as that which separated us from Great Britain. It is as radical, if in this transition our rights and privileges are endangered, and the sovereignty of the States be relinquished: And cannot we plainly see, that this is actually the case? The rights of conscience, trial by jury, liberty of the press, all your immunities and franchises, all pretensions to human rights and privileges, are rendered insecure, if not lost, by this change so loudly talked of by some, and inconsiderately by others. Is this same relinquishment of rights worthy of freemen? Is it worthy of that manly fortitude that ought to characterize republicans: It is said eight States have adopted this plan. I declare that if twelve States and an half had adopted it, I would with manly firmness, and in spite of an erring world, reject it. You are not to inquire how your trade may be increased, nor how you are to become a great and powerful people, but how your liberties can be secured; for liberty ought to be the direct end of your Government. Having premised these things, I shall, with the aid of my judgment and information, which I confess are not extensive, go into the discussion of this system more minutely. Is it necessary for your liberty, that you should abandon those great rights by the adoption of this system? Is the relinquishment of the trial by jury, and the liberty of the press, necessary for your liberty? Will the abandonment of your most sacred rights tend to the security of your liberty? Liberty, the greatest of all earthly blessings—give us that precious jewel, and you may take every thing else: But I am fearful I have lived long enough to become an old fashioned fellow: Perhaps an invincible attachment to the dearest rights of man, may, in these refined enlightened days, be deemed *old fashioned:* If so, I am contended to be so: I say, the time has been, when every pore of my heart beat for American liberty, and which, I believe, had a counterpart in the breast of every true American: But suspicions have gone forth—suspicions of my integrity—publicly reported that my professions are not real—23 years ago was I supposed a traitor to my country; I was then said to be a bane of sedition, because I supported the rights of my country: I may be thought suspicious when I say our privileges and rights are in danger: But, Sir, a number of the people of this country are weak enough to think these things are too true: I am happy to find that the Honorable Gentleman on the other side, declares they are groundless: But, Sir, suspicion is a virtue, as long as its object is the preservation of the public good, and as long as it stays within proper bounds: Should it fall on me, I am contented: Conscious rectitude is a powerful consolation: I trust, there are many who think my professions for the public good to be real. Let your suspicion look to both sides: There are many on the other side, who, possibly may have been persuaded of the necessity of these measures, which I conceive to be dangerous to your liberty. Guard with jealous attention the public liberty. Suspect every one who approaches that jewel. Unfortunately, nothing will preserve it, but downright force: Whenever you give up that force, you are inevitably ruined. I am answered by Gentlemen, that though I might speak of terrors, yet the fact was, that we were surrounded by none of the dangers apprehended. I conceive this new Government to be one of those dangers: It has produced those horrors, which distress many of our best citizens. We are come hither to preserve the poor Commonwealth of Virginia, if it can be possibly done: Something must be done to preserve your liberty and mine: The Confederation; this same despised Government, merits, in my opinion, the highest encomium: It carried us through a long and dangerous war: It rendered us victorious in that bloody conflict with a powerful nation: It has secured us a territory greater than any European Monarch possesses: And shall a Government which has been thus strong and vigorous, be accused of imbecility and abandoned for want of energy? Consider what you are about to do before you part with this Government. Take longer time in reckoning things: Revolutions like this have happened in almost every country in Europe: Similar examples are to be found in ancient Greece and ancient Rome: Instances of the people losing their liberty by their own carelessness and the ambition of a few. We are cautioned by the Honorable Gentleman who presides, against faction and turbulence: I acknowledge that licentiousness is dangerous, and that it ought to be provided against: I acknowledge also the new form of Government may effectually prevent it: Yet, there is another thing it will as effectually do: it will oppress and ruin the people. There are sufficient guards placed against sedition and licentiousness: For when power is given to this Government to suppress these, or, for any other purpose, the language it assumes is clear, express, and unequivocal, but when this Constitution speaks of privileges, there is an ambiguity, Sir, a fatal ambiguity;—an ambiguity which is very astonishing: In the clause under consideration, there is the strangest that I can conceive, I mean, when it says, that there shall not be more Representatives, than one for every 30,000. Now, Sir, how easy is it to evade this privilege? "The number shall not exceed one for every 30,000." This may be satisfied by one Representative from each State. Let our numbers be ever so great, this immence continent, may, by this artful expression, be reduced to have but 13 Representatives: I confess this construction is not natural; but the ambiguity of the expression lays a good ground for a quarrel. Why was it not clearly and unequivocally expressed, that they *should* be entitled, to have one for every 30,000? This would have obviated all disputes; and was this difficult to be done? What is the inference? When population increases, and a State shall send Representatives in this proportion, Congress *may* remand them, because the right of having one for every 30,000 is not clearly expressed: this possibility of reducing the number to one for each State, approximates to probability by that other expression, "but each State shall at least have one Representative." Now is it not clear that from the first expression, the number might be reduced so much, that some States should have no Representative at all, were it not for the insertion of this last expression? And as this is the only restriction upon them, we may fairly conclude that they *may* restrain the number to one from each State: Perhaps the same horrors may hang over my mind again. I shall be told I am continually afraid: But, Sir, I have strong cause of apprehension: In some parts of the plan before you, the great rights of freemen are endangered, in other parts absolutely taken away. How does your trial by jury stand? In civil cases gone—not sufficiently secured in criminal—this best privilege is gone: But we are told that we need not fear, because those in power being our Representatives, will not abuse the powers we put in their hands: I am not well versed in history, but I will submit to your recollection, whether liberty has been destroyed most often by the licentiousness of the people, or by the tyranny of rulers? I imagine, Sir, you will find the balance on the side of tyranny: Happy will you be if you miss the fate of those nations, who, omitting to resist their oppressors, or negligently suffering their liberty to be wrested from them, have groaned under intolerable despotism. Most of the human race are now in this deplorable condition: And those nations who have gone in search of grandeur, power and splendor, have also fallen a sacrifice, and been the victims of their own folly: While they acquired those visionary blessings, they lost their freedom. My great objection to this Government is, that it does not leave us the means of defending our rights; or, of waging war against tyrants: It is urged by some Gentlemen, that this new plan will bring us an acquisition of strength, an army, and the militia of the States: This is an idea extremely ridiculous: Gentlemen cannot be in earnest. This acquisition will trample on your fallen liberty: Let my beloved Americans guard against that fatal lethargy that has pervaded the universe: Have we the means of resisting disciplined armies, when our only defence, the militia is put into the hands of Congress? The Honorable Gentleman said, that great danger would ensue if the Convention rose without adopting this system: I ask, where is that danger? I see none: Other Gentlemen have told us within these walls, that the Union is gone—or, that the Union will be gone: Is not this trifling with the judgment of their fellow-citizens? Till they tell us the ground of their fears, I will consider them as imaginary: I rose to make enquiry where those dangers were; they could make no answer: I believe I never shall have that answer: Is there a disposition in the people of this country to revolt against the dominion of laws? Has there been a single tumult in Virginia? Have not the people of Virginia, when labouring under the severest pressure of accumulated distresses, manifested the most cordial acquiescence in the execution of the laws? What could be more awful than their unanimous acquiescence under general distresses? Is there any revolution in Virginia? Whither is the spirit of America gone? Whither is the genius of America fled? It was but yesterday, when our enemies marched in triumph through our country: Yet the people of this country could not be appalled by their pompous armaments: They stopped their career, and victoriously captured them: Where is the peril now compared to that? Some minds are agitated by foreign alarms: Happily for us, there is no real danger from Europe: that country is engaged in more arduous business; from that quarter there is no cause of fear: You may sleep in safety forever for them. Where is the danger? If, Sir, there was any, I would recur to the American spirit to defend us;—that spirit which has enabled us to surmount the greatest difficulties: To that illustrious spirit I address my most fervent prayer, to prevent our adopting a system destructive to liberty. Let not Gentlemen be told, that it is not safe to reject this Government. Wherefore is it not safe? We are told there are dangers; but those dangers are ideal; they cannot be demonstrated: To encourage us to adopt it, they tell us, that there is a plain easy way of getting amendments: When I come to contemplate this part, I suppose that I am mad, or, that my countrymen are so: The way to amendment, is, in my conception, shut. Let us consider this plain easy way: "The Congress, whenever two-thirds of both Houses shall deem it necessary, shall propose amendments to this Constitution, or, on the application of the Legislatures of two-thirds of the several States, shall call a Convention for proposing amendments, which, in either case, shall be valid to all intents and purposes, as part of this Constitution, when ratified by the Legislatures of three-fourths of the several States, or by Conventions in three-fourths thereof, as the one or the other mode of ratification may be proposed by the Congress. Provided, that no amendment which may be made prior to the year 1808, shall in any manner affect the first and fourth clauses in the ninth section of the first article; and that no State, without its consent, shall be deprived of its equal suffrage in the Senate." Hence it appears that three-fourths of the States must ultimately agree to any amendments that may be necessary. Let us consider the consequences of this: However uncharitable it may appear, yet I must tell my opinion, that the most unworthy characters may get into power and prevent the introduction of amendments: Let us suppose (for the case is supposeable, possible, and probable) that you happen to deal these powers to unworthy hands; will they relinquish powers already in their possession, or, agree to amendments? Two-thirds of the Congress, or, of the State Legislatures, are necessary even to propose amendments: If one-third of these be unworthy men, they may prevent the application for amendments; but what is destructive and mischievous is, that three-fourths of the State Legislatures, or of State Conventions, must concur in the amendments when proposed: In such numerous bodies, there must necessarily be some designing bad men: To suppose that so large a number as three-fourths of the States will concur, is to suppose that they will possess genius, intelligence, and integrity, approaching to miraculous. It would indeed be miraculous that they should concur in the same amendments, or, even in such as would bear some likeness to one another. For four of the smallest States, that do not collectively contain one-tenth part of the population of the United States, may obstruct the most salutary and necessary amendments: Nay, in these four States, six tenths of the people may reject these amendments; and suppose, that amendments shall be opposed to amendments (which is highly probable) is it possible, that three-fourths can ever agree to the same amendments? A bare majority in these four small States may hinder the adoption of amendments; so that we may fairly and justly conclude, that one-twentieth part of the American people, may prevent the removal of the most grievous inconveniences and oppression, by refusing to accede to amendments. A trifling minority may reject the most salutary amendments. Is this an easy mode of securing the public liberty? It is, Sir, a most fearful situation, when the most contemptible minority can prevent the alteration of the most oppressive Government; for it may in many respects prove to be such: Is this the spirit of republicanism? What, Sir, is the genius of democracy? Let me read that clause of the Bill of Rights of Virginia, which relates to this: third clause. "That Government is or ought to be instituted for the common benefit, protection, and security of the people, nation, or community: Of all the various modes and forms of Government, that is best which is capable of producing the greatest degree of happiness and safety, and is most effectually secured against the danger of mal-administration, and *that whenever any Government shall be found inadequate, or contrary to these purposes, a majority of the community hath, an undubitable, unalienable and indefeasible right to reform, alter, or abolish it, in such manner as shall be judged most conducive to the public weal.*" This, Sir, is the language of democracy; that a majority of the community have a right to alter their Government when found to be oppressive: But how different is the genius of your new Constitution from this? How different from the sentiments of freemen, that a contemptible minority can prevent the good of the majority? If then Gentlemen standing on this ground, are come to that point, that they are willing to bind themselves and their posterity to be oppressed, I am amazed and inexpressibly astonished. If this be the opinion of the majority, I must submit; but to me, Sir, it appears perilous and destructive: I cannot help thinking so: Perhaps it may be the result of my age; these may be feelings natural to a man of my years, when the American spirit has left him, and his mental powers, like the members of the body, are decayed. If, Sir, amendments are left to the twentieth or the tenth part of the people of America, your liberty is gone forever. We have heard that there is a great deal of bribery practiced in the House of Commons in England; and that many of the members raised themselves to preferments, by selling the rights of the people: But, Sir, the tenth part of that body cannot continue oppressions on the rest of the people. English liberty is in this case, on a firmer foundation than American liberty. It will be easily contrived to procure the opposition of one tenth of the people to any alteration, however judicious. The Honorable Gentleman who presides, told us, that to prevent abuses in our Government, we will assemble in Convention, recall our delegated powers, and punish our servants for abusing the trust reposed in them. Oh, Sir, we should have fine times indeed, if to punish tyrants, it were only sufficient to assemble the people. Your arms wherewith you could defend yourselves, are gone; and have no longer a aristocratical; no longer democratical spirit. Did you ever read of any revolution in any nation, brought about by the punishment of those in power, inflicted by those who had no power at all? You read of a riot act in a country which is called one of the freest in the world, where a few neighbours cannot assemble without the risk of being shot by a hired soldiery, the engines of despotism. We may see such an act in America. A standing army we shall have also, to execute the execrable commands of tyranny: And how are you to punish them? Will you order them to be punished? Who shall obey these orders? Will your Mace-bearer be a match for a disciplined regiment? In what situation are we to be? The clause before you gives a power of direct taxation, unbounded and unlimited: Exclusive power of Legislation in all cases whatsoever, for ten miles square; and over all places purchased for the erection of forts, magazines, arsenals, dock-yards, etc. What resistance could be made? The attempt would be madness. You will find all the strength of this country in the hands of your enemies: Those garrisons will naturally be the strongest places in the country. Your militia is given up to Congress also in another part of this plan: They will therefore act as they think proper: All power will be in their own possession: You cannot force them to receive their punishment: Of what service would militia be to you, when most probably you will not have a single musket in the State; for as arms are to be provided by Congress, they may or may not furnish them. Let me here call your attention to that part which gives the Congress power, "To provide for organizing, arming, and disciplining the militia, and for governing such part of them as may be employed in the service of the United States, reserving to the States respectively, the appointment of the officers, and the authority of training the militia, according to the discipline prescribed by Congress." By this, Sir, you see that their control over our last and best defence, is unlimited. If they neglect or refuse to discipline or arm our militia, they will be useless: The States can do neither, this power being exclusively given to Congress: The power of appointing officers over men not disciplined or armed, is ridiculous: So that this pretended little remains of power left to the States, may, at the pleasure of Congress, be rendered nugatory. Our situation will be deplorable indeed: Nor can we ever expect to get this government amended, since I have already shewn, that a very small minority may prevent it; and that small minority interested in the continuance of the oppression: Will the oppressor let go the oppressed? Was there ever an instance? Can the annals of mankind exhibit one single example, where rulers overcharged with power, willingly let go the oppressed, though solicited and requested most earnestly? The application for amendments will therefore be fruitless. Sometimes the oppressed have got loose by one of those bloody struggles that desolate a country. A willing relinquishment of power is one of those things which human nature never was, nor ever will be capable of: The Honorable Gentleman's observations respecting the people's right of being the agents in the formation of this Government, are not accurate in my humble conception. The distinction between a National Government and a Confederacy is not sufficiently discerned. Had the delegates who were sent to Philadelphia a power to propose a Consolidated Government instead of a Confederacy? Were they not deputed by States, and not by the people? The assent of the people in their collective capacity is not necessary to the formation of a Federal Government. The people have no right to enter into leagues, alliances, or confederations: They are not the proper agents for this purpose: States and sovereign powers are the only proper agents for this kind of Government: Shew me an instance where the people have exercised this business: Has it not always gone through the Legislatures? I refer you to the treaties with France, Holland, and other nations: How were they made? Were they not made by the States? Are the people therefore in their aggregate capacity, the proper persons to form a Confederacy? This, therefore, ought to depend on the consent of the Legislatures; the people having never sent delegates to make any proposition of changing the Government. Yet I must say, at the same time, that it was made on grounds the most pure, and perhaps I might have been brought to consent to it so far as to the change of Government; but there is one thing in it which I never would acquiesce in. I mean the changing it into a Consolidated Government; which is so abhorent to my mind. The Honorable Gentleman then went on to the figure we make with foreign nations; the contemptible one we make in France and Holland; which, according to the system of my notes, he attributes to the present feeble Government. An opinion has gone forth, we find, that we are a contemptible people: The time has been when we were thought otherwise: Under this same despised Government, we commanded the respect of all Europe: Wherefore are we now reckoned otherwise? The American spirit has fled from hence: It has gone to regions, where it has never been expected: It has gone to the people of France in search of a splendid Government—a strong energetic Government. Shall we imitate the example of those nations who have gone from a simple to a splendid Government? Are those nations more worthy of our imitation? What can make an adequate satisfaction to them for the loss they suffered in attaining such a Government for the loss of their liberty? If we admit this Consolidated Government it will be because we like a great splendid one. Some way or other we must be a great and mighty empire; we must have an army, and a navy, and a number of things: When the American spirit was in its youth, the language of America was different: Liberty, Sir, was then the primary object. We are descended from a people whose Government was founded on liberty: Our glorious forefathers of Great-Britain, made liberty the foundation of every thing. That country is become a great, mighty, and splendid nation; not because their Government is strong and energetic; but, Sir, because liberty is its direct end and foundation: We drew the spirit of liberty from our British ancestors; by that spirit we have triumphed over every difficulty: But now, Sir, the American spirit, assisted by the ropes and chains of consolidation, is about to convert this country to a powerful and mighty empire: If you make the citizens of this country agree to become the subjects of one great consolidated empire of America, your Government will not have sufficent energy to keep them together: Such a Government is incompatible with the genius of republicanism: There will be no checks, no real balances, in this Government: What can avail your specious imaginary balances, your rope-dancing, chain-rattling, ridiculous ideal checks and contrivances? But, Sir, we are not feared by foreigners: we do not make nations tremble: Would this, Sir, constitute happiness, or secure liberty? I trust, Sir, our political hemisphere will ever direct their operations to the security of those objects. Consider our situation, Sir: Go to the poor man, ask him what he does; he will inform you, that he enjoys the fruits of his labour, under his own fig-tree, with his wife and children around him, in peace and security. Go to every other member of the society, you will find the same tranquil ease and content; you will find no alarms or disturbances: Why then tell us of dangers to terrify us into an adoption of this new Government? And yet who knows the dangers that this new system may produce; they are out of the sight of the common people: They cannot foresee latent consequences: I dread the operation of it on the middling and lower class of people: It is for them I fear the adoption of this system. I fear I tire the patience of the Committee, but I beg to be indulged with a few more observations: When I thus profess myself an advocate for the liberty of the people, I shall be told, I am a designing man, that I am to be a great man, that I am to be a demagogue; and many similar illiberal insinuations will be thrown out; but, Sir, conscious rectitude, out-weighs these things with me: I see great jeopardy in this new Government. I see none from our present one: I hope some Gentleman or other will bring forth, in full array, those dangers, if there be any, that we may see and touch them.

7 June 1788

I have thought, and still think, that a full investigation of the actual situation of America, ought to precede any decision on this great and important question. That Government is no more than a choice among evils, is acknowledged by the most intelligent among mankind, and has been a standing maxim for ages. If it be demonstrated that the adoption of the new plan is a little or a trifling evil, then, Sir, I acknowledge that adoption ought to follow: But, Sir, if this be a truth that its adoption may entail misery on the free people of this country, I then insist, that rejection ought to follow. Gentlemen strongly urge its adoption will be a mighty benefit to us: But, Sir, I am made of such incredulous materials that assertions and declarations, do not satisfy me. I must be convinced, Sir. I shall retain my infidelity on that subject, till I see our liberties secured in a manner perfectly satisfactory to my understanding. . . .

You are told [by Governor Randolph] there is no peace, although you fondly flatter yourselves that all is peace—No peace—a general cry and alarm in the country—Commerce, riches, and wealth vanished—Citizens going to seek comforts in other parts of the world—Laws insulted—Many instances of tyrannical legislation. These things, Sir, are new to me. He has made the discovery—As to the administration of justice, I believe that failures in commerce, etc. cannot be attributed to it. My age enables me to recollect its progress under the old Government. I can justify it by saying, that it continues in the same manner in this State, as it did under former Government. As to other parts of the Continent, I refer that to other Gentlemen. As to the ability of those who administer it, I believe they would not suffer by a comparison with those who administered it under the royal authority. Where is the cause of complaint if the wealthy go away? Is this added to the other circumstances, of such enormity, and does it bring such danger over this Commonwealth as to warrant so important, and so awful a change in so precipitate a manner? As to insults offered to the laws, I know of none. In this respect I believe this Commonwealth would not suffer by a comparison with the former Government. The laws are as well executed, and as patiently acquiesced in, as they were under the royal administration. Compare the situation of the country—Compare that of our citizens to what they were then, and decide whether persons and property are not as safe and secure as they were at that time. Is there a man in this Commonwealth, whose person can be insulted with impunity? Cannot redress be had here for personal insults or injuries, as well as in any part of the world—as well as in those countries where Aristocrats and Monarchs triumph and reign? Is not the protection of property in full operation here? The contrary cannot with truth be charged on this Commonwealth. Those severe charges which are exhibited against it, appear to me totally groundless. On a fair investigation, we shall be found to be surrounded by no real dangers. We have the animating fortitude and persevering alacrity of republican men, to carry us through misfortunes and calamities. 'Tis the fortune of a republic to be able to withstand the stormy ocean of human vicissitudes. I know of no danger awaiting us. Public and private security are to be found here in the highest degree. Sir, it is the fortune of a free people, not to be intimidated by imaginary dangers. Fear is the passion of slaves. Our political and natural hemisphere are now equally tranquil. Let us recollect the awful magnitude of the subject of our deliberation. Let us consider the latent consequences of an erroneous decision—and let not our minds be led away by unfair misrepresentations and uncandid suggestions. There have been many instances of uncommon lenity and temperance used in the exercise of power in this Commonwealth. I could call your recollection to many that happened during the war and since—But every Gentleman here must be apprized of them.

. . . I have said that I thought this a Consolidated Government: I will now prove it. Will the great rights of the people be secured by this Government? Suppose it should prove oppressive, how can it be altered? Our Bill of Rights declares, "That a majority of the community hath an *undubitable, unalienable,* and *indefeasible right* to reform, alter, or abolish it, in such manner as shall be judged most conducive to the public weal." I have just proved that one tenth, or less, of the people of America, a most despicable minority may prevent this reform or alteration. Suppose the people of Virginia should wish to alter their Government, can a majority of them do it? No, because they are connected with other men; or, in other words, consolidated with other States: When the people of Virginia at a

future day shall wish to alter their Government, though they should
be unanimous in this desire, yet they may be prevented therefrom
by a despicable minority at the extremity of the United States:
The founders of your own Constitution made your Government
changeable: But the power of changing it is gone from you! Whither
is it gone? It is placed in the same hands that hold the rights of twelve
other States; and those who hold those rights, have right and power
to keep them: It is not the particular Government of Virginia: One
of the leading features of that Government is, that a majority can
alter it, when necessary for the public good. This Government is not
a Virginian but an American Government. Is it not therefore a
Consolidated Government? The sixth clause of your Bill of Rights
tells you, "That elections of members to serve as Representatives of
the people in Assembly, ought to be free, and that all men having
sufficient evidence of permanent common interest with, and
attachment to the community, have the right of suffrage, and *cannot
be taxed* or *deprived* of *their property* for public uses, without their own
consent, or that of their Representatives so elected, nor bound by
any law to which they have not in like manner assented for the public
good." But what does this Constitution say? The clause under
consideration gives an unlimited and unbounded power of taxation:
Suppose every delegate from Virginia opposes a law laying a tax,
what will it avail? They are opposed by a majority: Eleven members
can destroy their efforts: Those feeble ten cannot prevent the passing
the most oppressive tax law. So that in direct opposition to the spirit
and express language of your Declaration of Rights, you are taxed
not by your own consent, but by people who have no connection
with you. The next clause of the Bill of Rights tells you, "That all
power of suspending law, or the execution of laws, by any authority
without the consent of the Representatives of the people, is injurious
to their rights, and ought not to be exercised." This tells us that there
can be no suspension of Government, or laws without our own
consent: Yet this Constitution can counteract and suspend any of
our laws, that contravene its oppressive operation; for they have the
power of direct taxation; which suspends our Bill of Rights; and it
is expressly provided, that they can make all laws necessary for carrying
their powers into execution; and it is declared paramount to the laws
and constitutions of the States. Consider how the only remaining
defence we have left is destroyed in this manner: Besides the expences
of maintaining the Senate and other House in as much splendor as
they please, there is to be a great and mighty President, with very

extensive powers; the powers of a King: He is to be supported in extravagant magnificence: So that the whole of our property may be taken by this American Government, by laying what taxes they please, giving themselves what salaries they please, and suspending our laws at their pleasure: I might be thought too inquisitive, but I believe I should take up but very little of your time in enumerating the little power that is left to the Government of Virginia; for this power is reduced to little or nothing: Their garrisons, magazines, arsenals, and forts, which will be situated in the strongest places within the States: Their ten miles square, with all the fine ornaments of human life, added to their powers, and taken from the States, will reduce the power of the latter to nothing. The voice of tradition, I trust, will inform posterity of our struggles for freedom: If our descendants be worthy the name of Americans, they will preserve and hand down to their latest posterity, the transactions of the present times; and though, I confess, my exclamations are not worthy the hearing, they will see that I have done my utmost to preserve their liberty: For I never will give up the power of direct taxation, but for a scourge: I am willing to give it conditionally; that is, after non-compliance with requisitions: I will do more, Sir, and what I hope will convince the most sceptical man, that I am a lover of the American Union, that in case Virginia shall not make punctual payment, the control of our custom houses, and the whole regulation of trade, shall be given to Congress, and that Virginia shall depend on Congress even for passports, till Virginia shall have paid the last farthing; and furnished the last soldier: Nay, Sir, there is another alternative to which I would consent: Even that they should strike us out of the Union, and take away from us all federal privileges till we comply with federal requisitions; but let it depend upon our own pleasure to pay our money in the most easy manner for our people. Were all the States, more terrible than the mother country, to join against us, I hope Virginia could defend herself; but, Sir, the dissolution of the Union is most abhorent to my mind: The first thing I have at heart is American *liberty*; the second thing is American Union; and I hope the people of Virginia will endeavor to preserve that Union: The increasing population of the southern States, is far greater than that of New England: Consequently, in a short time, they will be far more numerous than the people of that country: Consider this, and you will find this State more particularly interested to support American liberty, and not bind our posterity by an improvident relinquishment of our rights. I would give the best security for a punctual compliance with requisitions; but I beseech Gentlemen, at all hazards, not to give up this unlimited power of taxation: The Honorable Gentleman has told us these powers given to Congress, are accompanied by a Judiciary which will connect all: On examination you will find this very Judiciary oppressively constructed; your jury trial destroyed, and the Judges dependent on Congress. In this scheme of energetic Government, the people will find two sets of tax-gatherers—the State and the Federal Sheriffs. This it seems to me will produce such dreadful oppression, as the people cannot possibly bear: The Federal Sheriff may commit what oppression, make what distresses he pleases, and ruin you with impunity: For how are you to tie his hands? Have you any sufficient decided means of preventing him from sucking your blood by speculations, commissions and fees? Thus thousands of your people will be most shamefully robbed: Our State Sheriffs, those unfeeling blood-suckers, have, under the watchful eye of our Legislature, committed the most horrid and barbarous ravages on our people: It has required the most constant vigilance of the Legislature to keep them from totally ruining the people: A repeated succession of laws has been made to suppress their inequitous speculations and cruel extortions; and as often have their nefarious ingenuity devised methods of evading the force of those laws: In the struggle they have generally triumphed over the Legislature. It is fact that lands have sold for five shillings, which were worth one hundred pounds: If Sheriffs thus immediately under the eye of our State Legislature and Judiciary, have dared to commit these outrages, what would they not have done if their masters had been at Philadelphia or New York? If they perpetrate the most unwarrantable outrage on your persons or property, you cannot get redress on this side of Philadelphia or New York: and how can you get it there? If your domestic avocations could permit you to go thither, there you must appeal to Judges sworn to support this Constitution, in opposition to that of any State, and who may also be inclined to favor their own officers: When these harpies are aided by excise men, who may search at any time your houses and most secret recesses, will the people bear it? If you think so you differ from me: Where I thought there was a possibility of such mischiefs, I would grant power with a niggardly hand; and here there is strong probability that these oppressions shall actually happen. I may be told, that it is safe to err on that side; because such regulations *may* be made by Congress, as shall restrain these officers, and because laws are made by our Representatives, and judged by righteous Judges: But, Sir, as these regulations may be made, so they may not; and many reasons there are to induce a belief that they will not: I shall therefore be an infidel on that point till the day of my death.

This Constitution is said to have beautiful features; but when I come to examine these features, Sir, they appear to me horridly frightful: Among other deformities, it has an awful squinting; it squints towards monarchy: And does not this raise indignation in the breast of every American? Your President may easily become King: Your Senate is so imperfectly constructed that your dearest rights may be sacrificed by what may be a small minority; and a very small minority may continue forever unchangeably this Government, although horridly defective: Where are your checks in this Government? Your strong holds will be in the hands of your enemies: It is on a supposition that our American Governors shall be honest, that all the good qualities of this Government are founded: But its defective, and imperfect construction, puts it in their power to perpetrate the worst of mischiefs, should they be bad men: And, Sir, would not all the world, from the Eastern to the Western hemisphere, blame our distracted folly in resting our rights upon the contingency of our rulers being good or bad. Shew me that age and country where the rights and liberties of the people were placed on the sole chance of their rulers being good men, without a consequent loss of liberty? I say that the loss of that dearest privilege has ever followed with absolute certainty, every such mad attempt. If your American chief, be a man of ambition, and abilities, how easy is it for him to render himself absolute: The army is in his hands, and, if he be a man of address, it will be attached to him; and it will be the subject of long meditation with him to seize the first auspicious moment to accomplish his design; and, Sir, will the American spirit solely relieve you when this happens? I would rather infinitely, and I am sure most of this Convention are of the same opinion, have a King, Lords, and Commons, than a Government so replete with such insupportable evils. If we make a King, we may prescribe the rules by which he shall rule his people, and interpose such checks as shall prevent him from infringing them: But the President, in the field, at the head of his army, can prescribe the terms on which he shall reign master, so far that it will puzzle any American ever to get his neck from under the galling yoke. I cannot with patience, think of this idea. If ever he violates the laws, one of two things will happen: He shall come to the head of his army to carry every thing before him; or, he will give bail, or do what Mr. Chief Justice will order him. If he be guilty, will not the recollection of his crimes teach him to make one bold push for the American throne? Will not the immense difference between being master of every thing, and being ignominiously tried and punished, powerfully excite him to make this bold push? But, Sir, where is the existing force to punish him? Can he not at the head of his army beat down every opposition? Away with your President, we shall have a King: The army will salute him Monarch; your militia will leave you and assist in making him King, and fight against you: And what have you to oppose this force? What will then become of you and your rights? Will not absolute despotism ensue? [Here Mr. Henry strongly and pathetically expatiated on the probability of the president's enslaving America and the horrible consequences that must result.]

What can be more defective than the clause concerning the elections?—The control given to Congress over the time, place, and manner of holding elections, will totally destroy the end of suffrage. The elections may be held at one place, and the most inconvenient in the State; or they may be at remote distances from those who have a right of suffrage: Hence nine out of ten must either not vote at all, or vote for strangers: For the most influential characters will be applied to, to know who are the most proper to be chosen. I repeat that the control of Congress over the *manner,* etc. of electing, well warrants this idea. The natural consequence will be, that this democratic branch, will possess none of the public confidence: The people will be prejudiced against Representatives chosen in such an injudicious manner. The proceedings in the northern conclave will be hidden from the yeomanry of this country: We are told that the yeas and nays shall be taken and entered on the journals: This, Sir, will avail nothing: It may be locked up in their chests, and concealed forever from the people; for they are not to publish what parts they think require secrecy: They *may* think, and *will think,* the whole requires it. Another beautiful feature of this Constitution is the publication from time to time of the receipts and expenditures of the public money. This expression, from time to time, is very indefinite and indeterminate: It may extend to a century. Grant that any of them are wicked, they may squander the public money so as to ruin you, and yet this expression will give you no redress. I say, they may ruin you;—for where, Sir, is the responsibility? The yeas and nays will shew you nothing, unless they be fools as well as knaves: For after having wickedly trampled on the rights of the people, they would act like fools indeed, were they to publish and devulge their iniquity, when they have it equally in their power to suppress and conceal it.—Where is the responsibility—that leading principle in the British government? In that government a punishment, certain and inevitable, is provided: But in this, there is no real actual punishment for the grossest maladministration. They may go without punishment, though they commit the most outrageous violation on our immunities. That paper may tell me they will be punished. I ask, by what law? They must make the law—for there is no existing law to do it. What—will they make a law to punish themselves? This, Sir, is my great objection to the Constitution, that there is no true responsibility—and that the preservation of our liberty depends on the single chance of men being virtuous enough to make laws to punish themselves. In the country from which we are descended, they have real, and not imaginary, responsibility—for there, maladministration has cost their heads, to some of the most saucy geniuses that ever were. The Senate, by making treaties may destroy your liberty and laws for want of responsibility. Two-thirds of those that shall happen to be present, can, with the President, make treaties, that shall be the supreme law of the land: They may make the most ruinous treaties; and yet there is no punishment for them. Whoever shows me a punishment provided for them, will oblige me. So, Sir, notwithstanding there are eight pillars, they want another. Where will they make another? I trust, Sir, the exclusion of the evils wherewith this system is replete, in its present form, will be made a condition, precedent to its adoption, by this or any other State. The transition from a general unqualified admission to offices, to a consolidation of government, seems easy; for though the American States are dissimilar in their structure, this will assimilate them: this, Sir, is itself a strong consolidating feature, and is not one of the least dangerous in that system. Nine States are sufficient to establish this government over those nine: Imagine that nine have come into it. Virginia has certain scruples. Suppose she will consequently, refuse to join with those States:—May not they still continue in friendship and union with her? If she sends her annual requisitions in dollars, do you think their stomachs will be so squeamish that they will refuse her dollars? Will they not accept her regiments? They would intimidate you into an inconsiderate adoption, and frighten you with ideal evils, and that the Union shall be dissolved. 'Tis a bugbear, Sir:—The fact is, Sir, that the eight adopting States can hardly stand on their own legs. Public fame tells us, that the adopting States have already heart-burnings and animosity, and repent their precipitate hurry: This, Sir, may occasion exceeding great mischief. When I reflect on these and many other circumstances, I must think those States will be fond to be in confederacy with us. If we pay our quota of money annually, and furnish our rateable number of men, when necessary, I can see no danger from a rejection. . . .

SPEECHES OF MELANCTON SMITH

20–27 June 1788

The New York State Convention concerning ratification of the Constitution met in June 1788. There was strong opposition to the new Constitution in New York, led by Governor George Clinton, an anti-Federalist. Reprinted here are speeches by delegate Melancton Smith, New York City businessman, politician, and a leading anti-Federalist. Smith's arguments, thoughtful and well expressed as they were, were rendered academic when New Hampshire became the ninth state to ratify on June 21, and Virginia the tenth on June 25. New York had no choice then but to ratify or simply refuse to join the new union, an unpalatable idea to everyone. Alexander Hamilton, Robert Livingston, and others skillfully led the debate on the Federalist side and New York duly ratified the Constitution on July 26, the eleventh state to do so. Rhode Island became the last of the original 13 states to ratify on May 29, 1790.

20 June 1788

. . . He [Smith] was as strongly impressed with the necessity of a Union, as any one could be: He would seek it with as much ardor. In the discussion of this subject, he was disposed to make every reasonable concession, and indeed to sacrifice every thing for a Union, except the liberties of his country, than which he could contemplate no greater misfortune. But he hoped we were not reduced to the necessity of sacrificing or even endangering our liberties to preserve the Union. If that was the case, the alternative was dreadful. But he would not now say that the adoption of the Constitution would endanger our liberties; because that was the point to be debated, and the premises should be laid down previously to the drawing of any conclusion. He wished that all observations might be confined to this point; and that declamation and appeals to the passions might be omitted.

Why, said he, are we told of our weakness? Of the defenceless condition of the southern parts of our state? Or the exposed situation of our capital? Of Long Island surrounded by water, and exposed to the incursions of our neighbours in Connecticut? Of Vermont having separated from us and assumed the powers of a distinct government; and of the North-West part of our state being in the hands of a foreign enemy?—Why are we to be alarmed with apprehensions that the Eastern states are inimical, and disinclined to form alliances with us? He was sorry to find that such suspicions were entertained. He believed that no such disposition existed in the Eastern states. Surely it could not be supposed that those states would make war upon us for exercising the rights of freemen, deliberating and judging for ourselves, on a subject the most interesting that ever came before any assembly. If a war with our neighbour was to be the result of not acceding, there was no use in debating here; we had better receive their dictates, if we were unable to resist them. The defects of the Old Confederation needed as little proof as the necessity of an Union: But there was no proof in all this, that the proposed Constitution was a good one. Defective as the Old Confederation is, he said, no one could deny but it was possible we might have a worse government. But the question was not whether the present Confederation be a bad one; but whether the proposed Constitution be a good one.

It had been observed, that no examples of Federal Republics had succeeded. It was true that the ancient confederated Republics were all destroyed—so were those which were not confederated; and all ancient Governments of every form had shared the same fate. Holland had undoubtedly experienced many evils from the defects in her government; but with all these defects, she yet existed; she had under her Confederacy made a principal figure among the nations of Europe, and he believed few countries had experienced a greater share of internal peace and prosperity. The Germanic Confederacy was not the most pertinent example to produce on this occasion:— Among a number of absolute Princes who consider their subjects as their property, whose will is law, and to whose ambition there are no bounds, it was no difficult task to discover other causes from which the convulsions in that country rose, than the defects of their

Confederation. Whether a Confederacy of States under any form be a practicable Government, was a question to be discussed in the course of investigating this Constitution.

He was pleased that thus early in the debate, the honorable gentleman had himself shown, that the intent of the Constitution was not a Confederacy, but a reduction of all the states into a consolidated government. He hoped the gentleman would be complaisant enough to exchange names with those who disliked the Constitution, as it appeared from his own concession that they were Federalists, and those who advocated it Anti-Federalists. He begged leave, however, to remind the gentleman, that Montesquieu, with all the examples of modern and ancient Republics in view, gives it as his opinion, that a confederated Republic has all the internal advantages of a Republic, with the external force of a Monarchical Government. He was happy to find an officer of such high rank recommending to the other officers of Government, and to those who are members of the Legislature, to be unbiassed by any motives of interest or state importance. Fortunately for himself, he was out of the verge of temptations of this kind, not having the honor to hold any office under the state. But then he was exposed, in common with other gentlemen of the Convention, to another temptation, against which he thought it necessary that we should be equally guarded:—If, said he, this Constitution is adopted, there will be a number of honorable and lucrative offices to be filled, and we ought to be cautious lest an expectancy of some of them should influence us to adopt without due consideration.

We may wander, said he, in the fields of fancy without end, and gather flowers as we go: It may be entertaining—but it is of little service to the discovery of truth:—We may on one side compare the scheme advocated by our opponents to golden images, with feet part of iron and part of clay; and on the other, to a beast dreadful and terrible, and strong exceedingly, having great iron teeth, which devours, breaks in pieces, and stamps the residue with his feet: And after all, said he, we shall find that both these allusions are taken from the same vision; and their true meaning must be discovered by sober reasoning.

He would agree with the honorable gentleman, that perfection in any system of government was not to be looked for. If that was the object, the debates on the one before them might soon be closed.— But he would observe that this observation applied with equal force against changing any systems—especially against material and radical changes.—Fickleness and inconstancy, he said, was characteristic of a free people; and in framing a Constitution for them, it was, perhaps the most difficult thing to correct this spirit, and guard against the evil effects of it—he was persuaded it could not be altogether prevented without destroying their freedom—it would be like attempting to correct a small indisposition in the habit of the body, by fixing the patient in a confirmed consumption.—This fickle and inconstant spirit was the more dangerous in bringing about changes in the government. The instance that had been adduced by the gentleman from sacred history, was an example in point to prove this: The nation of Israel having received a form of civil government from Heaven, enjoyed it for a considerable period; but at length labouring under pressures, which were brought upon them by their own misconduct and imprudence, instead of imputing their misfortunes to their true causes, and making a proper improvement of their calamities, by a correction of their errors, they imputed them to a defect in their constitution; they rejected their Divine Ruler, and asked Samuel to make them a King to judge them, like other nations. Samuel was grieved at their folly; but still, by the command of God, he hearkened to their voice; tho' not until he had solemnly declared unto them the manner in which the King should reign over them. "This, (says Samuel) shall be the manner of the King that shall reign over you. He will take your sons and appoint them for himself, for his chariots, and for his horsemen, and some shall run before his chariots; and he will appoint him captains over thousands, and captains over fifties, and will set them to ear his ground, and to reap his harvest, and to make his instruments of war, and instruments of his chariots. And he will take your daughters to be confectionaries, and to be cooks, and to be bakers. And he will take your fields, and your vine yards, and your olive yards, even the best of them, and give them to his servants. And he will take the tenth of your seed, and of your vineyards, and give to his officers and to his servants. And he will take your men servants and your maid servants, and your goodliest young men, and your asses, and put them to his work. He will take the tenth of your sheep: And ye shall be his servants. And ye shall cry out in that day, because of your King which ye have chosen you; and the Lord will not hear you in that day."—How far this was applicable to the subject he would not now say; it could be better judged of when they had gone through it.—On the whole he wished to take up this matter with candor and deliberation.

He would now proceed to state his objections to the clause just read (section 2 of article I, clause 3). His objections were comprised under three heads: 1st, the rule of appointment is unjust; 2d, there is no precise number fixed on below which the house shall not be reduced; 3d, it is inadequate. In the first place the rule of apportionment of the representatives is to be according to the whole number of the white inhabitants, with three fifths of all others; that is in plain English, each state is to send Representatives in proportion to the number of freemen, and three fifths of the slaves it contains. He could not see any rule by which slaves are to be included in the ratio of representation: The principle of a representation, being that every free agent should be concerned in governing himself, it was absurd to give that power to a man who could not exercise it—slaves have no will of their own: The very operation of it was to give certain privileges to those people who were so wicked as to keep slaves. He knew it would be admitted that this rule of apportionment was founded on unjust principles, but that it was the result of accommodation; which he supposed we should be under the necessity of admitting, if we meant to be in union with the Southern States, though utterly repugnant to his feelings. In the second place, the number was not fixed by the Constitution, but left at the discretion of the Legislature; perhaps he was mistaken; it was his wish to be informed. He understood from the Constitution, that sixty-five Members were to compose the House of Representatives for three years; that after that time a census was to be taken, and the numbers to be ascertained by the Legislature on the following principles: 1st, they shall be apportioned to the respective States according to numbers; 2d, each State shall have one at least; 3d, they shall never exceed one to every thirty thousand. If this was the case, the first Congress that met might reduce the number below what it now is; a power inconsistent with every principle of a free government, to leave it to the discretion of the rulers to determine the number of the representatives of the people. There was no kind of security except in the integrity of the men who were entrusted; and if you have no other security, it is idle to contend about Constitutions. In the third place, supposing Congress should declare that there should be one representative for every thirty thousand of the people, in his opinion it would be incompetent to the great purposes of representation. It was, he said, the fundamental principle of a free government, that the people should make the laws by which they were to be governed: He who is controlled by another is a slave; and that government which is directed by the will of any one or a few, or any number less than is the will of the community, is a government for slaves.

The next point was, how was the will of the community to be expressed? It was not possible for them to come together;

the multitude would be too great: In order, therefore to provide against this inconvenience, the scheme of representation had been adopted, by which the people deputed others to represent them. Individuals entering into society became one body, and that body ought to be animated by one mind; and he conceived that every form of government should have that complexion. It was true that notwithstanding all the experience we had from others, it had not appeared that the experiment of representation had been fairly tried: there was something like it in the ancient republics, in which, being of small extent, the people could easily meet together, though instead of deliberating, they only considered of those things which were submitted to them by their magistrates. In Great Britain representation had been carried much farther than in any government we knew of, except our own; but in that country it now had only a name. America was the only country, in which the first fair opportunity had been offered. When we were Colonies, our representation was better than any that was then known: Since the revolution we had advanced still nearer to perfection. He considered it as an object, of all others the most important, to have it fixed on its true principle; yet he was convinced that it was impracticable to have such a representation in a consolidated government. However, said he, we may approach a great way towards perfection by encreasing the representation and limiting the powers of Congress. He considered that the great interest and liberties of the people could only be secured by the State Governments. He admitted, that if the new government was only confined to great national objects, it would be less exceptionable; but it extended to every thing dear to human nature. That this was the case could be proved without any long chain of reasoning:—for that power which had both the purse and the sword, had the government of the whole country, and might extend its powers to any and to every object. He had already observed, that by the true doctrine of representation, this principle was established—that the representative must be chosen by the free will of the majority of his constituents: It therefore followed that the representative should be chosen from small districts. This being admitted, he would ask, could 65 men for 3,000,000, or 1 for 30,000, be chosen in this manner? Would they be possessed of the requisite information to make happy the great number of souls that were spread over this extensive country?—There was another objection to the clause: If great affairs of government were trusted to a few men, they would be more liable to corruption. Corruption, he knew, was unfashionable amongst us, but he supposed that Americans were like other men; and though they had hitherto displayed great virtues, still they were men; and therefore such steps should be taken as to prevent the possibility of corruption. We were now in that stage of society, in which we could deliberate with freedom;—how long it might continue, God only knew! Twenty years hence, perhaps, these maxims might become unfashionable; we already hear, said he, in all parts of the country, gentlemen ridiculing that spirit of patriotism and love of liberty, which carried us through all our difficulties in times of danger.—When patriotism was already nearly hooted out of society, ought we not to take some precautions against the progress of corruption? . . .

21 June 1788

To determine whether the number of representatives proposed by this Constitution is sufficient, it is proper to examine the qualifications which this house ought to possess, in order to exercise their powers discreetly for the happiness of the people. The idea that naturally suggests itself to our minds, when we speak of representatives is, that they resemble those they represent; they should be a true picture of the people; possess the knowledge of their circumstances and their wants; sympathize in all their distresses, and be disposed to seek their true interests. The knowledge necessary for the representatives of a free people, not only comprehends extensive political and commercial information, such as is acquired by men of refined education, who have leisure to attain to high degrees of improvement, but it should also comprehend that kind of acquaintance with the common concerns and occupations of the people, which men of the middling class of life are in general much better competent to, than those of a superior class. To understand the true commercial interests of a country, not only requires just ideas of the general commerce of the world, but also, and principally, a knowledge of the productions of your own country and their value, what your soil is capable of producing, the nature of your manufacturers, and the capacity of the country to increase both. To exercise the power of laying taxes, duties and excises with discretion, requires something more than an acquaintance with the abstruse parts of the system of finance. It calls for a knowledge of the circumstances and ability of the people in general, a discernment how the burdens imposed will bear upon the different classes.

From these observations results this conclusion that the number of representatives should be so large, as that while it embraces men of the first class, it should admit those of the middling class of life. I am convinced that this Government is so constituted, that the representatives will generally be composed of the first class in the community, which I shall distinguish by the name of the natural aristocracy of the country. I do not mean to give offence by using this term. I am sensible this idea is treated by many gentlemen as chimerical. I shall be asked what is meant by the natural aristocracy—and told that no such distinction of classes of men exists among us. It is true it is our singular felicity that we have no legal or hereditary distinctions of this kind; but still there are real differences: Every society naturally divides itself into classes. The author of nature has bestowed on some greater capacities than on others—birth, education, talents and wealth, create distinctions among men as visible and of as much influence as titles, stars and garters. In every society, men of this class will command a superior degree of respect—and if the government is so constituted as to admit but few to exercise the power of it, it will, according to the natural course of things, be in their hands. Men in the middling class, who are qualified as representatives, will not be so anxious to be chosen as those of the first. When the number is so small the office will be highly elevated and distinguished—the stile in which the members live will probably be high—circumstances of this kind, will render the place of a representative not a desirable one to sensible, substantial men, who have been used to walk in the plain and frugal paths of life.

Besides, the influence of the great will generally enable them to succeed in elections—it will be difficult to combine a district of country containing 30 or 40,000 inhabitants, frame your election laws as you please, in any one character; unless it be in one of conspicuous, military, popular, civil or legal talents. The great easily form associations; the poor and middling class form them with difficulty. If the elections be by plurality, as probably will be the case in this state, it is almost certain, none but the great will be chosen—for they easily unite their interest.—The common people will divide, and their divisions will be promoted by the others. There will be scarcely a chance of their uniting, in any other but some great man, unless in some popular demagogue, who will probably be destitute of principle. A substantial yeoman of sense and discernment, will hardly ever be chosen. From these remarks it appears that the government will fall into the hands of the few and the great. This will be a government of oppression. I do not mean to declaim against the great, and charge them indiscriminately with want of principle and honesty.—The same passions and prejudices govern all men. The circumstances in which men are placed in a great measure give a cast to the human character. Those in middling circumstances, have less temptation—they are inclined by habit and the company with whom they associate, to set bounds to their passions and appetites—if this is not sufficient, the want of means to gratify them will be a restraint—they are obliged to employ their time in their respective callings—hence the substantial yeomanry of the country are more temperate, of better morals and less ambition than the great. The latter do not feel for the poor and middling class; the reasons are obvious—they are not obliged to use the pains and labour to procure property as the other.—They feel not the inconveniences arising from the payment of small sums. The great consider themselves above the common people—entitled to more respect—do not associate with them—they fancy themselves to have a right of preeminence in every thing. In short, they possess the same feelings, and are under the influence of the same motives, as an hereditary nobility. I know the idea that such a distinction exists in this country is ridiculed by some—but I am not the less apprehensive of anger from their influence on this account.—Such distinctions exist all the world over—have been taken notice of by all writers on free government—and are founded in the nature of things. It has been the principal care of free governments to guard against the encroachments of the great. Common observation and experience prove the existence of such distinctions. Will any one say, that there does not exist in this country the pride of family, of wealth, of talents; and that they do not command influence and respect among the common people? Congress, in their address to the habitants of the province of Quebec, in 1775, state this distinction in the following forcible words quoted from the Marquis Beccaria. "In every human society, there is an essay continually tending to confer on one part of the height of power and happiness, and to reduce the other to the extreme of weakness and misery. The intent of good laws is to oppose this effort, and to diffuse their influence universally and equally." We ought to guard against the government being placed in the hands of this class.—They cannot have that sympathy with their constituents which is necessary to connect them closely to their interest: Being in the habit of profuse living, they will be profuse in the public expenses. They find no difficulty in paying their taxes, and therefore do not feel public burdens: Besides if they govern, they will enjoy the emoluments of the government. The middling class, from their frugal habits, and feeling themselves the public burdens, will be careful how they increase them.

But I may be asked, would you exclude the first class in the community, from any share in legislation? I answer by no means—they would be more dangerous out of power than in it—they would be factious—discontented and constantly disturbing the government—it would also be unjust—they have their liberties to protect as well as others—and the largest share of property. But my idea is, that the Constitution should be so framed as to admit this class, together with a sufficient number of the middling class to control them. You will then combine the abilities and honesty of the community—a proper degree of information, and a disposition to pursue the public good. A representative body, composed principally of respectable yeomanry is the best possible security to liberty.—When the interest of this part of the community is pursued, the public good is pursued; because the body of every nation consists of this class. And because the interest of both the rich and the poor are involved in that of the middling class. No burden can be laid on the poor, but what will sensibly affect the middling class. Any law rendering property insecure, would be injurious to them.—When therefore this class in society pursue their own interest, they promote that of the public, for it is involved in it.

In so small a number of representatives, there is great danger from corruption and combination. A great politician has said that every man has his price: I hope this is not true in all its extent—but I ask the gentlemen to inform, what government there is, in which it has not been practised? Notwithstanding all that has been said of the defects in the Constitution of the ancient Confederacies of the Grecian Republics, their destruction is to be imputed more to this cause than to any imperfection in their forms of government. This was the deadly poison that effected their dissolution. This is an extensive country, increasing in population and growing in consequence. Very many lucrative offices will be in grant of the government, which will be the object of avarice and ambition. How easy will it be to gain over a sufficient number, in the bestowment of these offices, to promote the views and purposes of those who grant them! Foreign corruption is also to be guarded against. A system of corruption is known to be the system of government in Europe. It is practised without blushing. And we may lay it to our account it will be attempted amongst us. The most effectual as well as natural security against this, is a strong democratic branch in the legislature frequently chosen, including in it a number of the substantial, sensible yeomanry of the country. Does the house of representatives answer this description? I confess, to me they hardly wear the complexion of a democratic branch—they appear the mere shadow of representation. The whole number in both houses amounts to 91—of these 46 make a quorum; and 24 of those being secured, may carry any point. Can the liberties of three millions of people be securely trusted in the hands of 24 men? Is it prudent to commit to so small a number the decision of the great questions which will come before them? Reason revolts at the idea.

The honorable gentleman from New York has said that 65 members in the house of representatives are sufficient for the present situation of the country, and taking it for granted that they will increase as one for 30,000, in 25 years they will amount to 200. It is admitted by this observation that the number fixed in the Constitution, is not sufficient without it is augmented. It is not declared that an increase shall be made, but is left at the discretion of the legislature, by the gentleman's own concession; therefore the Constitution is imperfect. We certainly ought to fix in the Constitution those things which are essential to liberty. If anything falls under this description, it is the number of the legislature. To say, as this gentleman does, that our security is to depend upon the spirit of the people, who will be watchful of their liberties, and not suffer them to be infringed, is absurd. It would equally prove that we might adopt any form of government. I believe were we to create a despot, he would not immediately dare to act the tyrant; but it would not be long before he would destroy the spirit of the people, or the people would destroy him. If our people have a high sense of liberty, the government should be congenial to this spirit—calculated to cherish the love of liberty, while yet it had sufficient force to restrain licentiousness. Government operates upon the spirit of the people, as well as the spirit of the people operates upon it—and if they are not conformable to each other, the one or the other will prevail. In a less time than 25 years, the government will receive its tone. What the spirit of the country may be at the end of that period, it is impossible to foretell: Our duty is to frame a government friendly to liberty and the rights of mankind, which will tend to cherish and cultivate a love of liberty among our citizens. If this government becomes oppressive it will be by degrees: It will aim at its end by disseminating sentiments of government opposite to republicanism; and proceed from step to step in depriving the people of a share in the government. A recollection of the change that has taken place in the minds of many in this country in the course of a few years, ought to put us upon our guard. Many who are ardent advocates for the new system, reprobate republican principles as chimerical and such as ought to be expelled from society. Who would have thought ten years ago, that the very men who risqued their lives and fortunes in support of republican principles, would now treat them as the fictions of fancy?—A few years ago we fought for liberty.—We framed a general government on free principles.—We placed the state legislatures, in whom the people have a full and fair representation, between Congress and the people. We were then, it is true, too cautious; and too much restricted the powers of the general government. But now it is proposed to go into the contrary, and a more dangerous extreme; to remove all barriers; to give the New Government free access to our pockets, and ample command of our persons; and that without providing for a genuine and fair representation of the people. No one can say what the progress of the change of sentiment may be in 25 years. The same men who now cry up the necessity of an energetic government, to induce a compliance with this system, may in much less time reprobate this in as severe terms as they now do the Confederation, and may as strongly urge the necessity of going as far beyond this, as this beyond the Confederation.—Men of this class are increasing—they have influence, talents and industry.—It is time to form a barrier against them. And while we are willing to establish a government adequate to the purposes of the union, let us be careful to establish it on the broad basis of equal liberty.

23 JUNE 1788

Honorable Mr. *Smith.* I did not intend to make any more observations on this article. Indeed, I have heard nothing to day, which has not been suggested before, except the polite reprimand I have received for my declamation. I should not have risen again, but to examine who has proved himself the greatest declaimer. The gentleman wishes me to describe what I meant, by representing the feelings of the people. If I recollect right, I said the representative ought to understand, and govern his conduct by the true interest of the people.—I believe I stated this idea precisely. When he attempts to explain my ideas, he explains them away to nothing; and instead of answering, he distorts, and then sports with them. But he may rest assured, that in the present spirit of the Convention, to irritate is not the way to conciliate. The gentleman, by the false gloss he has given to my argument, makes me an enemy to the rich: This is not true. All I said, was, that mankind were influenced, in a great degree, by interests and prejudices:—That men, in different ranks of life, were exposed to different temptations—and that ambition was more peculiarly the passion of the rich and great. The gentleman supposes the poor have less sympathy with the sufferings of their fellow creatures; for that those who feel most distress themselves, have the least regard to the misfortunes of others:—Whether this be reasoning or declamation, let all who hear us determine. I observed that the rich were more exposed to those temptations, which rank and power hold out to view; that they were more luxurious and intemperate, because they had more fully the means of enjoyment; that they were more ambitious, because more in the hope of success. The gentleman says my principle is not true; for that a poor man will be as ambitious to be a constable, as a rich man to be a governor:—But he will not injure his country so much by the party he creates to support his ambition.

The next object of the gentleman's ridicule is my idea of an aristocracy; and he indeed has done me the honor, to rank me in the order. If then I am an aristocrat, and yet publicly caution my countrymen against the encroachments of the aristocrats, they will surely consider me as one of their most disinterested friends. My idea of aristocracy is not new:—It is embraced by many writers on government:—I would refer the gentleman for a definition of it to the honorable John Adams, one of our natural aristocrats. This writer will give him a description the most ample and satisfactory. But I by no means intended to carry my idea of it to such a ridiculous length as the gentleman would have me; nor will any of my expressions warrant the construction he imposes on them. My argument was, that in order to have a true and genuine representation, you must receive the middling class of people into your government—such as compose the body of this assembly. I observed, that a representation from the United States could not be so constituted, as to represent completely the feelings and interests of the people; but that we ought to come as near this object as possible. The gentlemen say, that the exactly proper number of representatives is so indeterminate and vague, that it is impossible for them to ascertain it with any precision. But surely, they are able to see the distinction between twenty and thirty. I acknowledged that a complete representation would make the legislature too numerous; and therefore, it is our duty to limit the powers, and form checks on the government, in proportion to the smallness of the number.

The honorable gentleman next animadverts on my apprehensions of corruption, and instances the present Congress, to prove an absurdity in my argument. But is this fair reasoning? There are many material checks to the operations of that body, which the future Congress will not have. In the first place, they are chosen annually:—What more powerful check! They are subject to recall: Nine states must agree to any important resolution, which will not be carried into execution, till it meets the approbation of the people in the state legislatures. Admitting what he says, that they have pledged their faith to support the acts of Congress; yet, if these be contrary to the essential interests of the people, they ought not to be acceded to; for they are not bound to obey any law, which tends to destroy them.

It appears to me, that had economy been a motive for making the representation small, it might have operated more properly in leaving out some of the offices which this constitution requires. I am sensible that a great many of the common people, who do not reflect, imagine that a numerous representation involves a great expence:— But they are not aware of the real security it gives to an economical management in all the departments of government.

The gentleman further declared, that as far his acquaintance extended, the people thought sixty-five a number fully large enough for our State Assembly; and hence inferred, that sixty-five is to two hundred and forty thousand, as sixty five is to three millions.—This is curious reasoning.

I feel that I have troubled the committee too long. I should not indeed have risen again upon this subject, had not my ideas been grossly misrepresented.

The first part of the June 25 speech was in response to a suggestion limiting the time Senators could serve to six out of any 12 year period and giving state legislatures the right to recall Senators and elect replacements for them.

25 JUNE 1788

Mr. *Smith* . . . argued as follows. The amendment embraces two objects: First, that the senators shall be eligible for only six years in any term of twelve years: Second, that they shall be subject to the recall of the legislatures of their several states. It is proper that we take up these points separately. I concur with the honorable gentleman, that there is a necessity for giving this branch a greater stability than the house of representatives. I think his reasons are conclusive on this point. But, sir, it does not follow from this position that the senators ought to hold their places during life. Declaring them ineligible during a certain term after six years, is far from rendering them less stable than is necessary. We think the amendment will place the senate in a proper medium between a fluctuating and a perpetual body. As the clause now stands, there is no doubt that the senators will hold their office perpetually; and in this situation, they must of necessity lose their dependence and attachment to the people. It is certainly inconsistent with the established principles of republicanism, that the senate should be a fixed and unchangeable body of men. There should be then some constitutional provision against this evil. A rotation I consider as the best possible mode of affecting a remedy. The amendment will not only have a tendency to defeat any plots, which may be formed against the liberty and authority of the state governments, but will be the best means to extinguish the factions which often prevail, and which are sometimes so fatal in legislative bodies. This appears to me an important consideration. We have generally found, that perpetual bodies have either combined in some scheme of usurpation, or have been torn and distracted with cabals.— Both have been the source of misfortunes to the state. Most people acquainted with history will acknowledge these facts. Our Congress would have been a fine field for party spirit to act in.—That body would undoubtedly have suffered all the evils of faction, had it not been secured by the rotation established by the articles of the confederation. I think a rotation in the government is a very important and truly republican institution. All good republicans, I presume to say, will treat it with respect.

It is a circumstance strongly in favor of rotation, that it will have a tendency to diffuse a more general spirit of emulation, and to bring forward into office the genius and abilities of the continent.— The ambition of gaining the qualifications necessary to govern, will be in some proportion to the chance of success. If the office is to be perpetually confined to a few, other men of equal talents and virtue, but not possessed of so extensive an influence, may be discouraged from aspiring to it. The more perfectly we are versed in the political science, the more firmly will the happy principles of republicanism be supported. The true policy of constitutions will be to increase the information of the country, and disseminate the knowledge of government as universally as possible. If this be done, we shall have, in any dangerous emergency, a numerous body of enlightened citizens, ready for the call of their country. As the constitution now is, you only give an opportunity to two men to be acquainted with the public affairs. It is a maxim with me, that every man employed in a high office by the people, should from time to time return to them, that he may be in a situation to satisfy them with respect to his conduct and the measures of administration. If I recollect right, it was observed by an honorable member from New York, that this amendment would be an infringement of the natural rights of the people. I humbly conceive, if the gentleman reflects maturely on the nature of his argument, he will acknowledge its weakness. What is government itself, but a restraint upon the natural rights of the people? What constitution was ever devised, that did not operate as a restraint on their original liberties? What is the whole system of qualifications, which take place in all free governments, but a restraint? Why is a certain age made necessary? Why a certain term of citizenship? This constitution itself, sir, has restraints innumerable.— The amendment, it is true, may exclude two of the best men; but it can rarely happen, that the state will sustain any material loss by this. I hope and believe that we shall always have more than two men, who are capable of discharging the duty of a senator. But if it should so happen that the state possessed only two capable men, it will be necessary that they should return home, from time to time, to inspect and regulate our domestic affairs. I do not conceive the state can suffer any inconvenience. The argument indeed might have some weight were the representation very large: But as the power is to be exercised upon only two men, the apprehensions of the gentlemen are entirely without foundation.

With respect to the second part of the amendment, I would observe that as the senators are the representatives of the state legislatures, it is reasonable and proper that they should be under their control. When a state sends an agent commissioned to transact any business, or perform any service, it certainly ought to have a power to recall him. These are plain principles, and so far as they apply to the case under examination, they ought to be adopted by us. Form this government as you please, you must at all events lodge in it very important powers: These powers must be in the hands of a few men, so situated as to produce a small degree of responsibility. These circumstances ought to put us upon our guard; and the inconvenience of this necessary delegation of power should be corrected, by providing some suitable checks.

Against this part of the amendment a great deal of argument has been used, and with considerable plausibility. It is said if the amendment takes place, the senators will hold their office only during the pleasure of the state legislatures, and consequently will not possess the necessary firmness and stability. I conceive, sir, there is a fallacy in this argument, founded upon the suspicion that the legislature of a state will possess the qualities of a mob, and be incapable of any regular conduct. I know that the impulses of the multitude are inconsistent with systematic government. The people are frequently incompetent to deliberate discussion, and subject to errors and imprudencies. Is this the complexion of the state legislatures? I presume it is not. I presume that they are never actuated by blind impulses—that they rarely do things hastily and without consideration. The state legislatures were select bodies of men, chosen for their superior wisdom, and so organized as to be capable of calm and regular conduct. My apprehension is, that the power of recall would not be exercised as often as it ought. It is highly improbable that a man, in whom the state has confided, and who has an established influence, will be recalled, unless his conduct has been notoriously wicked.—The arguments of the gentleman therefore, do not apply in this case. It is further observed, that it would be improper to give the legislatures this power, because the local interests and prejudices of the states ought not to be admitted into the general government; and that if the senator is rendered too independent of his constituents, he will sacrifice the interests of the Union to the policy of his state. Sir, the senate has been generally held up by all parties as a safe guard to the rights of the several states. In this view, the closest connection between them has been considered as necessary. But now it seems we speak a different language.—We now look upon the least attachment to their state as dangerous.—We are now for separating them, and rendering them entirely independent, that we may root out the last vestige of state sovereignty.

An honorable gentleman from New York observed yesterday, that the states would always maintain their importance and authority, on account of their superior influence over the people. To prove this influence, he mentioned the aggregate number of the state representatives throughout the continent. But I ask him, how long the people will retain their confidence for two thousand representatives, who shall meet once in a year to make laws for regulating the heighth of your fences and the repairing of your roads? Will they not by and by be saying—Here, we are paying a great number of men for doing nothing: We had better give up all the civil business of our state with its powers to congress, who are sitting all the year round: We had better get rid of the useless burden. That matters will come to this at last, I have no more doubt than I have of my existence. The state governments, without object or authority, will soon dwindle into insignificance, and be despised by the people themselves. I am, sir, at a loss to know how the state legislatures will spend their time. Will they make laws to regulate agriculture? I imagine this will be best regulated by the sagacity and industry of those who practise it. Another reason offered by the gentleman is, that the states will have a greater number of officers than the general government. I doubt this. Let us make a comparison. In the first place, the federal government must have a complete set of judicial officers of different ranks throughout the continent: Then, a numerous train of executive officers, in all the branches of the revenue, both internal and external, and all the civil and military departments. Add to this, their salaries will probably be larger and better secured than those of any state officers. If these numerous offices are not at once established, they are in the power of congress, and will all in time be created. Very few offices will be objects of ambition in the states. They will have no establishments at all to correspond with some of those I have mentioned.—In other branches, they will have the same as congress. But I ask, what will be their comparative influence and importance? I will leave it, sir, to any man of candour, to determine whether there will not probably be more lucrative and honorable places in the gift of congress than in the disposal of the states all together. But the whole reasoning of the gentlemen rests upon the principle that the states will be able to check the general government, by exciting the people to opposition: It only goes to prove, that the state officers will have such an influence over the people, as to impel them to hostility and rebellion. This kind of check, I contend, would be a pernicious one; and certainly ought to be prevented. Checks in government ought to act silently, and without public commotion. I think that the harmony of the two powers should by all means be maintained: If it be not, the operation of government will be baneful—one or the other of the parties must finally be destroyed in the conflict. The constitutional line between the authority of each should be so obvious, as to leave no room for jealous apprehensions or violent contests.

It is further said, that the operation of local interests should be counteracted; for which purpose, the senate should be rendered permanent. I conceive that the true interest of every state is the interest of the whole; and that if we should have a well regulated government, this idea will prevail. We shall indeed have few local interests to pursue, under the new constitution; because it limits the claims of the states by so close a line, that on their part there can be little dispute, and little worth disputing about. But, sir, I conceive that partial interests will grow continually weaker, because there are not those fundamental differences between the real interests of the several states, which will long prevent their coming together and becoming uniform.

Another argument advanced by the gentlemen is, that our amendment would be the means of producing factions among the electors: That aspiring men would misrepresent the conduct of a faithful senator; and by intrigue, procure a recall, upon false grounds, in order to make room for themselves. But, sir, men who are ambitious for places will rarely be disposed to render those places unstable. A truly ambitious man will never do this, unless he is mad. It is not to be supposed that a state will recall a man once in twenty years, to make way for another. Dangers of this kind are very remote: I think they ought not to be brought seriously into view.

More than one of the gentlemen have ridiculed my apprehensions of corruption. How, say they, are the people to be corrupted? By their own money? Sir, in many countries, the people pay money to corrupt themselves: why should it not happen in this? Certainly, the congress will be as liable to corruption as other bodies of men. Have they not the same frailties, and the same temptations? With respect to the corruption arising from the disposal of offices, the gentlemen have treated the argument as insignificant. But let any one make a calculation, and see whether there will not be good offices enough, to dispose of to every man who goes there, who will then freely resign his seat; for, can any one suppose, that a member of congress would not go out and relinquish his four dollars a day, for two or three thousand pounds a year? It is here objected that no man can hold an office created during the time he is in congress—but it will be easy for a man of influence, who has in his eye a favorite office previously created and already filled, to say to his friend, who holds it—Here—I will procure you another place of more emolument, provided you will relinquish yours in favor of me. The constitution appears to be a restraint, when in fact it is none at all. I presume, sir, there is not a government in the world in which there is greater scope for influence and corruption in the disposal of offices. Sir, I will not declaim, and say all men are dishonest; but I think that, in forming a constitution, if we presume this, we shall be on the safest side. The extreme is certainly less dangerous than the other. It is wise to multiply checks to a greater degree than the present state of things requires. It is said that corruption has never taken place under the old government—I believe, gentlemen hazard this assertion without proofs. That it has taken place in some degree is very probable. Many millions of money have been put into the hands of government, which have never yet been accounted for: The accounts are not yet settled, and Heaven only knows when they will be.

I have frequently observed a restraint upon the state governments, which congress never can be under, construct that body as you please. It is a truth, capable of demonstration, that the nearer the representative is to his constituent, the more attached and dependent he will be.—In the states, the elections are frequent, and the representatives numerous: They transact business in the midst of their constituents, and every man may be called upon to account for his conduct. In this state the council of appointment are elected for one year.—The proposed constitution establishes a council of appointment who will be perpetual.—Is there any comparison between the two governments in point of security? It is said that the governor of this state is limited in his powers—indeed his authority is small and insignificant, compared to that of the senate of the United States.

27 JUNE 1788

Another idea is in my mind, which I think conclusive against a simple government for the United States. It is not possible to collect a set of representatives, who are acquainted with all parts of the continent. Can you find men in Georgia who are acquainted with the situation of New Hampshire? who know what taxes will best suit the inhabitants; and how much they are able to bear? Can the best men make laws for a people of whom they are entirely ignorant? Sir, we have no reason to hold our state governments in contempt, or to suppose them incapable of acting wisely. I believe they have operated more beneficially than most people expected, who considered that those governments were erected in a time of war and confusion, when they were very liable to errors in their structure. It will be a matter of astonishment to all unprejudiced men hereafter, who shall reflect upon our situation, to observe to what a great degree good government has prevailed. It is true some bad laws have been passed in most of the states; but they arose more from the difficulty of the times, than from any want of honesty or wisdom. Perhaps there never was a government, which in the course of ten years did not do something to be repented of. As for Rhode Island, I do not mean to justify her—she deserves to be condemned.—If there were in the world but one example of political depravity, it would be hers: And no nation ever merited or suffered a more genuine infamy, than a wicked administration has attached to her character. Massachusetts also has been guilty of errors: and has lately been distracted by an internal convulsion. Great Britain, notwithstanding her boasted constitution, has been a perpetual scene of revolutions and civil war.—Her parliaments have been abolished; her kings have been banished and murdered. I assert that the majority of the governments in the union have operated better than any body had reason to expect: and that nothing but experience and habit is wanting, to give the state laws all the stability and wisdom necessary to make them respectable. If these things be true, I think we ought not to exchange our condition, with a hazard of losing our state constitutions. We all agree that a general government is necessary: But it ought not to go so far, as to destroy the authority of the members. We shall be unwise, to make a new experiment in so important a matter, without some known and sure grounds to go upon. The state constitutions should be the guardians of our domestic rights and interests; and should be both the support and the check of the federal government. . . .

Sir, has any country which has suffered distresses like ours, exhibited within a few years, more striking marks of improvement and prosperity? How its population has grown; how its agriculture, commerce and manufactures have been extended and improved! How many forests have been cut down; how many wastes have been cleared and cultivated; how many additions have been made to the extent and beauty of our towns and cities! I think our advancement has been rapid. In a few years, it is to be hoped, that we shall be relieved from our embarrassments; and unless new calamities come upon us, shall be flourishing and happy. . . .